100 THINGS BRAVES FANS SHOULD KNOW & DO BEFORE THEY DIE

Jack Wilkinson

Library of Congress Cataloging-in-Publication Data
Wilkinson, Jack, 1950–
100 things Braves fans should know and do before they die / Jack Wilkinson.
p. cm.
Includes bibliographical references.
ISBN 978-1-60078-555-9
1. Atlanta Braves (Baseball team)—History—Miscellanea. 2. Baseball—Georgia—Atlanta—History—Miscellanea. 3. Atlanta Braves (Baseball team)—History—Anecdotes. 4. Baseball—Georgia—Atlanta—History—Anecdotes. I. Title. II. Title: One hundred things Braves fans should know and do before they die.
GV875.A8W56 2011
796.357'6409758231–dc22
2010046992

This book is available in quantity at special discounts for your group or organization. For further information, contact:

Triumph Books
542 South Dearborn Street, Suite 750
Chicago, Illinois 60605
(312) 939-3330 | Fax (312) 663-3557
www.triumphbooks.com

Printed in U.S.A.
ISBN: 978-1-60078-555-9
Design by Patricia Frey
Page production by Prologue Publishing Services, LLC
All photos courtesy of AP Images unless otherwise specified

This is dedicated to the ones I love:

My sister, Kathleen, the funny one, whose love and long-distance friendship are two of the great joys of my life.

Tommy, our late, great brother, who left us much too soon but left us much to cherish…and miss.

My blessed trinity, Janet, Dr. K, and the Ballerina, again and always.

And to those I respect:

The Professor, Pete Van Wieren.
Chip Caray, a real friend who carries on the family name.
And Leonard Smith, a true hero.

And, finally, to Braves fans everywhere.

Contents

1 A+, as in Aaron

The ball, like the Hammer himself, is larger than life. Much, much larger. How much? Try 100 feet in diameter. Try looking up, up, four or five stories up. Those are the measurements of an enormous color photograph of a baseball. The very ball Henry Aaron lined over the left-field wall one long-ago April evening and into the Atlanta Braves bullpen, into the record and history books, and on into posterity.

It's the 715 ball. The one that broke the Babe's career home run record. In terms of sheer size and significance, the photo is baseball's ultimate tape-measure shot.

Much like that photograph, which looms over the Fan Plaza at Turner Field, Henry Louis Aaron still hovers over his franchise and his adopted hometown. He is a towering presence in Atlanta, and remains so nearly four decades after breaking baseball's most hallowed record.

Aaron played here, brilliantly. He made history here, heroically. He continues to live and thrive here, financially and personally. More than any other citizen of the South's flagship city, Aaron and Atlanta are conjoined at the A. No one else comes close. Not Ted Turner. Not Jimmy Carter. Not Bobby Cox or Beyoncé. Someone says *Atlanta*, you think *Aaron*.

To get to Turner Field, you drive or walk from the golden dome of the state capitol building down a street that begins as Capitol Avenue but soon becomes—what else?—Hank Aaron Drive. You can see the photo of the ball nearly a quarter-mile away. The closer you get to the ballpark, the bigger the ball and the man who hammered it become.

The dimensions of the photograph, of course, are just that: merely dimensions. And Aaron, the very best of all Braves, one of baseball's greatest all-around players and now once again the peoples' choice as the legitimate home run king, was anything but one-dimensional as a player.

His greatness is spread all over baseball's hit lists. Aaron holds more major league batting records than any player in the game's long history. He drove in 2,297 runs. He lashed out 1,477 extra-base hits. He amassed 6,856 total bases. He finished in the top 10 in six other major career categories and compiled a lifetime batting average of .305. Yet Aaron also won four RBI titles, three Gold Gloves, two batting titles and the 1957 National League MVP Award, and led the NL in homers four times.

"About the only thing I didn't do," he once said, "is win a stolen base title."

However, it's his home runs we immediately think of when we think of Henry Aaron.

He hit this historic 715th off the Dodgers' Al Downing on April 8, 1974, in Atlanta to surpass Babe Ruth, and endured hell en route to that milestone. The 755th and last he belted back in Milwaukee, where Aaron began his big-league career in 1954 and ended it in 1976. The 109th, in September of 1957, which Aaron later acknowledged was his most satisfying, even more so than the 715th. That 11th-inning walk-off blast, one of the young Aaron's National League–leading 44 homers that season, that clinched the pennant for the Braves. Milwaukee went on to win its only World Series championship.

"I galloped around the bases, and when I touched home plate, the whole team was there to pick me up and carry me off the field," Aaron later reflected. "I had always dreamed about a moment like Bobby Thomson had in '51, and this was it."

We know where we were when "Bad Henry," as Don Drysdale, the late Dodgers Hall of Fame pitcher, admiringly called Aaron during

A street vendor sets up shop outside Turner Field with the photo mural of Hank Aaron's 715th home run ball serving as the perfect backdrop.

their playing days, hit No. 715. Much like we recall where we were when JFK was assassinated, when Neil Armstrong took a small step for man on the Moon, or when the Berlin wall came tumbling down. We remember 715. Long gone. Never forgotten.

It wasn't until Aaron surpassed Ruth, though, that the awful truth eventually came out: the racism he'd endured, the pure hatred and vitriol, the hate mail and death threats aimed squarely at the color of a man's skin. It began in the 1972 season and built throughout '73 as Aaron, at age 39, hit 40 homers to finish the year with 713, one shy of Ruth's record.

"All I've got to do this winter," he said at season's end, "is stay alive."

Of course, long before he challenged Ruth, Aaron had encountered racism in baseball. As a teenager, the young infielder from Mobile, Alabama, briefly played for the Indianapolis Clowns of the Negro Leagues. One weekend, their doubleheader in Washington, D.C., at Griffith Stadium—home of the Washington Senators—was rained out. As Aaron recalled in his autobiography *I Had a Hammer*, written with Lonnie Wheeler: "We had breakfast while they were waiting for the rain to stop, and I can still envision sitting with the Clowns in a restaurant behind Griffith Stadium and hearing [restaurant employees] break all the plates in the kitchen after we were finished eating. What a horrible sound. Even as a kid, the irony of it hit me: here we were in the capital in the land of freedom and equality, and they had to destroy the plates that had touched the forks that had been in the mouths of black men. If dogs had eaten off those plates, they'd have washed them."

A quarter-century and untold anguish later, at 9:07 PM on a Monday night, 715 finally took flight. In his second at-bat, when the rain subsided as if on cue, Aaron lined the historic homer into the Braves' bullpen, into the glove of teammate Tom House. The reliever ran toward home plate and hand-delivered the historic ball to Aaron. His father, Herbert, hugged his son. Then his mother, Estella, finally embraced him. A crowd of 53,775 roared its approval. Henry Aaron could finally exhale and say, "Thank God."

Vin Scully, the Dodgers' iconic broadcaster, said this to his Los Angeles audience: "Fastball…there's a high drive to deep left-center field. Buckner goes back to the fence, it is…GONE!"

Scully paused, for one minute, 44 seconds. The only sounds: the cheering of the crowd and fireworks exploding in the night air. Then: "What a marvelous moment for baseball! What a marvelous moment for Atlanta and the state of Georgia! What a marvelous moment for the country and the world! A black man is getting a standing ovation in the Deep South for breaking the record of an all-time baseball idol."

And later, tellingly, this: "Aaron is being mobbed by photographers. He's holding his right hand high in the air. And for the first time in a long time that poker face of Aaron's shows the tremendous strain, and relief, of what it must have been like to live with for the last several months."

Watching the telecast that night was a young Atlantan named Arington Hendley. Twenty-three years later, by then an accomplished photographer, Hendley was hired by a design firm to shoot the 715 ball for use at Turner Field. He drove to Aaron's home in southwest Atlanta, and wound up in the slugger's trophy room in the basement.

"He introduced himself as Henry Aaron," Hendley said. "I've shot the top golfers and some movie stars. Those guys, I couldn't have cared less about. But Hank Aaron was entirely different. I was shaking like a leaf."

Not that it was Aaron's fault. On the contrary, "He was just this quiet, unassuming, and accommodating gentleman," Hendley said, "and he was just treated like dirt [during the home run chase]. I mean, I felt guilty being white. I just desperately wanted to apologize to him for the entire white race."

Hendley said nothing, then did something regrettable. "I was so intimidated," he said. "Here it was, I was with the guy who I thought hung the Moon, and I screwed up the job. I blew it. I didn't expose the film properly.

"The photograph's a picture of a baseball. Almost anybody could've done it, and they probably wouldn't have screwed it up the first time. It became this piece of art I was trying to make. I wanted to hit a home run with his ball."

The first shots weren't detailed enough, and the significance of the 715 shot is not just in its size but in the details. "You could see where the ball was hit, which I discovered when we took the ball out of its case," Hendley said. "I showed it to Hank, and he said, 'Yeah, that's it.'"

Aaron agreed to let the ball be photographed once more. This time, Hendley hit his homer. Now anytime anyone comes to Turner Field, they can see the ball and precisely where Aaron's bat launched No. 715. It's not bad for Hendley's business. "In advertising," he said, "people ask what I've taken pictures of, and I say, 'Hank Aaron's ball at the stadium.' They go, 'Ooooh!'"

And the photo also befits Aaron's stature in his sport, his city, and history, especially now that steroids are no longer baseball's dirty secret. McGwire. A-Rod. Does anyone believe Bonds or Clemens? But people can still believe in Aaron. And they do.

As Dwight Garner wrote in his May 2010 *New York Times* book review of *The Last Hero: A Life of Henry Aaron*, Howard Bryant's superb biography: "In an era in which home runs are now a discredited commodity, Henry Aaron looms larger than ever: a nation has returned its lonely eyes to him."

2 "FINALLY!"

It was a sign of the times and nigh perfect. Rarely has one sign captured a moment, a city's psyche and sense of joy and relief, a team and a time so perfectly. All in just one word:

"...FINALLY!"

That's how the homemade sign read, the one a fan held aloft on the evening of October 28, 1995—the night the Atlanta Braves won the World Series at blessed last.

"Guys, that says it all right there," Joe Morgan, the Hall of Famer–turned-broadcaster, told his on-air TV partners at game's end. "Finally."

"The team of the '90s has its world championship," play-by-play man Bob Costas declared after the Braves beat Cleveland 1–0 in Game 6 of the 1995 World Series, behind Tom Glavine's eight-inning, one-hit pitching masterpiece and a solo homer by the lightning rod David Justice. With that, the Atlanta Braves joined their 1957 Milwaukee and 1914 Boston forebears as the only clubs in franchise history to win the Fall Classic.

This, after so many seasons of atrocious baseball in Atlanta. This, after losing 106 games in 1988, then back-to-back 97-loss seasons. This, after the worst-to-first wonder of '91, only to suffer Kirby Puckett's 11th-inning walk-off homer in Game 6, then a 1–0, 10th-inning heartbreak to Jack Morris and the Minnesota Twins in Game 7 of the greatest World Series ever. The Francisco Cabrera–Sid Bream miracle in the ninth inning of Game 7 of the 1992 NLCS was trumped by Dave Winfield's 11th-inning double to give Toronto the World Series title. In '93, after prevailing in a magnificent NL West pennant race with San Francisco, an exhausted Atlanta was no match for Philadelphia in the NLCS.

"So many disappointments," Tom Glavine said.

Not after the strike-shortened 1994 season. In 1995 the Braves won the NL East by a staggering 21 games. They dispatched wild-card Colorado in the initial NL Division Series then swept Cincinnati. In the World Series Braves pitchers would hold Cleveland's potent lineup to a .179 batting average. Despite losing Game 5 at Jacobs Field, the Braves returned home up 3–2.

On the off day, Justice teed off on Atlanta fans. "They'll probably burn down our houses if we don't win," he told reporters. "They're not behind us like the Cleveland fans, who were standing and cheering even when they were three runs down."

This infuriated Atlanta fans. Justice was booed fiercely, angrily when the starting lineups were announced, and again before his first at-bat. All that changed with one swing of the bat in the sixth inning, when Justice led off with a home run. This, after Glavine had surrendered a bloop single to Tony Pena in the top half, Cleveland's only hit of the night.

"Just get me one!" Glavine screamed as he walked into the dugout. One run. Justice obliged. As he crossed home plate, Bob Costas said, "Dave Justice, all is forgiven in Atlanta."

That was all the run support Glavine needed. That, and ninth-inning relief help from closer Mark Wohlers, who began by getting speedy Kenny Lofton to foul out to Pac Man—aka shortstop Rafael Belliard, who'd gobbled up everything all year. Paul Sorrento flied out, and that brought Carlos Baerga to the plate and the Braves to the brink.

"In the ninth inning, Mark [Wohlers] is in, and I just remember sitting there in the dugout, knowing we were on the verge of doing what we wanted to do—finally winning the World Series," Glavine said. "It's just an eternity for that inning to end. It's taking forever: *Come on, hurry up!* I thought to myself.

"I think the key to that inning was Raffy running down the line to get Lofton's ball. The key was to keep Lofton off base. We get the next out, and then there's that fly ball…"

"When Baerga hit it," Justice said, "I thought, *Oh my God!* I thought it was out." He was not alone.

Skip Caray's call said it all: "Fly ball, deep left-center...Grissom on the run…Yes! Yes! YES! The Atlanta Braves have given you a world championship!!!"

Each "Yes!" reverberated with an echo courtesy of Caray's colleague Joe Simpson, who was standing behind him in the broadcast booth and yelling "Yes!" in concert with Skip. Simpson wasn't working the ninth inning. But like all of Atlanta, he was celebrating. Finally.

"It was like the weight of the world was off of our shoulders," Justice said. "We'd finally won the World Series!"

"In the short time it took for that ball to settle into Marquis' glove, there were so many emotions," said Glavine. "I played it out from the start of the season. This is what we came to spring training

Finally! The Atlanta Braves celebrate after Game 6 of the World Series, where they beat the Cleveland Indians 1–0 to win the best-of-seven series 4–2.

for, to win the World Series and to run out on the field with my buddies.

"We'd had so many disappointments. We had this group of guys, all these guys who'd played together and been around each other in the system and then the major leagues, and we'd finally tasted success after so many disappointments. That's what made it so special."

Finally.

3 Frankie, Sid, and Skip

With genuine respect and all due apologies to Henry Aaron, the most dramatic moment in Braves franchise history was not his record-breaking home run. No. 715 was a foregone conclusion by that point, a matter of when, not if. But no one could have foreseen what unfolded on the evening of October 14, 1992.

For the second straight season, the Braves and Pittsburgh Pirates met in the National League Championship Series. Once again, it came down to a decisive Game 7. John Smoltz, who'd beaten the Bucs in Game 7 of the 1991 NLCS, had already defeated Doug Drabek twice in this series. Yet it was Drabek, not Smoltz, who carried a 2–0 lead into the bottom of the ninth inning as he walked to the mound in Atlanta-Fulton County Stadium.

In NLCS play Terry Pendleton had gone 0-for-15 against Drabek. But he led off with a double to right. This, after all, was Pendleton, the 1991 NL Most Valuable Player who later admitted, "I thought I had a better year in '92." An All-Star Game starter that year, the third baseman finished second in the MVP voting despite batting .311 with 21 homers, a career-high 105 RBIs and 199 hits (including an Atlanta-record 39 doubles). Still, he didn't repeat as the MVP.

"Pittsburgh had this guy named Barry Bonds," Pendleton said, smiling.

Pendleton advanced to third base when, on a ground ball by David Justice, Pirates second baseman Jose "Chico" Lind made a very uncharacteristic error. "I backed up on the ball," confessed Lind, who won a Gold Glove Award that year after making just six errors during the regular season. When Drabek walked lumber-legged Sid Bream on four pitches to load the bases, manager Jim Leyland brought in side-winding reliever Stan Belinda.

Ron Gant's sacrifice fly put Atlanta on the board, down 2–1. Although Damon Berryhill walked to reload the bases, Brian Hunter popped up softly. The Berryhill walk included a tight call on one pitch by umpire Randy Marsh. He had moved behind the plate early in the game after John McSherry—a superb ball-strike umpire—hyperventilated and had to be taken to Piedmont Hospital.

One out from elimination, with reliever Jeff Reardon due up, Braves manager Bobby Cox made the easy choice of pinch-hitting Francisco Cabrera. Never mind that Cabrera spent most of the year in the minors and played in just 12 big-league games during the regular season. In his lone career at-bat against Belinda, the Dominican homered on July 29, 1991.

"I remember it was very loud, so loud that [third-base coach] Jimy Williams had to walk up and almost kiss my ear to tell me what he was saying," Justice later told me. "He wasn't really saying anything. Just pretending, where they might think a squeeze was on."

After Cabrera ripped a line drive foul down the third-base line, Justice remembers what he was thinking. "Exactly: *He's going to hit a home run right here*," he said. "He was one of the best fastball hitters ever."

So with two out and Atlanta still trailing 2–1, Skip Caray called the next pitch: "A double, an error, and a walk, and the bases are full of Braves. Bream carries the winning run...two balls, one strike. What tension...the runners lead. A lotta room in right-center. If he hits one there, we can dance in the streets. The 2–1...

"Swing...line drive left field! One run is in! Here comes Bream, here's the throw to the plate. He iiiiiiiisssssssss...SAFE!!! Braves win! Braves win! Braves win! Braves win!"

Pause.

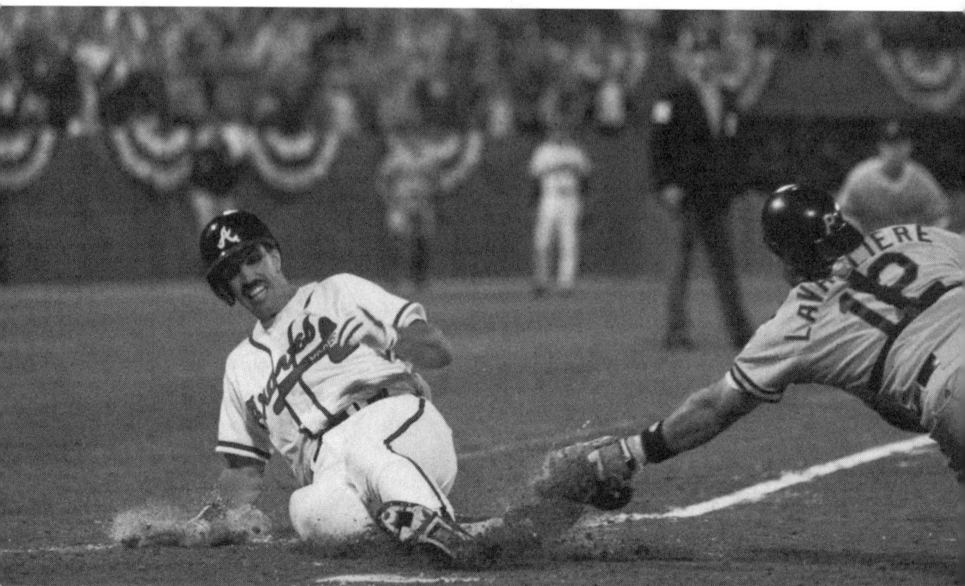

Sid Bream scores the winning run as Mike LaValliere of the Pittsburgh Pirates misses the tag during Game 7 of the NLCS on October 14, 1992, in Atlanta.
Photo courtesy Getty Images

"BRAVES WIN!"

Any Atlantan, any bona fide Braves fan knows that Skip screamed "Braves Win!" five times with a pregnant pause before the fifth. It's a perfect call, one that Stan Kasten, then the president of the Braves and now also the former president of the Washington Nationals, says should be taught in college broadcast journalism courses.

"I score, and I turn around and see Barry," Justice later said of Bonds. "He's going toward left-center, took a little angle. I'm thinking, *Sid's got this easy.* I'm not even waving my arms [down]. All of a sudden, I see Sid coming and the ball coming, and Sid's got a monkey on his back. I start jumping up and down, yelling, 'Get down! Get down!'"

Bonds' throw was slightly to the first-base side of home plate. Catcher Mike LaValliere caught the ball, then lunged back toward the plate—just as Bream slid on the outside corner, barely avoiding the swipe tag. And the capacity crowd of 51,975 went bonkers. The Braves had just become the first team in major league history to win a decisive postseason game while trailing before the final pitch.

Bonds sank to one knee in left field, stunned. Andy Van Slyke simply sat down in center, in shock. "I remember jumping on Sid, and I roll over and my feet are straight up in the air in the pile," Justice said of the mosh pit at the plate. "Everybody's jumping up in the air, and my feet are straight up in the air in the pile."

With a background soundtrack of delirium, Caray continued his classic call: "They may have to hospitalize Sid Bream! He's down at the bottom of a huge pile at the plate. They help him to his feet. Frank Cabrera got the game-winner. The Atlanta Braves are National League champions again! This crowd is going berserk!"

Indeed, no one left the stadium, it seemed, for the longest time. The Braves ran around deliriously, screaming and pumping their fists. The fans did the Tomahawk Chop and raised the Chant to new decibel levels. The streets of Atlanta rocked the night away in celebration.

"Oh, my God, it was pandemonium," Justice said. "Unbelievable."

And high drama, the likes of which the Braves had never seen.

715

The end was in sight now, the long road to Ruth and 715 nearly over. After coming so close in 1973, just one homer shy of a tie, just two more to "Move over, Babe," Henry Aaron wanted to be done with it all.

His winter had been relatively quiet, with little hassle from the press. His happiest moment? Aaron had remarried. Billye Williams was a widow, active in the Civil Rights movement, and the host of a morning TV talk show, *Today in Atlanta*, where the two had met. Billye and her new husband were very happy.

Aaron had hit his 713th homer off Houston left-hander Jerry Reuss the previous September. In that season finale at home, on a rainy day in Atlanta, Aaron failed to go deep against a regular foil, Astro Dave Roberts. Afterward, he apologized to those in attendance: "I'm sorry I couldn't hit one for them, sitting in the rain like that. I was going for the home run. I wasn't trying to hit singles."

The Braves opened the 1974 season in Cincinnati. Aaron, who wanted to break the record back in Atlanta, said he wanted to play only in the second game of the Reds series and sit out the other two. Baseball Commissioner Bowie Kuhn wasn't pleased. He told Braves chairman Bill Bartholomay the Braves had to play Aaron "in the same pattern of 1973, when he started approximately two of every three games."

Aaron was angry, saying, "I live in Atlanta, and that's where I want to hit the home run that ties the record and the home run that breaks the record. I feel I owe it to the fans."

In his first at-bat in Cincinnati, with his first swing of the season, Aaron hit No. 714 off Jack Billingham. It was his only hit of the opener. Braves manager Eddie Mathews, Aaron's old slugging partner in their Milwaukee days, said he wouldn't play Aaron again in Cincinnati: "Right or wrong, this is my decision." Kuhn's response? Aaron must play in Sunday's series finale.

Mathews issued a statement before the game: "The commissioner has unlimited powers to issue very serious penalties on individuals or the ballclub itself. For the first time, I realize these penalties are not only fines but also suspensions and other threats to the franchise itself. Because of this order and the threatened penalties, I intend to start Hank Aaron [today]."

Hank Aaron belts his 715th home run over the left-field fence against the Reds' Al Downing on April 8, 1974, in Atlanta, breaking Babe Ruth's record and putting the anticipation and dread of this moment behind him.

The Reds' Clay Kirby held Aaron hitless that day, striking him out twice before Mathews pulled him in the seventh. Everyone was satisfied with the outcome. No one had lost face or been disciplined. More important, the stage was now perfectly set for Monday, back home in Atlanta.

In his second at-bat, on Al Downing's second pitch and Aaron's first swing of the evening, the Hammer lined a rising laser over the left-field fence for No. 715. With that, Henry Aaron had the record, and America finally had to acknowledge his greatness throughout his career.

In his 1991 autobiography *I Had a Hammer*, Aaron wrote, "The most basic motivation was the pure ambition to break such an important and long-standing barrier. Along with that would come the recognition that I thought was long overdue me: I would be out of the shadows."

Aaron's daughter, Gaile, could not be in Atlanta-Fulton County Stadium. She was back at Fisk University in Tennessee, watching on TV. So, too, were FBI agents assigned to protect her against a kidnapping plot. When Estella Aaron ran out to home plate and hugged her son, it seemed a beautiful moment of maternal love. Actually, Mrs. Aaron was serving as a human shield, in case someone in the crowd carried an assassin's weapon.

"Thank God it's over," were Henry Aaron's first words said into a microphone.

5 Worst to First

With a nod to Dickens, it was the best of times, it was the worst-to-first of times. Twenty years later, the memory of the 1991 season is preserved for what it was and will always be: the greatest in Atlanta history.

For years, the Braves were Dickensian in the very worst sense. In Atlanta-Fulton County Stadium, Major League Baseball had its own Bleak House, filled with 90-, even 100-loss seasons and very few fans. All that changed in '91, when the Braves captured the NL pennant, captivated the city, and nearly won the greatest World Series ever played.

"It was like your wedding night," broadcaster Skip Caray recalled of the entire turnaround. "It's the first time, and everything's great."

"We captured a city," John Smoltz said on the 10-year anniversary of the '91 miracle. "It was hysterical, kind of like Elvis was back."

"It's the booster rocket for a great—so far—10-year run," said then–general manager John Schuerholz, the architect of the turnaround and now the Braves' team president.

Even Terry Pendleton, who'd played in America's best baseball city for the St. Louis Cardinals before coming to Atlanta as a free agent, understood the essence of worst-to-first. "It's my most satisfying season," said the third baseman and hot cornerstone in Schuerholz's grand redesign of baseball's most maligned franchise. Pendleton was voted the National League's Most Valuable Player that season, winning the batting title with a .319 average while showing the Braves how to win.

"You won't find many situations where you ask players what their favorite year was, and you have a choice between winning a World Series and another year," said Tom Glavine, who won the first of his two NL Cy Young Awards that season. "It's a toss-up here. 1995 was the ultimate. But had we won the World Series in '91, there'd be no way to top that."

It was Glavine who beat Cleveland 1–0 in Game 6 of the '95 World Series to give Atlanta its only world championship. Yes, 1995 was triumphant. But '91 is timeless.

"Nineteen ninety-one is second but not by much," he said. "Second separated by one game. One more win and '91 is a hands-down winner."

For Rafael Belliard, the memory lingered almost daily. "Sometimes I wear my '95 ring, but this one I wear more," he said on the 10th anniversary. He extended his left hand, with the '91 National League Champions ring on his ring finger. "This is my favorite one."

As a shortstop with Atlanta from 1991 to 1998, Belliard won seven championship rings of varying significance. When he later worked as a roving minor league fielding instructor in the Braves organization, he kept his '95 World Series ring in a safe-deposit box. He wore his '91 ring instead.

"The people of Atlanta wrapped their arms around us and just rode it like a wave," said catcher Greg Olson, an unlikely hitting star of the '91 postseason. "It was like you were a prince, the president. We were kings of the town. By the end of the year, where we used to have 4,000 fans in the stands, it got to where a mouse couldn't get in because he'd get trampled."

After the All-Star break, the Braves began their move to catch Los Angeles. Dodgers manager Tommy Lasorda was the pitchman for a diet supplement that summer that helped him lose a great deal of weight. One fan's sign, with a photo of Lasorda, played off that ad as Atlanta closed in on L.A.: "I lost 9½ games in only nine weeks! And I owe it all to the Braves plan."

On the next-to-last day of the season, a capacity crowd in Atlanta-Fulton County Stadium celebrated twice: first when the Braves beat Houston to clinch a tie for the NL West title, again when the Giants' victory over the Dodgers was shown on the stadium video screen.

"You take a picture like that, it's like a sigh of relief," manager Bobby Cox said of a famous photo of himself, gazing up at the video board after the final out. "It was a special feeling. We'd won. Gone through hell, but we'd done it."

They'd do it again in the NLCS, winning Games 6 and 7 to oust the Pirates. They nearly did it again in the World Series, only to lose Game 6 on an 12th-inning Kirby Puckett homer, then the magnificent 10-inning Game 7. Smoltz matched his boyhood idol, Jack Morris, that night with 7⅓ scoreless innings before the Twins scored off Alejandro Pena in the 10th to win 1–0.

Smoltz was crestfallen that night. Much later, he said, "To go from worst to first, then have the chance to go to the World Series? Wow! We played in some of the greatest games ever. Ever. Ever. How can there be a better game than the seventh game of the '91 Series?"

"Did it matter we lost? Sure," Olson said. "Did I feel bad about losing? Absolutely not. It was a once-in-a-lifetime experience. And every day, I still think about it."

"I really believe that '91 brought Atlanta closer together," said Terry Pendleton, now a Braves coach. "It brought those outside the city and inside together. I really believe it brought the races together. It didn't matter where you were from or what kind of job you had. Whether you were young or old, black or white, it was special for everyone."

It remains so to this day, and always will.

6 "Thanks, Bobby!"

That's how the big banner read, the one hanging in front of the Chop House all season long. That's the name of a website—www.thanksbobby.com—and Facebook page that got far more hits than the Braves did last year. And that's essentially what the 2010 baseball season was: a prolonged good-bye and a thank you to Bobby Cox from Atlanta, Braves fans everywhere, and all of Major League Baseball.

You know the essentials: fourth-winningest manager of all time, with 2,504 victories. An unparalleled 14 consecutive division

During Bobby Cox's quarter-century with the Braves, he led the team to a run of 14 straight division titles beginning in 1991, including the 1995 World Series title.

titles from 1991 to 2005. Five National League pennants, one World Series championship (1995). A total of 158 regular season ejections and three more in the playoffs for a record 161. That's one game shy of a full season's worth of heave-hoes for Coxie. Or as ESPN's Stan Verrett said, "He's been ejected more times than a cassette tape."

You know how it all ended: the injury-riddled Braves clinching the NL wild-card on the last day of the regular season to give their beloved manager one more October. This, a day after Bobby Cox Day, when some 75 former Braves who played for Cox came in from all around the country to honor him in a spectacular, packed-house tribute. The next day, after staving off the Phillies 8–7, and once San Diego was eliminated, Cox returned to the field, and his players joyously carried him aloft on their shoulders.

You know how the NLDS panned out. It didn't. Not for poor Brooks Conrad and not, alas, for No. 6. That's Cox's number—and the reason this item is No. 6 on this list—which will surely be retired by the Braves, whether before or after he's inducted into Cooperstown.

You saw how Cox, trying to compose himself in the clubhouse, came back onto the field to wave good-bye to the thousands still chanting, "Bob-by! Bob-by!" And how the San Francisco Giants, celebrating their advance to the NLCS, stopped and applauded for Bobby Cox. In a postgame press conference, Cox began to break down and had to stop speaking, biting his lip. One of the game's greatest managers had managed his last.

How will we remember him? Let's let those who knew him best do that, beginning with that wonderful Saturday ceremony, emceed by Braves' longtime former broadcaster Pete Van Wieren:

"He changed the baseball culture in Atlanta forever.... Hundreds of players passed through here, and only one manager.... Bobby, I know you're not real proud of that record [most ejections in baseball history]. But we are." A crowd of 54,296 roared.

"I've been trying to make you proud for 20 years," said the injured Chipper Jones, who leaned over and whispered, "I love you," and brought a tear to his manager's eye.

"You never heard a player who was traded to Atlanta say, 'Oh, I don't want to go there and play for him,'" said team president John Schuerholz, who was the general manager throughout that 14-season title run. "Bobby, you are truly the best ever, a gift and a blessing to us all."

"Looking back on all you've accomplished, it's hard to believe I let you go," said Ted Turner, who, as a young, naïve owner fired Cox in 1981. Fortunately, Cox came down from his GM's office to resume managing in mid-1990. "The greatest manager in baseball history," Turner said in his end-of-the-season video tribute.

You won't get any argument from these people about that—a series of first-person tributes to Cox, compiled by *Atlanta Journal-Constitution* Braves writers Carroll Rogers and David O'Brien.

Terry Pendleton: "I always said he has more patience than grandma.... He just believes in his players. If you're his, you're his."

Brian McCann: "If you're young and you make a mistake, he doesn't bury you. He doesn't call you out in the paper, he doesn't call you out in front of teammates.... I get to say I played for the best manager of all time, or one of the best."

John Holland, visiting clubhouse manager: "You can't count the number of times I've been in here [with opposing players], and they can hear Bobby on the television—'Come on, now,'—cheering, rah-rah from the dugout. And the people who know what he's about, they say, 'I'd like to hear more of that. I'd like to be in that dugout.'"

Tom Glavine: "After a game in Pittsburgh, there might have been a ball that was dropped because nobody called it, and he came in after the game, and everybody is getting undressed and getting ready to eat, and he comes out of his office and just tips the table over with all the food on it, like, 'All right, none of you guys are even trying.' When he did stuff like that, it went a long way and people took notice.

"You knew you didn't want to piss him off. At the same time, you knew it took a lot to do that. But more than anything else, you didn't want to feel like you let him down."

Bobby Dews, former Braves coach: "He makes it so that everybody on the ballclub, top to bottom, feels important. I don't know how you do that. If I knew, I'd be a good manager. He's a great manager."

Fredi Gonzalez, once Cox's third-base coach, now his successor: "I always came out during media time on the road. It was either my first year or second when Kelly Johnson [was struggling], and Bobby told the media he reminded him of Stan Musial. I almost spilled the coffee.

"Stan Musial, skipper? Kelly was so bad, like he'd never swung a bat in his life. Then all of sudden it was like he was hitting off a tee. Whether Kelly read it or one of the writers went over and said, 'Bobby [says] you remind him of Stan Musial,' or it was just coincidence. He went on to win Player of the Week; he just completely went off. You couldn't get him out. The old gray fox."

Umpire Dan Iassogna: "The most difficult managers to work with are the guys who pat you on the back, and they've got the knife in the other hand. Bobby is not like that. He will protect his players at all times. What a lot of people don't realize, he gets thrown out of a lot of games, but his players don't....

"I've thrown him out one time. It was a balk call in Montreal. I was going up and down, kind of like a Triple A player going between Triple A and the big leagues. John Burkett was pitching. He started and stopped and threw to first and picked off the guy, and I called a balk. Bobby yelled from the dugout, 'Go back to [expletive] Double A.' So I ran him. And he came out; we had a little bit of an argument. And then he left. It was the only time I ever ran him. That was in 2001....

"I didn't get hired [full-time] until 2004. He was very typical Bobby. The hat comes off, goes back on, hat comes off, goes back on. He screamed a little bit, and I yelled at him. But as a young umpire, there are certain managers you don't feel like you've made it to the big leagues until you've had a situation with him. Throwing Bobby Cox out of a game, you know you are absolutely in the big leagues. The nice thing was, the next day was a brand new day with him. After the game, in the tunnel, he's the friendliest guy you've ever met in your life. He's like your grandfather."

Jeff Francoeur, once a Braves rookie, now with Kansas City: "In '06, when I got off to that awful start, I remember Bobby calling me into his office and telling me, 'You're going to play right field for me every day for the rest of this year. Just go out there, relax, and have fun.' For him to say that meant the world to me.

"Probably the greatest story was when I got tossed [that year] out in San Diego right after the All-Star break. I'll never forget it. I got tossed, and Bobby got tossed, and we come in and I'm like, 'What do I do now?' He said, 'Go have a couple of cold beers and get in the tub or something and relax. And then you'll probably have to write a $500 check. Or you can do what I do: write a $10,000 one and tell them when it runs out, let me know.'"

Leo Mazzone: "Being by his side in the dugout for 16 years, every single game was as good as it gets for a pitching coach. It don't get any better than that. It was a privilege to be by his side for that many years....

"I wish I could do it again. It went too fast. [Mazzone paused, all choked up]. It flew by. But I had the opportunity to be the pitching coach for one of the greatest individuals I've ever met."

Could Cox have won more than one World Series? Absolutely. Should he have? Sure. Even Tom Glavine admits the Braves blew one in 1996. Everyone knows that.

But Glavine realizes this: "I know it's real easy for people on the outside to criticize Bobby, to blame Bobby that we didn't win more World Series. What I always found curious, when we were winning division after division, and winning 100 games every year, you'd always hear the same comments from people on talk radio or in the newspaper: 'Geez, how hard is it for Bobby, look at the lineup he's throwing out there every day. Then you throw in Maddux and Smoltz and Glavine and Avery, how hard is it?' When we get to the postseason and throw the same lineup out there and don't win, somehow that was Bobby's fault."

No. Tom Glavine is grateful for those seasons in the sun. And thankful for Bobby.

7 Spahn

It was 102 degrees in the midday sun that August 2003 afternoon in Broken Arrow, Oklahoma. Felt like it, too, to Warren Spahn, once he'd slowly made his way to the back door and gingerly stepped outside. On the grass, baseball's winningest left-handed pitcher—and, many still insist, its greatest—was handed a baseball by a photographer. A prop to enhance a photo op.

The great Spahn, then 82 and in failing health, held the ball in his left hand. He gripped it the way he always had, with his now-wrinkled left thumb and his index and middle fingers. Looking at the ball, Spahn said in a whisper, "Damn thing's heavy."

An official baseball, according to the rules of the game, "Shall not weigh less than five nor more than 5¼ ounces." Spahn studied the ball for a moment, smiled and said, "I'm glad I don't have to make my living with this now."

But, oh, what a living he made, what a legacy he created by throwing a baseball.

Pitching for the Braves in Boston and Milwaukee for 19 of his 20 seasons, Spahn won 363 games, the most of any lefty. He's fifth on the all-time list behind Cy Young (511), Walter Johnson (416), and Christy Mathewson and Grover Cleveland Alexander (373 apiece). He also won a Purple Heart during World War II. He threw 63 career shutouts and 382 complete games. He had 13 20-win seasons, including six consecutive from 1956 to 1961. The 1957 Cy Young Award winner in Milwaukee's only world championship season, Spahn was the runner-up in 1958, '60, and '61.

He threw a no-hitter at age 39 against Philadelphia on September 16, 1960. The next April, six starts later, the 40-year-old Spahn threw another no-no against San Francisco. Yet his most incredible start came on July 2, 1963, at age 42.

For 15 scoreless innings, Spahn matched the Giants' young Juan Marichal zero for zero. But in the 16th, Spahn threw a screwball that didn't screw. It was his 201st pitch—yes, 201—and Willie Mays parked it for a game-winning solo homer.

"It became rhythmic that one out followed another," Spahn told me that summer day in 2003. "I thought I had to get ahead of Mays, and I hung that screwball. Afterward, I was beat. Oh, man. Gangrene set in after I got in the clubhouse. Marichal was 25 and said the only reason he stayed in was because he didn't want an old guy to beat him.

"Today, everybody's afraid they're gonna hurt a guy's arm," he continued. "A guy gets a hangnail, and [he's] out for a week. I had aches and pains, but I never had an arm I couldn't throw with. Now, guys are on the disabled list forever. I don't think we even had a disabled list."

A large part of Spahn's longevity was his delivery. The full windup and especially the incomparable leg kick his father taught

Milwaukee Braves hurler Warren Spahn rears back to fire one from the mound early in an October 5, 1958, World Series game at Yankee Stadium. The Braves won the game 3–0 to take the lead in series play, but New York would win three straight games to take the series 4–3.

him in Buffalo, New York. "I wasn't a big guy—175, 180 pounds," said the 6′ Spahn. "My dad said to get all the momentum you could. So I kept my weight back, transferred it from my back leg to my front leg, and I think that's why I didn't hurt my arm. I see some guys pitch now and think, 'Gad!'"

Somewhere, Spahn was surely smiling while watching Tim Lincecum in the 2010 playoffs and World Series. The undersized Giants right-hander, himself a two-time Cy Young Award winner, doesn't have a sky-high Spahnian leg kick. But "the Freak" uses his distinctive, almost contorted delivery to create torque, bring heat, and confound hitters.

Spahn's majestic leg kick was captured perfectly by Oklahoma sculptor Shan Gray. He created the nine-foot bronze statue of Spahn that was unveiled at the 2003 Braves Hall of Fame Luncheon and Induction. That was due to the devotion of Gary Caruso, a lifetime Spahn acolyte, one-time Atlanta newspaperman, and the publisher of *Chop Talk*, the Braves' fan magazine. It was Caruso who raised the funds for the sculpture. It was Spahn—who died four months later—who raised his right leg toward the sky and the art of pitching to new heights. A legacy now on permanent display at Turner Field's Monument Grove.

8 Long Ball, Literally

The Braves are the longest continuously operating franchise in Major League Baseball. You could look it up—simply look up and out at a portion of the right field wall in Turner Field, just to the left (and in front) of the Braves bullpen. The words of the franchise are written on the outfield wall: The Longest Continuously Operating Franchise in Major League Baseball.

Others may have opened for business before the Braves, most notably the Cincinnati Reds, but the team that dawned as the Boston Red Stockings has been in business every season since 1871.

Consistency, thy name is Red Stockings...or simply Reds, as the club came to be known. On January 20, 1871, the first meeting of the Boston Red Stockings Club was held at the Parker House in Boston. The club was incorporated for $15,000, with a baseball-mad businessman named Ivers Whitney Adams as president. The Red Stockings were one of 10 charter members of the new National Association of Professional Base Ball Players. Membership fee: $10.

Only the Red Stockings played continuously through all five years of the National Association before joining its successor, the National League, in 1876. The Boston franchise has fielded a team every season since 1871. From 1872 to 1875, they finished in first place each year, going a combined 205–50. Star pitcher Al Spalding, who would later make his fortune in sporting goods, won 185 of those 205 victories. In 1875—the year the catcher's mask was introduced—Boston won 71 of 79 games, including all 37 at home.

At various times, the club was called the Doves, the Rustlers, the Bees, and, eventually, the Braves. In 1883 they became known as the Beaneaters, a name concocted by some Boston sportswriters for the city's fondness for baked beans.

"I'm a bean-eater, too," proclaimed Mike "King" Kelly, one of baseball's earliest and biggest stars. He'd been sold from the Chicago White Stockings to Boston for the ungodly sum of $10,000 and commanded a $5,000 salary, a fortune in those days. The Babe Ruth of his time, Kelly caroused, loved the nightlife, drank, often played while hungover, and was the game's first great superstar. Teammate Hugh Duffy, who played with Honus Wagner and Napoleon Lajoie, called Kelly "the greatest player ever to put on a uniform."

After the 1875 season, William A. Hulbert, owner of the Chicago White Stockings, led a movement to establish a new professional league. He convinced the presidents of seven other teams—including Boston's Nathaniel T. Apollonio—to join in creating the National League of Professional Base Ball Clubs. Annual membership fee: $100. The original eight cities in the

National League: Boston, Philadelphia, Chicago, Cincinnati, New York, St. Louis, Hartford, and Louisville.

Boston played in the first game in National League history on April 22, 1876, at Philadelphia. The Red Stockings scored twice in the top of the ninth inning to beat the Athletics 6–5. Boston center fielder Jim O'Rourke got the first hit in National League annals, a single. Catcher Tim McGinley scored the first NL run on right fielder Jack Manning's sacrifice fly. Some 3,000 people paid the 50¢ admission to catch all the action at the ballground at 25th Street and Jefferson.

From 1890 to 1901, under manager Frank Selee, the Beaneaters won five National League pennants. The 1898 champs were led by pitcher Kid Nichols, who won 31 games; third baseman Jimmy Collins, who led the NL with 15 homers; and outfielder Billy Hamilton, who hit .369 and stole 54 bases. But in 1901 the American League was formed, which included the Boston Somersets. Several Beaneaters left for the AL, including Jimmy Collins, who became manager of the Somersets, which became Boston's fan favorites. Although the Beaneaters slashed admission in half to 25¢ to match the Somersets' ticket price, they drew about 200,000 fewer fans.

A fifth-place finish cost Selee his job and began an awful stretch from 1902 to 1913 in which Boston finished a collective 465 games under .500. Not even a name change helped. When the Dovey Brothers bought the team in 1907, they changed the nickname to the Doves, a perfectly peaceful, pacifist name for a club that would suffer four straight 100-loss seasons from 1909 to 1912.

By then, the Doveys had sold the team following the 1910 season. William Russell, the new owner, renamed the club the Rustlers. He died the following off-season, but not before the legendary Cy Young ended his career as a Boston Rustler. On September 22 the 44-year-old Young beat Pittsburgh 1–0 for his 511th and final career victory.

Another ownership change resulted in yet another nickname in 1912: the Braves. In 1914 they would become "the Miracle Braves."

And after controversial moves to Milwaukee in 1953, then Atlanta in 1966, the Braves remain the longest continuously operating franchise in Major League Baseball.

You could look it up.

9 Chipper

When the city fathers of DeLand, Florida, the hometown of Larry Wayne Jones Jr., finally and fully get around to honoring their most famous native son, perhaps they should think outside the box—the left-hand batter's box, where Chipper Jones did most of his damage. Even as a boy, Jones was learning to master the art of switch-hitting in his backyard.

His father, Larry Sr., was pitching to his namesake, and Chipper was ripping it: right-handed, left-handed, either side, depending on which big-league lineup he was mimicking that day. Larry Sr., once a pretty fair player himself and then a college baseball coach at Stetson University, finally took a breather. He walked inside and told his wife, Lynn, "I can't get him out."

Major League Baseball has been saying that for nearly two decades now.

In the pantheon of switch-hitters, a small and very select group in baseball, Chipper Jones is on the medal stand. He's one of the three best switch-hitters of all time. There's Mickey Mantle, of course, not only the gold standard for switch-hitters but one of the game's all-time, all-around greats. There's Eddie Murray, the dour but redoubtable Baltimore Oriole, second on the career switch-hitting home run list, with 504 to Mantle's 536. And in third, with 436 and counting, is Chipper Jones. A chip off the old man's block and as pure an all-around hitter as baseball has seen in years.

With 436 home runs to date, Chipper Jones is one of the three best switch-hitters in baseball history.

Let's do the numbers: a .306 career average and 1,491 RBIs to augment those 436 homers. A World Series ring in 1995, a six-time National League All-Star, two Silver Sluggers and, most impressively, a 1999 NL Most Valuable Player season. Jones batted .319 that year, hit a career-high 45 homers, and drove in 110 runs in leading the Atlanta Braves back to the World Series.

Nine years later, at the age of 36, the third baseman flirted with .400 for much of the season before winning the NL batting crown with a .364 average. At 36, he was the oldest switch-hitter ever to win a batting title, his .364 finishing one percentage point behind Mantle's record .365 average. Jones also had an on-base percentage of .470 that year and hit an ungodly .399 in Turner Field.

Let's do more numbers: his .306 career average is second all-time among switch-hitters to Hall of Famer Frankie Frisch (.316). Jones is the only switch-hitter in baseball history with a career average of .300 or better and at least 400 home runs. His '99 MVP campaign was epic. How so? He became the first player to hit over .300 (.319) with 40 or more homers (45) and 40 or more doubles (41) while drawing 100 or more walks (126), driving in 100 or more runs (110), scoring at least 100 runs (116), and stealing 20 or more bases (25). Got all that? That's hitting.

Fast forward to August 10, 2010. In a game in Houston, Jones tore the ACL in his left knee, ending his season. He leaped to make an acrobatic throw, then landed awkwardly on his left leg. It was the same ACL he tore in 1994, causing him to miss what would have been his rookie season in Atlanta.

In an August 13 press conference Jones said, "I don't want the fans' final image of me to be one of me hurt on the field."

So in part inspired by the Braves' spirited run to the NL wild-card and the postseason, Jones began rehabbing his knee over the winter. He hoped to come back. April 24, 2011, marks his 39th birthday. He has more money than he'll ever need, a wife and four kids, and owns a Texas-sized ranch in Texas where people—including the owner—enjoy deer-hunting.

Whatever Jones decides, what DeLand should do is this: commission and erect a statue of Chipper right downtown. Of two Chippers, actually. One standing in the right-hand batter's box, the other in the left. Both with bat cocked, prepared to unload on the next pitch from the poor guy on the mound. Forget the extra expense of two Chippers. How cool would that be? As cool as watching Chipper Jones at work in either batter's box once again.

10 "Just Get Me One!"

Call it what it was that night and remains so to this day: the best game ever pitched in franchise history. It wasn't just Tom Glavine's excellence that October evening, but the game's significance and the opposition's potency. Those '95 Cleveland Indians? Those boppers could hit.

"My defining game," Glavine calls Game 6 of the 1995 World Series. "The greatest game I pitched." Which is saying something for the guy who won two National League Cy Young Awards and 305 games and is a sure-fire, first-ballot lock for the Baseball Hall of Fame.

"I guess from a pitching standpoint, statistically, it's as good or maybe better than any game I've ever had," Glavine once said. "But when you combine the whole package—what the game meant, and what we'd all gone through—that's as good as it gets. To pitch that game, in that situation, that's the greatest thing I could have asked for."

By the mid-'90s, Glavine had established himself as one of the two best left-handers in baseball. Yet unlike Randy Johnson, the overpowering, 6′11″ "Big Unit," Glavine was a crafty little lefty who changed speeds, lived on the outside corner of the plate, and thrived with his circle change-up. Asked once what nickname he might give himself, Glavine told Atlanta writer Mark Bradley, "The little twerp?"

Having edged Cleveland 4–3 in Game 2, then having seen Steve Avery beat the Indians in Game 4 for a 3–1 series advantage, Glavine hoped that opening-game winner Greg Maddux would close out Cleveland in Game 5. Instead, the Indians' 5–4 victory sent the series back to Atlanta.

"When you have an opportunity to win it all, you want to win it and put it to bed," said Glavine, who no longer found himself in baseball limbo. "You go through the disappointment of not winning the series. You have to start gearing up to pitch a game you hoped you wouldn't have to pitch.

"It really kind of hit me when we flew back from Cleveland to Atlanta and we landed. And I realized I had to pitch," he continued. "I looked at it as a great opportunity, though, not a disappointment.

Tom Glavine fires one home during the first inning of Game 6 of the 1995 World Series with the Cleveland Indians in Atlanta. Glavine calls that night his "defining game."

It was the game that helped provide the championship we all wanted desperately."

This, after losing 1–0 to Minnesota and Jack Morris in 10 innings in a magnificent Game 7 of the 1991 World Series. And then to Toronto in Game 6 of the '92 Fall Classic. And then to Philadelphia in the '93 NLCS. Critics were starting to call the

Braves "the Buffalo Bills of baseball." The Braves were not amused. But Glavine was enthused about Game 6.

"I started to embrace the opportunity," he recalled. Especially when he took the mound in Atlanta-Fulton County Stadium. "I knew I had good stuff warming up in the bullpen," Glavine said. "But for me, so many times, well, you just don't know. I warmed up well that night. Everything was crisp. You try to carry everything over, from the bullpen warm-up to the game's first pitch."

But there are no guarantees, not even for a Tom Glavine. Some actors have notorious opening-night jitters. Glavine often had first-inning futility. "The first inning for me has always been my Achilles heel," he said. "But when I got through the first inning that night, I thought, *Okay, that's the same stuff I had in the bullpen. Here we go.*"

Not so fast. No assumptions, not against a lineup featuring six .300 hitters. The Indians led the American League that season with 207 homers, including 50 from Albert Belle.

"I never envisioned throwing a one-hitter," Glavine said. "That's the most dangerous, most-balanced lineup I ever faced. Even their seventh-place hitter, Jim Thome, had 25 home runs. But as each inning went on, and I got through it and I hadn't given up a hit yet, everything was snowballing. I got more and more confident."

But after Glavine gave up a bloop single to catcher Tony Pena, the No. 8 hitter, in the top half of the sixth inning for Cleveland's first and only hit.

"It was first time I'd faced any kind of adversity that night, but I got through it," Glavine said to me. "The no-hitter was certainly out there, but I didn't anticipate it. In that setting, [losing a no-hitter] was probably a relief. I didn't have to worry about it. I was kind of feeling good about myself. I came into the dugout after Pena's hit, and I remember screaming, 'Just get me one! 'Cause they're not getting any runs tonight!'

"As a pitcher, you sometimes say things to rally the troops," he said. "It just so happened it worked that time. David hit the home run." In the bottom half of the inning David Justice homered off Indians reliever Jim Poole to give the Braves a 1–0 lead. It was all Glavine needed.

Two innings later Glavine left, having thrown eight scoreless innings. He'd walked three men—Belle twice—and struck out eight Indians. He'd thrown 109 pitches but knew he was through. Enter closer Mark Wohlers, who worked a 1-2-3 ninth. The two Braves had thrown the first combined one-hitter in World Series history. They'd faced just 30 batters—three over the minimum. It was Cleveland's first 1–0 loss since 1992—556 games ago.

A year after many Braves fans began booing Glavine as the face and voice of the 1994 players strike—and some continued through the strike-shortened, 144-game '95 season—a capacity crowd of 51,875 cheered him boisterously that Saturday night. Atlanta finally had its first World Series title courtesy of Tom Glavine, and the best game ever pitched in franchise history.

11 The Fire

It was a fire sale, inadvertently so, yet in the most literal and alarming sense of the term.

On July 18, 1993, Braves general manager John Schuerholz, baseball's best GM, pulled off a three-for-one coup. Before the trading deadline, he acquired slugging first baseman Fred McGriff from San Diego for three minor league prospects. Schuerholz knew the cash-poor, salary-dumping Padres coveted Melvin Nieves, an outfielder in Atlanta's farm system. He knew McGriff's $4.25

million salary was no problem. What Schuerholz couldn't know was exactly how McGriff's arrival would ignite the Braves.

On July 20, the "Crime Dog" walked into Atlanta-Fulton County Stadium, said hello to familiar faces in the clubhouse, and introduced himself to other new teammates. Suddenly, a team security guard rushed in and shouted, "Fire! Fire! There's a fire upstairs. Everybody get out on the field!"

An introductory press conference for McGriff was scheduled for 4:00 PM in the ballpark's press lounge before that night's 7:40 game against the St. Louis Cardinals. McGriff was running a little late, so the press conference was switched to the clubhouse. Up in the radio booth, broadcasters Skip Caray and Pete Van Wieren were talking about the trade and whether it would help Atlanta catch the rampaging Giants in the NL West.

Shortly before 6:00, Skip and Pete noticed some smoke coming from the WSB-AM radio hospitality suite, three booths away. The hors d'oeuvres, as usual, were being heated by Sterno burners. Apparently, it turned out, part of a paper tablecloth was blown by a breeze into one of the burners.

The smoke thickened. The plot, too. Something was burning. Looking through glass dividers, Van Wieren and Caray saw flames in the hospitality suite. A stadium worker carrying a fire extinguisher walked along the front edge of the press box toward the fire. Good luck with that. All this as the Braves assembled on the field for batting practice.

Writing down the starting lineups in their scorebooks, the broadcasters quickly left the press lounge. The fire was now two booths away, raging. With thick black smoke billowing through the press lounge, Skip and Pete suddenly heard a tremendous *boom!* They later learned it was a steel beam above the drop ceiling in the press box area exploding from intense heat.

Down on the field, the scene was surreal, something out of *The Towering Inferno*. Players, club officials, and media looked up at the radio booth now engulfed in flames, as was most of the press box. Firefighters had arrived to fight the blaze. The stadium would be evacuated. Batting practice was put on hold.

But not before Jeff Blauser and Mark Lemke posed for one of the most memorable photos in franchise history. It was taken by legendary team photographer Walter Victor. Near home plate, Blauser and the Lemmer stood smiling, holding their bats, arms around each other's shoulder as an inferno blazed high overhead.

Nearby, team owner Ted Turner told local TV sportscaster Jeff Hullinger, "Put the fire out, we'll play. Hopefully, the Braves will get this hot."

They played that evening, starting about 90 minutes late. Once the fire was brought under control, radio and TV engineers rigged up impromptu broadcast facilities in a club-level seating area beyond the charred area. A couple thousand seats were roped off below the press box for the fans' safety. At 9:00 the game began, and Atlanta warmly welcomed Fred McGriff. He responded in kind.

Down 5–0 early, the Braves rallied for five runs of their own in the sixth inning to win 8–5. The big blast in the sixth? McGriff's two-run homer. "Like lightning striking," Terry Pendleton said, no pun intended. Still nine games behind surging San Francisco, the Crime Dog and the Braves would finally catch the Giants to win the Last Great Pennant Race. For now, the heat was on.

12 Game 161 in '91

It was an unscheduled, unintentional doubleheader of sorts. The second game, played nearly 2,500 miles away, lasted less than an

Catcher Greg Olson jumps into the arms of pitcher John Smoltz as the Braves celebrate their division-clinching NL West victory in 1991.

inning back in Atlanta, yet long enough to last a lifetime for those who watched it. Right up there on the center-field video screen.

On Saturday, October 5, 1991, more than 45,000 fans filled Atlanta-Fulton County Stadium. The mood was jubilant and expectant, justifiably so. The surging Braves held a one-game lead over the Dodgers in the National League West with two games to play. A victory over Houston would clinch at least a tie for the division title. That, coupled with a Dodgers loss on the Left Coast would...

Well, no one in Atlanta wanted to get ahead of themselves, even in this most unbelievable of seasons.

The easy part was the Braves' 5–2 win over the Astros. It was Atlanta's eighth consecutive victory and guaranteed, at worst, a one-game playoff for the NL West crown. There are two lasting images from the grand celebration that ensued:

Catcher Greg Olson, pulling off his mask, racing toward the mound and leaping into winning pitcher John Smoltz's embrace. That was Atlanta's answer to Yogi Berra's leap into Don Larsen's arms after Larsen's perfect game in the 1956 World Series.

And then, a short while later, there was manager Bobby Cox, standing on the mound, tinted glasses on, gazing up at the video screen's confirmation.

Here's Pete Van Wieren's call of the final out in Atlanta: "One ball, two strikes. The stretch by Smoltz, the pitch to Cedeno...high fly ball, right field. It's fairly deep. Back goes Justice...he's got it! And the magic number for Atlanta is down to one!"

Van Wieren wasn't even supposed to work that ninth inning. Neither was his longtime, on-air partner Skip Caray, who was out of town, preparing to call a football game for TNT. Skip's oldest son, Chip, was supposed to call the historic ninth. Instead, he told his audience, "There's a couple of guys [Pete and Skip] who have waited nearly 10 years for this [since Atlanta's 1982 NL West title]. So it's only apropos as we go to the top of the ninth...here's Pete."

With that, Chip Caray stood up and walked out of the broadcast booth.

"That was very classy of him to let me call that ninth inning," Van Wieren would say years later. "And it's something I'll always appreciate."

Now, Van Wieren and everyone else in the ballpark turned their attention to the video screen. The Giants were accommodating Atlanta, shutting out their hated rivals, the Dodgers. TBS had stayed on the air to put up that game on the big board. And when Eddie Murray grounded out to Giants second baseman Robby Thompson, it was over. Again, Van Wieren: "The Braves are the National League West champions! The San Francisco Giants have just beaten the Los Angeles Dodgers 4–0! Let the celebration begin, Atlanta!"

It was already in full swing. The look on Bobby Cox's face was almost beatific. He'd been fired in 1981, in his first go-round as Braves manager, before returning as the general manager who rebuilt the organization and then resumed managing in mid-1990. All about Cox, his players went nuts, as players are wont to do.

"We shook up the world!" Ron Gant yelled in a delirious clubhouse. The clincher was Atlanta's eighth straight victory. After the All-Star break, the Braves had gone 55–28, winning 21 of their last 29 games. They set Atlanta records with 94 wins and a season attendance of 2,140,217. And that memorable Saturday, they set Atlanta afire with an unexpected two-for-one celebration of their Braves.

13 The Key? TP

He set the tone. He did so with his glove and bat, his wise words and follow-me manner. Of the myriad changes the Atlanta Braves made in the winter of 1990, the most important was the acquisition of a 29-year-old third baseman coming off the worst season of his career. TP.

"The greatest free-agent signing in history," then Braves president Stan Kasten later called the signing of Terry Pendleton. In a whirlwind of off-season change, Pendleton quickly became change you could believe in.

Bobby Cox was back in his spikes full-time now, managing. The new general manager, John Schuerholz, came in from Kansas City with a plan: shore up the National League's worst infield in every sense. Bring in first baseman Sid Bream from Pittsburgh; also Rafael Belliard, a little Pirates shortstop nicknamed "Pac-Man" for his propensity to eat up ground balls. Import groundskeeper Ed Mangan to turn a rock-hard playing surface into a big-league infield to aid all those fine young pitching arms.

And finally, let TP show the way.

Not everyone was a believer, however. Not initially. Pendleton was coming off the worst year of his career. He hit .230 for St. Louis with six home runs and 58 RBIs. The Yankees were his only other suitor, even offering more money. Pendleton signed with the Braves largely because he felt his family would be more comfortable living in Atlanta. He was met with a relative civic yawn, while at least one new teammate was skeptical.

"Here's a guy who St. Louis was throwing away," Mark Lemke later said. "Todd Zeile was playing third base for them, and I'm thinking, *We're signing this guy for four years? What are we doing?*"

Outfoxing everyone, that's what. "You've got to see him every day," Lemke's uncle, who lived in St. Louis, told him. "You're going to love Pendleton."

By May, everyone did in Atlanta, if not around the league. TP was rejuvenated and reborn as a Brave. "The anchor of our team," Schuerholz called him. The switch-hitter became the first Brave to lead the NL in both average and hits (187) since Ralph Garr in 1974.

"I'd have to put '91 at the top, as my most satisfying season," said Pendleton, "and not because of my accolades." He was honored

Terry Pendleton watches his solo home run in the third inning of Game 4 of the 1991 World Series in Atlanta against the Minnesota Twins. He won the NL's MVP and batting title that year.

as the National League's Most Valuable Player and its Comeback Player of the Year. Pendleton won the NL batting crown with a .319 average, hitting 22 homers and driving in 86 runs.

He drove the young Braves, too, to unexpected places and heights. When they dropped five of seven games to the Dodgers to fall 9½ games back at the All-Star break, Pendleton paced in the visitors dugout at Dodger Stadium, repeating, "This isn't over. This isn't over."

The Braves, with a rejuvenated John Smoltz on the mound and TP in everyone's ear, won seven of eight while L.A. dropped seven straight. The division was a two-horse race again, and the love affair between Atlanta and its ballclub was at an all-time, ear-shattering high.

"I remember getting into the batter's box one night after Sid Bream hit a grand slam," Pendleton recalled. "I had to step out. I couldn't think; my concentration's gone. My ears were just ringing from the crowd noise—and I wore a double-flapped helmet."

"He showed the rest of the team how to act in a pennant race," said second baseman Jeff Treadway, who was lost to an injury in September and gave way to Lemke. Pendleton hit .353 in his last 28 games. His homer beat San Diego 1–0 in the September 11, three-man no-hitter thrown by Kent Mercker, Mark Wohlers, and Alejandro Pena. In the World Series Pendleton hit .367 in a true Fall Classic. If only Lonnie Smith had scored on TP's double in the eighth inning of a scoreless Game 7. When Minnesota finally won 1–0 in the 10th, he came back out of the clubhouse to shake the Twins' hands.

Pendleton hit .311 the next year, with 21 homers, 199 hits, and 105 RBIs, finishing second in that MVP balloting. After a slow April in '93, he sizzled and helped Atlanta win the Last Great Pennant Race, if not the NLCS.

He was a Florida Marlin in 1995 when the Braves finally won the World Series. Back with Atlanta in '96, TP got just nine at-bats as the Braves blew that World Series against the Yankees. He retired in '99 but returned as the Braves' hitting coach in 2002, a position he held until the end of the 2010 season. He's now the club's first-base coach. He's forever TP, the guy who showed the way in 1991.

"Terry is probably the greatest baseball player I've ever played with," Lemke said 15 years after that transformational season. "I always tell Chipper [Jones] he's the most talented player I ever played with. But on and off the field, in the clubhouse, as a mentor, a leader, Terry's the greatest."

14 The Only Boston, Milwaukee, and Atlanta Brave

That would be the one and only Eddie Mathews, a singular talent and the only man in franchise history to play for the Braves in each of the three cities in which the club was based. Yet that was hardly his lone mark of distinction on his sport.

Mathews was a fine-fielding, slugging third baseman and *Sports Illustrated*'s very first cover boy who later managed the Atlanta Braves and was eventually enshrined in the Baseball Hall of Fame. He was also possessed of one of the sweetest swings the game has ever seen. Says who? Said none other than Ty Cobb.

"I've seen three or four perfect swings in my time," the legendary Georgia Peach proclaimed after watching the young Mathews in spring training one year. "This lad has one of them."

In 1952, the team's last season in Boston, the rookie Mathews became the starting third baseman. He held that role for 15 consecutive seasons, including 1966, when the club moved to Atlanta. But it was during his 13 sweet summers in Milwaukee that Mathews made his indelible mark on baseball.

He belted 512 home runs, the most by a third baseman in baseball history until Mike Schmidt arrived in Philadelphia. Of those 512, 493 came in a Braves uniform, with 47 coming in 1953, the Braves' first season in Milwaukee. Those 47 led the National League and were tied with Hank Aaron for the most homers in a season by a Brave until Andruw Jones hit 51 in 2005. Those 47 homers began a streak of nine consecutive seasons in which Mathews hit at least 31, including four with 40 or more.

With Aaron, Mathews formed the most prolific home run hitting duo in baseball history. They hit 863 homers as teammates, more than the Giants' Willie Mays and Willie McCovey (800), more even than the New York Yankees' immortal Babe Ruth and Lou Gehrig (772). In Milwaukee, Aaron and Mathews were the two-headed toast of the town throughout their time together in Sudsville. But it was Mathews, young, handsome, and single, who was Milwaukee's matinee idol—and, at times too often, its nightlife connoisseur.

On August 16, 1954, Eddie Mathews graced the cover of the maiden issue of *Sports Illustrated.* The cover boy was an action figure. The nighttime photo showcased his graceful, powerful left-handed swing as another capacity crowd in Milwaukee County Stadium looked on expectantly. Mathews rarely failed to deliver.

As staggering as Aaron's statistics remain, Mathews' were unquestionably great, too. A nine-time National League All-Star, he twice led the league in homers (those 47 in '53, and with 46 in 1959). In each of those seasons, Mathews finished second in the NL Most Valuable Player voting—first to Brooklyn's Roy Campanella, later to Mr. Cub, Ernie Banks. Yet Mathews was also renowned for his fielding—due, in part, to a desire to out-do every third baseman he faced.

"I wanted to beat him in every department—fielding, hitting, running the bases," Mathews once said. "I played that game all my life, and it kept me on my toes." He led all NL third basemen in assists three times.

Yet Mathews is best remembered for what he did with his bat, not his glove. The Yankees were sufficiently impressed that they walked him eight times in the 1957 World Series—but not, alas, in

Eddie Mathews slugs his 400th major league homer in the eighth inning of the Milwaukee Braves' 5–0 victory over the Philadelphia Phillies, on April 16, 1963. Mathews played for the Braves from 1952 to 1966, spanning the three cities the Braves called home.

the 10th inning of Game 4. Mathews' two-run homer in the bottom of the 10th inning beat the Yanks 7–5 and tied the series at two games apiece. Four days later Lew Burdette beat the Yankees for the third time, 5–0, and Mathews and Milwaukee celebrated the city's first and only World Series title.

In his only season in Atlanta, during the club's 1966 debut, Mathews hit his last 16 home runs in a Braves uniform. In 1967 he was traded to Houston, where he hit his 500th career home run. He did so as an aging first baseman for the Astros in windswept Candlestick Park in San Francisco against the Giants' Juan Marichal. He did so despite striking out in his previous at-bat after an unexpected distraction: a mouse had scampered out from beneath the field boxes, then darted all over the infield and into the outfield before Willie Mays finally shooed it under the center-field fence.

Rodent-free, Mathews homered in his next at-bat off Marichal. He became just the seventh player to reach the 500-homer plateau, joining Babe Ruth, Jimmie Foxx, Ted Williams, Mel Ott, Mickey Mantle, and Mays. Mathews hit three more homers for Houston, then was traded to Detroit, where he hit another six.

Used sparingly by the Tigers in 1968, Mathews still hit three home runs to conclude his career with 512—one more than Ott. He even managed a single and a walk in the Tigers' World Series triumph over St. Louis before retiring.

Mathews returned to Atlanta in 1971 as a coach under manager Luman Harris. When Harris was fired in '72, Mathews succeeded him and managed into the 1974 season. In the first series of that season Mathews planned to sit Hank Aaron for the last two games in Cincinnati so his old teammate could break Babe Ruth's home run record back home in Atlanta. "Right or wrong," Mathews said, "this is my decision." Commissioner Bowie Kuhn, however, forced Mathews to start Aaron in Sunday's game.

Mathews capitulated, Aaron went hitless, then came home and hit No. 715 in Atlanta. Mathews was fired later that season. In 1978 he was inducted into the Baseball Hall of Fame. His No. 41, retired in 1969, is one of seven Braves numbers retired by the club.

When Eddie Mathews died in 2001, he still held franchise records for most RBIs in a season (135), career walks (1,376), and home runs on the road in one season (30, in his 47-homer campaign in 1953). To this day, many Braves fans—particularly older Milwaukee or Wisconsin natives—wonder why there isn't a statue of Mathews out in Monument Grove. What better swing to preserve for posterity than one of the most perfect the game has ever seen?

15 Smoltzie

If, as F. Scott Fitzgerald famously pronounced, "There are no second acts in American lives," well, Scotty never knew Smoltzie. But why stop at second chances? John Smoltz fashioned a novel three-act career, the likes of which the national pastime had never seen and, in all likelihood, won't ever see again.

Smoltz is the only player in Major League Baseball history to compile 200 victories and 150 saves. He's just the second pitcher to record both a 20-victory season and a 50-save season. The first? Hall of Famer Dennis Eckersley, the template for Smoltz's two-role act. But Eck did it the traditional way, moving from the starting rotation to the bullpen, a more conventional switch for an older pitcher.

Smoltz, of course, did nothing conventionally. In part because he was so talented, but also because he was so headstrong and, at times, injury-prone. After sitting out the 2000 season after Tommy John surgery [one of his four elbow surgeries], Smoltz returned to the rotation in 2001. But he reinvented himself later that year as the Braves' closer to help the club win another divisional title.

In 2002 the Michigan kid who grew up playing the accordion—he always had good hands—merely became the closer of all National League closers. In 75 relief appearances Smoltz recorded an NL-record 55 saves. He notched 45 more in '03 and finally another 44 in 2004. That gave him 154 career saves. The 40th of that season, the 150th save of Smoltz's unparalleled career, came on September 21, in a 5–4 win over the Reds in Atlanta. The hometown crowd roared its approval. Three days later, Smoltz became Atlanta's all-time strikeout leader.

John Smoltz pitches in the 1996 All-Star Game in Philadelphia. Smoltz won the Cy Young Award that year and is today one of 16 pitchers in history to record 3,000 strikeouts.

And the following season, unlike Eckersley, the chameleon-like Smoltz went back into the rotation.

Following this? Just checking. Wait. It gets better.

In 2005, at the age of 38, Smoltz made 33 starts and threw 229⅔ innings in going 14–7 with a 3.06 ERA and helping the Braves win their 14th consecutive division title. Two years later, in his last full season in the rotation, Smoltz rewrote the record book. On the night of May 24 he beat his longtime friend and former-teammate-turned-Met Tom Glavine 2–1 for his 200th career victory. Another Turner Field crowd roared its approval, but it was a tough emotional evening for Smoltz. For Glavine, too.

"It's pretty neat," Smoltz said of No. 200. "It's just a number. But it's a nice number....

"There's something special about knowing the other guy is going to battle harder than you or just as hard."

"I know how important to him it is," Glavine said after losing to Smoltz for the third time that season. "And under normal circumstances, I'd be thrilled for him. But on a day like this, if you get what you want, your buddy ends up with a loss."

Uncharacteristically, Smoltz came back out of the dugout at game's end and acknowledged the crowd of 36,660.

"I can't say who I beat for my 200th," Glavine said. "But I'm sure John will remember who he beat for his 200th."

Just as Smoltz will remember pitching the division-clincher in 1991. And the pennant winner in that '91 NLCS. And the magnificent pitching duel he had with Minnesota's Jack Morris in Game 7 of the incomparable 1991 World Series. And, of course, all those moments in his Cy Young season of 1996, when Smoltz went 24–8, struck out 276, won a franchise-record 14 straight decisions, won four more times in the postseason, and, with his victory in the All-Star Game, finished the year with 29 wins. He's one of 16 pitchers in baseball history to reach 3,000 strikeouts.

Now a Braves broadcaster who tells god-awful puns on the air, Smoltz is one of the most philanthropic Atlantans. A staunch advocate for the Atlanta Community Food Bank, he's received baseball's Roberto Clemente Award, the Lou Gehrig Award, and the 2007

Branch Rickey Award. He'll get his own reward in Cooperstown as soon as he's eligible for the Baseball Hall of Fame. His No. 29 will be retired by the Braves, but never forgotten by his fans. Smoltzie's fans.

16 Knucksie

It ended where it all began, where it should have all along. It ended much like the beginning, with not a whole lot of money involved. Phil Niekro, who started out in the Braves organization, thankfully bowed out a Brave, too. Something about his last set of work clothes back in '87 just didn't look right.

"I thought, *I can't leave this game wearing a Toronto shirt,*" Niekro said. "So I went down to the Braves and worked out a deal with them to pitch one last game. Then I signed a contract for $1."

By 1987, Niekro's Hall of Fame career was all over but the accounting. The numbers boggled the mind, nearly as much as Knucksie's knuckleball had flustered batters for years: 318 victories, 268 of them as a Brave from 1964 to 1983. Of his 3,342 strikeouts, 2,912 came in a Braves uniform. He compiled 14 straight seasons with 10 or more victories, including three 20-win seasons. He pitched more than 300 innings four times, including a staggering 342 in 1979. He fluttered a no-hitter against San Diego in 1973.

All this from an Ohio coal miner's son who learned how to grip and throw a knuckleball from his father, Phil Sr., known to all as "Primo." It took awhile, but eventually Junior's dancing knuckler was just like his dad's nickname: primo.

In 1958 a scout at an open tryout held by the Milwaukee Braves noticed that knuckleball. Niekro, who was working in a factory at the time and pitching on weekends against coal-mining

Phil Niekro, seen here pitching in a 1982 NLCS game in St. Louis, is one of the most popular Braves of all time. He played for the team from 1964 to 1983, and returned in 1987 for a single game, retiring as a Brave.

teams, finally accepted a Braves minor league contract in '59 that included a $500 signing bonus.

The Braves would get their money's worth. Niekro was selected to five All-Star Games (four as a Brave), won five Gold Gloves (all as a Brave), and, at the time of his retirement, his 318 wins were 14th all-time. His Atlanta Braves records for games pitched (740), complete games (226), and shutouts (43) will likely never be broken.

But beyond that, Niekro was one of the most popular Atlanta Braves of all time, and remains so to this day. A treasured teammate, too.

"Phil," Bob Horner said one afternoon in upstate New York, "was the greatest teammate you could ever have."

On that August Sunday in 1987, Horner was just one of many who'd come to Cooperstown for Niekro's induction into the Baseball Hall of Fame. Four busloads of folks from his hometown of Lansing had made the trip to Cooperstown. Thirty-five members of the Braves 400 Club, that fan club's true believers, were there for Knucksie. How often does a state governor come to Cooperstown for the festivities? Georgia's Zell Miller was in the house that afternoon. And, of course, Horner, the 1978 NL Rookie of the Year, as well as several other former teammates. They all recalled 1969.

"Probably my best season," said Niekro, originally a reliever who didn't become a part-time starter until 1967, then a full-time member of the rotation in '68, and finally a first-time All-Star in 1969. His 23 victories that season were an Atlanta record until John Smoltz won 24 in 1996. Niekro's 23rd win was especially sweet; it clinched the very first NL West Division title for the Braves. It would be 13 long years before the next one. No matter. Knucksie soldiered on, even from 1975 to 1979, when Atlanta won as many as 70 games just once.

"It's always tough, the losing," Niekro later said. "If I knew guys who weren't trying or were trying to lose, I'd be furious. But I never believed in getting on guys' asses. I knew they were trying. Even when I was a veteran, I wouldn't expect anybody to get on my ass if I made a bad pitch."

After going 11–10 in 1983, Knucksie was released by the Braves at age 44. He signed a two-year contract with the Yankees, winning 16 games each season. While he was pitching for the Yanks in 1984, the Braves retired Niekro's No. 35. He played for Cleveland in 1986 and most of '87 before finishing his career with two losses as a Blue Jay. Or so he thought.

On September 27, for a team that finished 69–92, Niekro made the 716th and last start of his big-league career. He worked three innings, walked six, and allowed six hits and five earned runs. It wasn't pretty, but it was perfect. "Then, that was it," said Knucksie, who ended his career as it began. As a Brave. Everyone got their dollar's worth that day.

17 "This Great, Grand Organization..."

He's 70 now and a grandfather. Huh? Johnny Suhspenduz, a seventy-something? Of course, the old high school English teacher would call himself a septuagenarian. But Gramps? Can you picture the dapper, longtime dean of baseball execs answering to "Grandpa?" How in the name of Brooks Brothers did all this happen?

Yet there was John Schuerholz last October 1, standing in his box at Turner Field with a big grin and two thumbs up, acknowledging 70th-birthday wishes from a capacity crowd as stadium organist Matthew Kaminski played "Happy Birthday." And a thought arose: good for you, Grandpa, after all the great work you did all those years and all the unforgettable moments you helped give Atlanta.

Of course, when Schuerholz first came to the Atlanta Braves from Kansas City in the winter of 1990, his baseball brethren wanted to give him something: a sanity test. "When I took this job," Schuerholz told Thomas Stinson of the *Atlanta Journal-Constitution* in a memorable profile in 2000, "I got calls from my friends in the business who thought I had lost my mind."

On the contrary, Atlanta proved to be hardball paradise found. Was Schuerholz vain? Absolutely. You'd be, too, if you'd made Kansas City a model franchise. But in Atlanta, he found a bigger-city, bigger-market, long-dreadful club nearly dressed for success. Schuerholz not only gussied them up—acquiring Sid Bream, Rafael Belliard, and especially Terry Pendleton—but quickly made the

Braves the blueprint for other teams and general managers to follow. He said he'd make the Braves winners, and he did.

Schuerholz would later famously refer to the franchise as, "This great, grand organization," once it had become the envy of baseball. And you know what? He was right.

It took Schuerholz one worst-to-first year to be officially acknowledged as the best GM in baseball. In 1991 he was honored by UPI as baseball's executive of the year. He never needed any other awards. His reward was watching his teams win a record 14 consecutive division titles while others looked on enviously. From his background in K.C. and, before that, with Baltimore, Schuerholz knew and appreciated the value of scouting and development. He knew his stuff, too.

"Unless you've ever been on the inside and worked with him," Paul Snyder, Atlanta's legendary scout and former personnel director, once said, "there's no way you can appreciate the man's baseball intelligence."

Each interview with Schuerholz was a vocabulary lesson. His wardrobe was as impressive as his command of the English language. Were he ever to retire, he might even have to dress...casually. "So I'll go to counseling, I guess, for that," Schuerholz told Stinson in 2000. "Maybe there's a Good Dressers Anonymous or something, where we can put on suspenders and ties and go talk. 'Hi, I'm John. I used to dress up. And I miss it.'"

He missed virtually nothing in his 17-year tenure as the Braves' GM from 1991 to 2007. In 1993, with the Braves drawing 3,884,720 in attendance and the coffers bulging, Schuerholz acquired Padres slugger Fred McGriff at the trade deadline. The year before, he'd pulled off his Greg Maddux coup, signing him as a high-priced free agent. Atlanta finally won the World Series in 1995, only to blow the '96 Series to the Yankees. That the Braves won just one World Series in his GM tenure is one of the very few minuses on the Schuerholz ledger.

The controversial, end-of-spring training trade dispatching David Justice and Marquis Grissom to Cleveland in 1997? That was done to free up the $91 million needed to re-sign Maddux and Tom Glavine to new five-year contracts. Justice felt betrayed by that deal. For Schuerholz, who was never reluctant to turn over the roster, it was simply business. Now in his fourth year as team president, the business of baseball and the game itself still stirs Schuerholz.

Atlanta's 14 straight division titles may become the team-record equivalent of DiMaggio's 56-game hitting streak—unapproachable. The three consecutive 100-win seasons in 1997 through 1999 are matched by only three other teams in baseball history: the 1929 through 1931 Philadelphia Athletics, the 1942 through 1944 St. Louis Cardinals, and the 1969 through 1971 Baltimore Orioles. And Johnny Suhspenduz even sings doo-wop.

In Naples, Florida, during the off-season, John and Karen Schuerholz always get together with four of their favorite couples. For the guys, it's the chance to harmonize again as "The Napletones," as they call themselves. Schuerholz loved '50s music as a kid and teenager. He still does. As he told Tom Stinson, "The greatest song ever written is 'Come Go with Me' by the Del-Vikings." He paused. "My apologies to Beethoven."

None needed, Grandpa. Certainly not to Atlanta.

18 Going, Going, Going, Going...Gone Again!

The *Sporting News* long ago proclaimed it "baseball's greatest single-game accomplishment." Only 15 major leaguers have hit four home runs in a game. The 11th? Bob Horner of the Atlanta Braves.

"What I remember about it," Horner said, "is every time I came up we were losing."

Which was not unusual—more like business as usual—for the Braves back in the awful '80s. On July 6, 1986, a steamy Sunday in Atlanta, Horner homered four times—and still the Braves lost 11–8 to Montreal. It's one of only two times a player has hit four home runs in a losing effort.

By then, for both ballplayer and ballclub, what a long, strange trip it'd been.

"Horner," Ted Turner predicted, "is destined for stardom—Cooperstown." He made that prediction after the Braves made Horner the No. 1 overall pick of the 1978 baseball draft. He was a slugging third baseman at Arizona State and the College Player of the Year. A strong, outrageously talented hitter, Horner went straight from the ASU campus to third base at Atlanta-Fulton County Stadium.

In his major league debut, in his third at-bat, Horner homered off Bert Blyleven, an eventual 287-game winner. Afterward, Horner deferentially referred to the pitcher as "Mr. Blyleven."

"I was 20 years old," Horner recalled years later. "I wasn't old enough to drink alcohol. The whole world was 'Mister' to me."

The whole world seemed his oyster, too. After hitting a collegiate record 25 homers at ASU, Horner was the first player honored as both the College Player of the Year and NL Rookie of the Year in the same season.

In just 89 games as a rookie, Horner belted 23 home runs. He averaged one homer every 14.04 at-bats, the best ever by a Rookie of the Year. "Another Harmon Killebrew," said Montreal manager Dick Williams.

But Horner was injury-prone, chronically so. He and his agent, Bucky Woy, were also often at war with front-office management. Horner played nine seasons in Atlanta, missing 390 games—most due to injury, some to suspension. Although he hit 215 homers as a Brave, Horner didn't realize the great expectations almost everyone had for him—most of all, Horner himself.

But on that one Sunday afternoon, everything came together.

"I'd hit three homers in a game in college," Horner told me. "I'd hit two in a game with the Braves. But never four."

Then the Expos came to the ballpark known as the Launching Pad. Quickly, we had liftoff.

"It was a Sunday getaway game in Atlanta," said Horner. "We were taking off afterward, going to Philadelphia." Not, however, until Horner made some real, rare baseball history.

All four of his home runs, Horner recalled two decades later, "were just pitchers making mistakes—hanging breaking balls—more than [anything I did]. But they could afford to make them; they were ahead. They kept throwing them, and I kept hitting them. And we lost.

"The first three homers, off Andy McGaffigan, were hanging breaking balls," he said. "Hanging breaking balls are mistakes. You're not always going to get great pitches to hit. You might get one great pitch to hit an at-bat. That day, I hit mistakes.

"I don't know if I'd ever faced McGaffigan before. I didn't know much about him, and he didn't know much about me. I don't think any of the home runs I hit even tied it up, much less put us ahead. I hit three in a row in my first three at-bats. All four were to left field, or left-center."

Montreal's Tim Burke, a sinkerballer, relieved McGaffigan after Horner's third homer. "He broke my bat," Horner recalled. "I popped out to first base."

Expos reliever Jeff Reardon came on in the bottom of the eighth, leading 11–7. With two out in the ninth and Horner at bat, Reardon—a fastball pitcher—pitched to his strength. A heater. "He threw it, and I hit it," Horner said. Home run No. 4. History…at Reardon's expense.

Uh, about HR Ball No. 4...

The letter was dated September 24, 2010. It was written by a man from Dacula, Georgia, named Eric Moore. It began:

"Mr. Wilkinson, I am a lifelong Atlanta Braves fan and..." That was clear from the first part of his email address: emoore755.

He continued:

> Part of my Atlanta Braves experience included time on the Braves ground crew from 1985 to 1990 (I quit too soon)....I was there the Sunday afternoon Bob Horner hit his four home runs. If you recall, at old Atlanta-Fulton County Stadium, the ground crew watched the games from behind the right-field fence, in the corner along the foul pole.
>
> In the old stadium, there was about 20 feet between the outfield fence and the foundation wall of the outfield seats. Along that wall were the football bleachers that were pushed up against the wall. The ground behind the fence was about three feet of dirt, then concrete, which extended to the foundation wall.
>
> There was a track built into the ground, about a foot deep and one or two feet wide that allowed the bleachers to move from left to right. Spaced intermittently along those tracks were drains, about six to eight inches in diameter, most of which did not have covers for some reason
>
> You guessed it. The fourth home run ball fell into the opened drain.
>
> When Horner came to bat that last time, we were well aware of the significance of the moment. When he hit the home run, I was one of three or four guys who chased after it. We were about 10 feet away when we saw it roll into the drain. We gave it a quick look, but no one was up to reaching their hand down into the yuck, and the ball wasn't visible from the surface.
>
> I remember the clubhouse calling, asking for the ball as they always did whenever a milestone home run was hit for either team, as most landed behind the fence and not in the seats as they now do at Turner Field. I hope this brings some clarification to the missing fourth home run ball. It would have been a great addition to the Braves museum.

Oops. As Horner told me in 2006, a man—he wasn't sure if it was someone from the ground crew or a fan—gave him the purported fourth home run ball after that game. It's been displayed, along with Horner's bat, in the Braves Museum and Hall of Fame in Turner Field for several years.

"Jeff didn't mind," Horner said. "He got the save and won the game. He didn't lose a minute's sleep over it. McGaffigan and I never talked about it. Our paths never crossed."

It had been a decade since the previous four-homer game. On April 17, 1976, Philadelphia's Hall of Fame third baseman Mike Schmidt accomplished the feat in Chicago. He went deep four times in Wrigley Field, where the wind was blowing out in the Phillies' 18–16 slugfest win over the Cubs.

Horner's home run derby was different. "It was a strange day," he said. "Yeah, I'd done it. It was a wonderful feeling. But it's a team game, in a team sport, and there wasn't much to celebrate about because we lost. After the game, we showered and packed and boarded the bus and flew to Philadelphia.

"When you get your butt kicked, there's not much to celebrate."

Horner did, however, manage some keepsakes from his record-tying day. "I have both my bats and the [last home run] ball from that game," he said. "I hit the first three homers with one bat. I gave that one to Cooperstown. The bat I hit the fourth home run with, I have. I liked it so much, I kept using it until I broke it. Then I taped it up and hung onto it."

Someone, either a fan or a member of the Braves grounds crew—Horner isn't sure who—retrieved home run ball No. 4 and gave it to him. Early in the last decade, Horner donated that ball and his bat to the Braves Museum and Hall of Fame at Turner Field.

"I figured it'd be better to have it there," Horner said. "It was just sitting here gathering dust in my house. I figured someone might enjoy it and remember the day."

A footnote: Horner was the third player in Braves history to hit four homers in a game. On July 31, 1954, Joe Adcock, the first baseman for the Milwaukee Braves, belted four against the Brooklyn Dodgers. The first player in franchise history to do so was also baseball's first four-homer man. On May 30, 1894, Bobby Lowe hit four against the Cincinnati Reds while playing for the

Boston Beaneaters (who eventually changed their nickname to the Braves). Fans were reportedly so excited by Lowe's feat, they threw $160 in silver coins on the field.

19 Dr. Jack's Red Shirt

By the 1991 All-Star break, the Braves were clearly improved. But the habitually last-place club—four straight seasons in the NL cellar—was still 9½ games behind Tommy Lasorda's Dodgers at the break, a game under .500 at 39–40. This, despite the worst half-season of John Smoltz's young career.

"I had lost my confidence," Smoltz, now a Braves broadcaster and an MLB analyst for TBS, told the *Wall Street Journal* in 2010. Stan Kasten, then the team president, put it more succinctly. "He couldn't find the plate," Kasten recalled last summer.

Smoltz was wild. Walking batters, throwing wild pitches. He had the best stuff of any of the Braves' Young Guns, but he kept misfiring. He worked too hard, found himself rushing things, and, as only Smoltz can, overanalyzed every single mistake he made.

"My teammates, my manager, and my coaches are sick of seeing this," Smoltz said back then. Help was on the way. No dummies, Braves management hired Dr. Jack Llewellyn, a local sports psychologist, to work with Smoltz.

Initially, some people were skeptical. Especially one Atlanta writer who, later in the season after countless hosannas were tossed Llewellyn's way, summarily dismissed the good doctor as "Sigmund Fraud." Smoltz and the Braves knew better.

In their sessions, the pitcher and the psychologist talked about focus, among many topics. Llewellyn was big on positive reinforcement. He put together a two-minute videotape for Smoltz of six pitches he'd thrown absolutely perfectly.

Whenever he made a bad pitch in a game later that season, Smoltz told the *Journal*, "I would literally not step back on the mound until I had pulled up that positive file in my mind."

Then there was the shirt. Whenever Smoltz made a start in the second half, Dr. Jack wore a red checkered shirt and sat in the good seats, right behind home plate. The better and easier for his most famous patient to see him. Smoltz would spot the shirt, relax, and focus on what Llewellyn had preached. Seeing the red shirt was not only a reinforcement, but a little oasis of calm in a sold-out, loud-as-hell ballpark. In all but one park, that is.

As Pete Van Wieren, the longtime, now-retired Braves broadcaster, recalled in his 2010 autobiography *Of Mikes and Men*, "This worked everywhere but St. Louis, where everybody wore red shirts. But the association had the desired effect."

Come the second half, Smoltz was positively lights-out. Immediately after the All-Star break, the Braves went 9–2. Smoltz won three of those games, one more than he'd managed in the entire first half. The Dodgers went 2–9, and Atlanta suddenly found itself in a pennant race.

And Smoltz, having rediscovered his confidence and command of his pitches, was the primary pitching catalyst. He went 12–2 after the break and was nigh unhittable. It was Smoltz who was on the mound in Game 161—and Dr. Jack in the box seats behind the plate, red shirt and all—when the Braves beat Houston to clinch a tie for the NL West title. About 20 minutes later, the Braves watched on the video screen as the Giants eliminated the Dodgers out west. Pandemonium.

In the NLCS and World Series, the CBS-TV cameras located Llewellyn and focused in on him and his trusty shirt whenever Smoltz pitched. In his two NLCS wins, including the Game 7 clincher, and especially during his World Series starts against

Minnesota, the red shirt helped transform Smoltz, and very nearly turned the Braves into the unlikeliest of world champions.

20 The Miracle Braves of 1914

Wonder of wonders, miracle of miracles. Ladies and gentlemen, Boston's Miracle Braves of 1914. Nearly a century later, their turnaround still astounds. It's on par with the 1969 Miracle Mets and Atlanta's 180-degree, worst-to-first Braves of '91 for sheer incredulity.

How unbelievable? Boston began the 1914 season 4–18. After dropping a July 4 doubleheader to Brooklyn, the Braves remained 14 games under .500, at 26–40 and trailing the first-place New York Giants by 15 games. The Braves were still eighth and dead last in the National League.

A day or so later, at the start of a western road trip, Boston played an exhibition game against a minor league, or town team, from Buffalo. They lost 15–2. "We lost to a soap-manufacturing team," Johnny Evers later recalled. "That's how bad we were."

This was the same Evers of Tinker-to-Evers-to-Chance fame, the Chicago Cubs' double-play combo celebrated in verse. They'd helped the Cubbies win three straight NL pennants from 1906 to 1908. Evers was their player/manager in 1913, but was fired as manager at season's end for losing the City Series to the White Sox. He agreed to a trade to the doormat Braves, however, using the bargaining chip of the new Federal League to wrangle a $25,000 bonus from Boston.

Evers quickly became the Braves' fiery leader. "Anybody that comes to this team," he told legendary sportswriter Grantland Rice, "will either hustle with the rest of us or we'll drive him off the team." Evers, who was baseball's best second baseman in the early 20th century, was also a real grouch. His teammates nicknamed him "the Crab."

The mastermind behind the Braves' resurgence was the well-dressed man always wearing a suit in the dugout. By October, manager George Stallings would be hailed as the "Miracle Man." He was a master psychologist who'd made the long-moribund Braves at least respectable in 1913, revamping the roster. By 1914, only four holdovers remained from those 101-game losers of 1912 (the year the team became the Braves, following yet another ownership change): shortstop Rabbit Maranville, catcher Hank Gowdy, pitcher Lefty Tyler (part of an essentially three-man rotation), and Otto Hess, a reserve outfielder born in Switzerland. Stallings also platooned brilliantly.

When Boston started 4–18, though, he moaned, "This bunch of mine is the worst looking ballclub I've ever seen. They can't do anything right. I've never seen such luck. But don't think we're a tail-end team. It'll take us a month to get back in shape, but we're going to be hard to beat."

On July 19 Boston finished a series sweep in Cincinnati and escaped the NL cellar. After scoring three runs in the ninth inning of the finale to win 3–2, the happy Braves mobbed Stallings. "Now we'll catch New York," he vowed. "We're playing 30 percent better ball than any team in the league. They won't be able to stop us."

On to Pittsburgh, where Maranville, with the bases loaded in a scoreless tie, leaned into a pitch with his forehead. "If you can walk to first base," umpire Charlie Moran told him, "I'll let you get away with it." Dazed, the Rabbit got up and somehow got to first base, where he was replaced by a pinch runner. Boston won 1–0.

After winning a season-high nine straight games, the Braves took over second place on August 10. In New York they swept a three-game series from the Giants in the Polo Grounds, with Tyler outpitching Christy Mathewson in a 2–0 shutout to complete the sweep. This was all part of the season's surreal second half in which Boston went 61–16 (a .792 winning percentage), 34–10 down the stretch (.773).

By September 2, the Braves were in first place. Returning home from a 16–6 road trip, they faced the Giants in a Labor Day doubleheader—and did so in Fenway Park. The AL Red Sox had offered the use of their larger ballpark to the rampaging Braves for the rest of the season. An estimated 75,000 fans—35,000 for the morning game, 40,000 in the afternoon—saw the teams split. Once the Braves won the rubber game behind Bill James (one of his 26 wins, the same as teammate Dick Rudolph), they never looked back.

In a doubleheader sweep of Philadelphia the next day, George "Iron" Davis threw the fourth no-hitter in franchise history. Davis, a Harvard law student, won seven games in his career, six in three seasons with the Braves. The no-hitter was his only shutout. It was also one of Boston's 19 shutouts that season, 18 coming in the second half.

When third baseman Red Smith broke his leg while sliding on the season's last day, Stallings switched to defensive whiz Charlie Deal. Then the Miracle Braves prepared to face Connie Mack's mighty Philadelphia Athletics in the World Series. Their "$100,000 infield" included second baseman Eddie Collins (.344) and third baseman Frank "Home Run" Baker, who led the AL with nine homers. The A's had won the World Series in 1910, 1911, and 1913. The Braves hadn't won a pennant since 1898. Their 94–59 turnaround was their first winning season since 1902.

Few bookmakers would even take bets on what seemed to be a mismatch. They were right. It was no contest. The Braves killed 'em.

To boost his team's confidence, Stallings predicted the Braves would not only win but sweep the A's. He insulted them, treating Mack's men with scorn. The Braves harangued Wally Schang so mercilessly, the young catcher was charged with two passed balls and allowed nine runners to steal.

In the opener at Shibe Park, Boston battered A's ace Chief Bender 7–1. In Game 2, James threw a two-hit masterpiece to edge eventual Hall of Famer Eddie Plank 1–0. Before leaving Philadelphia, Stallings ordered all the club's equipment, including the road uniforms, shipped to Boston: "We won't be coming back."

Before 35,520 fans at Fenway Park, the A's scored twice in the 10th inning to lead 4–2. But in the bottom half Gowdy, the light-hitting catcher, homered, and then the Braves scored again to tie it. In the 12th Gowdy got things started with a leadoff double. A throwing error enabled Boston to win 5–4. Stallings promptly canceled the Braves' train reservations back to Philadelphia.

Game 4 was almost a forgone conclusion. The Braves won 3–1 to complete the first four-game World Series sweep in history. Gowdy, who hit just .243 in the regular season, batted .545. Braves pitchers held the mighty A's to a .172 average and five earned runs. A raucous, on-field celebration engulfed Fenway Park. Hundreds of fans and many players marched around Fenway with a band, then paraded through the streets of Boston.

Did they believe in miracles? Yes!

"Every man did his share," Stallings said. "It was team play that won. Stars couldn't have done it. There's no substitute in baseball for fighting spirit, and this team had it."

21 "Bushville Wins!"

In the 107-year history of the modern World Series, there have been few Odd Couple pairings as polar-opposite as the 1957 Fall Classic between the New York Yankees and Milwaukee Braves.

There were the imperial, pinstriped Yanks of New York City, then winners of 17 World Series titles, six in the previous eight years alone. And there were the Braves, long second-class citizens in Boston with one other-worldly world championship, now midwestern transplants in a town that liked its beer, brats, and now baseball.

These were Casey Stengel's mighty Yankees of Mickey, Yogi, and Whitey Ford. Fred Haney's Braves belonged in such company with 21-game winner Warren Spahn; bound-for-glory right-hander Lew Burdette; bound-for-glory slugger Eddie Mathews; and 1957 National League MVP Hank Aaron, with 44 homers, 132 RBIs, and a .322 average.

It was Aaron who hit what he'd call "the most important home run I ever hit"—his pennant-clinching, 11th-inning, walk-off homer that beat St. Louis 4–2. "My first thought," Aaron said, "was Bobby Thomson's homer," the legendary Shot Heard Round the World that beat Brooklyn in a playoff game and gave the Giants the 1951 pennant.

"That had always been my idea of the most important homer," said Aaron, who'd played with Thomson in Milwaukee before the veteran was traded in the off-season. "Now I got one for myself." The Braves got their first pennant since '48, and the city of Milwaukee its first ever. The town went appropriately nuts. These were heady times in Sudsville, especially when the Yankees arrived for Game 3 of the World Series.

They'd split the first two games in the Bronx, Ford besting Spahn 3–1 before Burdette beat Bobby Shantz 4–2. A visit from the Yankees was big stuff in small-town Wisconsin. When the Yankees' train stopped outside of Racine, in the little town of Sturtevant, the townspeople were waiting along with their mayor and a marching band. The Yanks were expected to merely say hello. Instead, arrogant as usual, they continued on without a word.

Once in Milwaukee, thousands of people were waiting at the downtown train station. A giant front-page headline in the *Milwaukee Journal* declared, "Today We Make History." The news that Russia had launched *Sputnik* that day to beat the U.S. to outer space? Fuhgedaboutit. The Yankees were coming! The Yankees were coming!

But not stopping to chat. The team ignored official welcoming parties downtown, too, as well as the crowd. They boarded the bus to their hotel, shunned local reporters who asked to ride along, and rode off. The Milwaukee media persisted, and one Yankees official was heard shouting, "Come on, stop acting bush! Get off the bus!"

Bush league. That's how the following day's newspaper stories characterized the Yankees' dismissal of Milwaukee. The *Journal*'s front-page headline? "Bushville!"

The Yankees were booed and cursed viciously the next day when the teams were introduced. Especially Stengel, who'd been misidentified as the source of the "Bush" slur. Hadn't he managed the minor league Milwaukee Brewers to a championship in 1944? No matter. The fans booed. Casey blew them a kiss. The Yanks cruised to a 12–3 win.

The famous Nippy Jones shoe polish incident saved Game 4. Having blown a 4–1 lead in the ninth inning, Milwaukee trailed 5–4 in the bottom of the 10th. Jones was hit in the foot by a curveball, but home plate umpire Augie Donatelli said it bounced in the dirt and was therefore a ball. Jones simply showed the ump the ball, and the black shoe polish scuff mark. Take your base, Nippy.

Johnny Logan, the combative shortstop, doubled Nippy home, then scored on Mathews' game-winning homer. Burdette's "sinker"—opponents swore it was a spitball—beat Ford in a 1–0 classic, thanks to Wes Covington's homer-saving catch. The Braves went back to the Bronx up 3–2. But when Bob Turley beat them 3–2, and Spahn was still suffering from the flu, Fred Haney had no choice but to start Burdette on two days' rest.

"There wasn't any way I was going to say no," said Burdette. Not in Game 7 of the World Series. Not against the team that traded him to the Braves in 1951.

It was a breeze, even against Don Larsen, the Game 3 winner who'd pitched a perfect game in the 1956 World Series. With a four-run cushion in the fourth inning, Burdette shut out the Yanks for the second straight time, 5–0, extending his Series scoreless string to 24 consecutive innings. He was the easy choice as the World Series MVP.

Back home in Milwaukee, a huge victory parade down Wisconsin Avenue included a banner reading, "Rest in peace, Yankees." The best photo captured a woman raising another banner. It read: "Bushville Wins!"

22 13 and 0!

The evidence is framed and hanging on the den wall. It's a now-yellowing placard with an oversized No. 12 and above it these words: I Was There…

Below it, more info:

Atlanta Braves vs. Cincinnati Reds
Atlanta Fulton County Stadium
Atlanta, Georgia. April 20, 1982

There's a signature, too. A nutty notary of sorts: "Brother Francis."

That was the name of a fan who, dressed as a monk, used to climb up on the dugout roof and root on the Braves. He was not alone that April. All of Atlanta went nuts over the Braves, who opened the '82 season with a record 13 consecutive wins. It was the best start in major league history at the time, and an ideal one for new Braves manager Joe Torre. After the wretched decade of the

'70s, it set Atlanta afire and led—barely—to the Braves' first NL West division title since 1969.

"I think the reason we won 13 games in a row is because I was on the DL," Phil Niekro once said, laughing all the way. "I was a horrible Opening Day pitcher."

Knucksie was 43 then, yet his knuckleball still fluttered and flummoxed batters. But after he was drilled in the ribs by a batting-practice line drive by teammate Rick Mahler during spring training, Niekro was on the disabled list when Atlanta opened the season in San Diego.

With seven rookies on the roster and Mahler on the mound that day, the Braves won 1–0 thanks to Glenn Hubbard's RBI double and Mahler's first career shutout. Torre's debut as the successor to Bobby Cox, who owner Ted Turner had fired after the '81 season, was a success.

"This is Bobby's team," Torre said repeatedly that year. Hired in 1978 after Atlanta went 61–101 in '77, Cox rebuilt and led the Braves to an 81–80 record in 1980. But he was fired after a 50–56 finish in the strike-shortened '81 season. Torre, who played in Atlanta from 1966 to 1968, was the early beneficiary of Cox's good work.

In the second game Dale Murphy's first homer and rookie leadoff man Brett Butler's decisive RBI enabled Bob Walk to beat the Padres 6–4. In their home opener the Braves jumped on Houston for five runs in the first inning. The losing pitcher: Don Sutton, who'd later become a Braves broadcaster. Murphy homered again. Atlanta won 6–2. Tommy Boggs got the win with relief help from Al Hrabosky, who knew what the Braves were getting in Joe Torre.

After Ted Turner had fired Cox, general manager John Mullen urged him to hire Eddie Haas, the manager of the Triple A Richmond Braves. Four other top front-office officials agreed. But Turner wanted a more magnetic TV personality, with the Braves always playing on TBS. So he hired Torre.

Hrabosky rejoiced. As he said to Steve Wulf of *Sports Illustrated*, who came to Atlanta during the record-setting run, "I told a club official over the winter, 'You may have hired him because of a TV decision, but you're going to be thankful you did.' I played with Joe in St. Louis, so I know what kind of guy he is."

No team ever responded to a new manager better than the Braves did to Torre. They swept the Astros, winning 8–6, then 5–0. For Mahler, his second start of the season resulted in his second career shutout. Murphy homered again in that game. So did Bob Horner. Brother Francis danced with delight on the dugout. Make it five in a row.

In Cincinnati, the Braves began by beating the Reds 6–1. Not that Dave Concepcion was impressed. "They're not going to win the division," scoffed the shortstop.

The seventh win was heavenly, despite Claudell Washington's first-inning beaning. Rufino Linares, his replacement, went 4-for-4 in an 8–5 win. Linares was still in left field the next day, in the ninth inning of a tied game, when a liner to left-center seemed a certain game-winning hit. Linares, who like Michael Jackson often wore a glove for no apparent reason, dove, stuck out his mitt, and somehow caught the ball.

His postgame recollection: "I dive for ball. I look to left, no ball. I look to right, no ball. I look in glove, ball. I say, 'Rufi, you one lucky guy.'" Atlanta scored three in the 10th to win 5–2. Make it eight in a row.

In the Astrodome the streak seemed over when Nolan Ryan took a 3–0, one-hitter into the sixth inning. Instead, Atlanta scored five runs in the sixth to win 5–3. The Braves had tied the 1888 Boston Beaneaters for the best start in franchise history. "The way we came back tonight," Rick Camp said, "especially against Ryan, there's no telling when we'll lose."

Not the next night, when the Braves tied the NL record for consecutive season-opening victories. Their 10th came on Horner's two-run double and terrific relief from Gene Garber. He retired the last nine Astros in that 2–1 win without a ball leaving the infield. When Biff Pocoroba—who now lives in the Atlanta suburb of Conyers and is known as "the Sausage King" for his homemade meat delicacies—hit a two-run, pinch-hit double in the eighth inning to edge the Astros 6–5, the Braves had tied Oakland's record of 11 consecutive season-opening victories. The A's set that mark in 1981. Hrabosky got that win for his buddy Torre.

When the Braves flew home that night, a crowd of more than 3,000 fans welcomed them at the airport. One held a sign reading: "Torre! Torre! Torre!—162–0"

The following evening, a crowd of 37,268 roared its approval. Washington, back from his beaning and in center field, tripled in the winning run in a 4–2 victory over Cincy. This, after rookie Steve Bedrosian worked 4⅓ scoreless innings after Tommy Boggs struggled early. When Murphy caught a fly ball for the final out, hundreds of fans ran onto the field. Brother Francis? Up on the dugout again.

"We wanted the record because it was an immediate goal that would help us get the respect we desire," first baseman Chris Chambliss said afterward.

"Considering no one else in baseball history has done it," said Torre, "considering that baseball has been around more than 100 years, it's incredible." Make it 12 in a row.

The next night, trailing 3–2 in the ninth, with one out and runners on first and second, Butler grounded toward short, where the slick-fielding Concepcion waited to turn a double play. Instead, the ball hit rookie catcher Matt Sinatro, who was running from second base toward third. He was called out. With men on first and second, a wild pitch by Reds reliever Jim Kern advanced the runners. When Pocoroba was intentionally walked, the bases were loaded for Washington.

Enter left-hander Joe Price. Washington stroked a two-run single for a thrilling 4–3 victory and the historic 13th straight win. The streak finally ended the next game, when Cincinnati won 2–1.

That 13–0 start was later tied by the 1987 Brewers. But it ignited the city of Atlanta and legitimized the Braves, who'd need every one of those wins. They promptly lost five straight. Over the rest of the season, they were just 76–73. But they held on to finish 89–73, a game ahead of the Dodgers to win the NL West.

23 The Brief Reign and Long Rain of '82

After their 13–0 start, the Braves were nine games up in the NL West on July 29. Cue the disaster music: losing 19 of the next 21 games, Atlanta fell behind L.A. A few fans speculated that Chief Noc-a-Homa, the Braves' mascot, had cast a retaliatory spell after his teepee was taken down to make room for extra seats.

The Braves and Dodgers kept trading places in the standings until the final week, when San Francisco was suddenly a player, too.

The Giants, once 13½ games out, were now tied with Atlanta, a game behind L.A. The Braves, who'd end the regular season on the West Coast, did so with a flourish. Phil Niekro, a kid of 43 whose last and only playoff appearance was in '69, threw his first shutout of the season. The Braves beat Frisco again, and then, after the Dodgers lost their seventh straight, Atlanta beat them in 12 innings to lead by two games.

In San Diego, in Game No. 160, Knucksie's knuckler confounded the Padres in a 4–0 win. In his two West Coast starts he'd pitched 18 shutout innings, allowing five hits. That night Niekro also hit his first homer since 1976, a two-run shot in the eighth to blow open a 1–0 nail-biter.

Niekro would later recall Padres players saying before the game even began, "We're gonna try and beat you guys. But we don't want the Dodgers to win." In his eighth-inning at-bat he took a fat, belt-high fastball from Padres starter Eric Show. When Niekro didn't swing, Show grinned widely. Niekro thought, *Why do you throw that ball right there?*

When he looked again at Show's smiling face, "It's like [asking], 'Why didn't you swing at that?'" Niekro remembered. And he thought, *He's gonna throw it again.*

He did. Knucksie lifted his leg for some power and parked that two-run homer.

Atlanta clinched a tie for the NL West title with Saturday's 4–2 win and the Dodgers cruising 15–2 to stay alive. On Sunday the Braves despaired after a 5–1 loss raised the possibility of a one-game playoff with L.A. When Jerry Royster jogged back to a quiet dugout after flying out in the ninth, manager Joe Torre told him, "Don't worry about a thing. Joe Morgan just hit a home run."

That three-run homer in the seventh made for a 5–2 Giants lead, a euphoric Braves clubhouse, and a fine flight to St. Louis. When L.A.'s rally came up short, Bob Horner toasted the NL West title with champagne. Knucksie wept sweet tears. "I've always wanted to pitch in a World Series," he said in the clubhouse. "Hopefully, this is the year."

On the flight to St. Louis, Dale Murphy, who'd win his first of two consecutive NL MVP Awards, went to every teammate, telling him how he'd won a particular game that season, and how that win made the difference in Atlanta's one-game margin of victory.

But there was nothing to celebrate in St. Louis. In Game 1 of the NLCS at Busch Stadium, Niekro had a 1–0 lead with two outs in the bottom of the fifth inning. Niekro needed one more out to make it an official game, but it was raining hard. After umpire Billy Williams walked over and talked to baseball commissioner Bowie Kuhn, the game was stopped for a rain delay. It never continued.

"They didn't want a playoff game decided in five innings," Niekro said more than two decades later. "So they stopped and waited. It rained and rained." And rained out the opener.

Game 1 would be started over, not resumed. The Cards breezed through it 7–0. After another day lost to rain, Game 2 began with Niekro back on the mound and leading 3–2 through six innings. "And Torre pinch-hits for me," Niekro later said. "Gene Garber comes in, and we lose 4–3. I was pitching well in St. Louis. I had 'em where I wanted them."

The next day in Atlanta the Cards completed the sweep with an easy 6–2 win. Phil Niekro never did get to pitch in his World Series after all.

24 Ave

What if? Imagine if Steve Avery had never been hurt, or at least not until much, much later. If we'd never heard the term "oblique muscle" until Avery's career was over. If the youngest of the Young Guns had stayed healthy and pitched longer. What if, indeed?

What was it Andy Van Slyke called him? "Poison Avery," one of the most clever and apt baseball nicknames ever. This was in October 1991, when baseball was agog over Ave, the 6′4″ Michigan kid who not only fired his fastball but commanded it, too. His over-the-top curveball? A dead-man's curve for hitters when the young lefty was on his game.

And especially so when he was on top of the world, as in '91. He'd turned 21 that April after a predictable 3–11 rookie year on an awful team. In 1991 Avery gave Atlanta's worst-to-first Braves their first win of the season, a 7–5 victory over the reigning world champion Reds. It was the first of his 18 regular season victories. Two more came in mid-September, five days apart in the heat of an unexpected pennant race. Avery beat Los Angeles 9–1 on September 15, completing a four-hitter to keep Atlanta in first place. Five days later he shut out the Dodgers in L.A., saying, "I can't understand why I match up with them so well."

The Dodgers couldn't figure him out, either. Nor could the Astros; in Avery's last regular season start he pitched a no-hitter through 6⅔ innings. In the NLCS Avery absolutely dumbfounded the potent Pittsburgh Pirates.

"We could've played another two hours and we still wouldn't have scored on Avery," manager Jim Leyland said after Avery evened the series at 1–1. In Game 2 in Three Rivers Stadium he shut out Pittsburgh through eight innings and, at age 21, became the youngest pitcher ever to win a playoff game.

After issuing a leadoff double to Bobby Bonilla, Avery induced a pop-out from Barry Bonds, who shattered his bat in disgust on the artificial turf. When Alejandro Pena came on to get the last two outs and the save, Atlanta had evened the NLCS.

And Avery had a new nickname. "Poison Avery," Van Slyke said, laughingly but admiringly.

Back home, the Braves easily won the third game 10–3, but two one-run defeats sent them back to Pittsburgh down 3–2. For eight innings, Avery went head-to-head against Pirates ace Doug Drabek. Neither team scored. The Pirates never got a runner beyond first base. Greg Olson's RBI double gave Atlanta a 1–0 lead in the ninth. In came Pena. With the tying run on third and two out, he threw Van Slyke a change-up after five straight fastballs. The change was, well, pure poison. Van Slyke swung right through it.

Pitcher Steve Avery wipes champagne from his face after the Braves defeated the Pittsburgh Pirates 4–0, winning Game 7 of the 1991 NLCS in Pittsburgh. Avery was named MVP of the series.

"I've seen a lot of good pitchers," said Ray Miller, Pittsburgh's highly regarded pitching coach. "Gibson…Koufax…and if Avery's not up there with them, he will be soon."

Avery had extended his scoreless streak against the Bucs to 16⅓ innings, an NLCS record, and Cox was uncharacteristically effusive. "Steve is unflappable, and he's got all the qualities to be an All-Star for years to come," he said. "He's as good as I've ever seen."

The next night, John Smoltz beat Pittsburgh 4–0 for his second win in the NLCS and the Braves' first pennant since 1958. Yet Avery was clearly the NLCS Most Valuable Player. Presented the MVP trophy in a jubilant clubhouse, Avery shut his eyes to protect them against the celebratory champagne. But his mouth was open, and his tongue stuck out to drink in the bubbly. It was the perfect photo, capturing a kid surely destined for a long, champagne-kissed career.

"The man can bring it, I'm aware of that," Kirby Puckett said before the Minnesota-Atlanta World Series. "I've watched Avery, and I know you don't have to meet him halfway with the fastball. He'll bring it right to you."

In Game 3 Avery left in the eighth inning leading 4–2, but got no decision in either Atlanta's 11-inning, 5–4 win or the wrenching 12-inning, 4–3 loss in Game 6.

In 1992, victimized by a lack of run support, Avery went just 11–11 yet lowered his ERA to 3.20. In Game 2 of the NLCS he held the Pirates scoreless through the first six innings of a 13–5 rout, extending his record NLCS scoreless streak to 22⅓ innings, shattering Ken Holtzman's record of 18. Avery was battered in Game 5, though, with Pittsburgh scoring four runs in the first inning of a 7–1 loss.

"I just didn't have it, and if you don't they'll hit you every time," said Avery, done after throwing 30 pitches, getting one Pirate out and allowing four runs on five hits. "I really have no explanation."

In the '92 World Series Avery was the Game 3 loser, 3–2 in Toronto, one of Atlanta's four losses, each by one run. The following year, it all came together—at least until mid-September.

The 1993 season was the pinnacle of Avery's career. He made the All-Star team and was 16–4 before a September 12 start against San Diego. He not only lost but suffered an injury to a muscle on his left side, under his armpit. The oblique. It would be a recurring problem. Although Avery ended the season 18–6 with a 2.94 ERA as the club's fourth starter, he was never the same again.

Many in baseball wondered if it was the workload. Avery had made 135 big-league starts (including postseason) before the age of 24. Poison Avery was no longer toxic to the opposition. From the beginning of the 1991 season until September 12, 1993, he'd been 45–23. Afterward: 48–49. The old, or rather young, Avery resurfaced periodically. Despite going 7–13 with a 4.67 ERA in 1995, he blanked Cincinnati 6–0 in Game 4 to complete the NLCS sweep. Avery even won Game 4 of the '95 World Series, limiting Cleveland to one run in six innings of a 5–2 victory.

But injured again and sidelined for two months in 1996, Avery went 7–10, his ERA 4.47. His last appearance in a Braves uniform was painful to watch: Game 4 of the '96 World Series, after the Braves blew a 6–0 lead over the Yankees and lost not only an 8–6 decision but control of the series. In the top of the 10th inning, the game tied 6–6, Avery allowed a hit, three walks, and the go-ahead run—which scored on the third walk to Wade Boggs. This, after Cox had Avery intentionally walk Bernie Williams to face the left-handed Boggs.

Avery signed with Boston the following January and went 16–14 in two seasons. But his ERA ballooned to 5.64. Poison Avery was old history. A 6–7 season with Cincinnati in 1999 was cut short by injury. A brief 2003 comeback with the Tigers, the team of his childhood, resulted in 19 relief appearances, the last on July 20. Poison Avery was done at 33.

In 11 seasons, Avery was 96–83 with an ERA of 4.19 and 980 strikeouts in 1,554⅔ innings pitched. He lives in Dearborn, Michigan, with his wife and children. And still…what if?

25 Miracle Braves II

The 1948 Boston Braves were not exactly the out-of-nowhere wonders of those 1914 Miracle Braves. Yet their 1948 National League pennant, the foundation for which was laid two years earlier, was remarkable in its own right.

From 1935 through 1945, the Braves were abysmal, beginning with the 38–115 obscenity of '35 (a mere 61½ games out of first place) and continuing through 10 more years in which Boston had just two winning seasons—barely—never finishing better than fifth. The Braves went 714–961 during that 11-year nightmare, 247 games under .500. On average, they finished 33 games out. Ouch.

In 1946 owner Lou Perini lured manager Billy Southworth away from the St. Louis Cardinals. He got his man with cold cash: a $35,000 salary and incentives for finishing fourth ($5,000), third ($10,000), second ($15,000), and first ($20,000). In '48 Southworth would cash in on every bonus.

The new manager was dictatorial, instituting rules, penalties, fines, and a curfew. The '46 Braves went 81–72 and finished fourth. In 1947 third baseman Bob Elliott, acquired from Pittsburgh, was named the National League's MVP after batting .317 with 22 homers and 113 RBIs. Warren Spahn and Johnny Sain each won 21 games for those third-place Braves, nearly half of the club's 86 wins.

"Spahn and Sain, and pray for rain" became the club's down-the-stretch mantra in 1948, Sain winning 24 games and Spahn 15. Yet there was more to those Braves, who quickly overcame a 1–6 start. The new middle infielders were a kid shortstop named Alvin Dark and veteran second baseman Eddie "the Brat" Stanky, acquired from Brooklyn. When Stanky broke his ankle in July, Sibby Sisti filled in admirably. Pitchers Bill Voiselle and Vern Bickford combined for 24 victories. Spahn and Sain were spectacular in September. The Braves easily led the NL in team ERA (3.38). Elliott (23 homers, 100 RBIs), Tommy Holmes (.325), and left fielder Jeff Heath (.319, 20 homers, and 76 RBIs, acquired from Cleveland) enabled the Braves to lead the league in hitting (.275).

On June 11 the Braves moved into first place for the first time. Timing is everything: on June 15, in the team's first televised game from Braves Field, Boston beat the Cubs 6–3.

By then, fans began flocking to the ballpark. By season's end, total attendance was a club-record 1,455,439. In a city where the Braves were perennial second bananas to the Red Sox, Braves Field

The Boston Braves meet the Cleveland Indians in Game 1 of the 1948 World Series before 40,135 spectators at Braves Field in Boston. Boston won 1–0 in the pitching duel between Boston's Johnny Sain and Cleveland's Bob Feller. The Indians went on to win the Series 4–2.

became the place to be. For the first time in 34 years, they were back in the World Series, this time against the Cleveland Indians of shortstop/manager Lou Boudreau and Bob Feller of the estimated (radar guns didn't exist then) 95-mph fastball. Hence the nickname "Rapid Robert."

A capacity, standing-room-only crowd of 40,135 crammed into Braves Field and was treated to a classic pitching duel. For eight innings, Sain shut down the Indians. For seven, Feller shut down the Braves. In the bottom of the eighth, with runners on first and second, Feller and Boudreau executed a pickoff, the "daylight" play, to perfection. Or so they thought.

But after Boudreau clearly tagged out pinch-runner Phil Masi, the second-base umpire called Masi safe. The Indians were livid. Game films later showed that the call was, indeed, incorrect. Tommy Holmes' two-out single scored Masi, and Sain completed the 1–0 victory.

Bob Lemon beat Spahn 4–1 in Game 2 for a split, and then the Series moved to Cleveland's cavernous Municipal Stadium. The Indians took two tight games 2–0 and 2–1 and needed just one more victory to win the World Series. That prospect drew a record crowd of 86,288 for Game 5, still the largest in American League history. They left disappointed after the Braves teed off on Feller. Bob Elliott—"Mr. Team," as he was know in Boston—homered in successive at-bats, and Boston scored six times in the seventh to win 11–5.

But the Braves badly missed Heath's bat. Heath had broken his ankle sliding just four days before the regular season ended. In the five World Series games besides the Game 5 breakout, the Braves scored just six runs. Half came in the 4–3, Game 6 loss that made the Indians world champions. They haven't won a World Series since.

A year or two later Spahn said this: "The 1948 team was a conglomeration of experienced players in the twilight of their careers. It was strictly a one-shot proposition, and nobody talked much about repeating the next year."

Warren Spahn, a hell of a pitcher, was also one smart man.

26 The SuperStation

It began with one little weak-signal TV station. In 1975 a pecan pie–in-the-sky Atlanta entrepreneur named Ted Turner owned WTCG, a distant fourth in a four-station market. WTCG's staples were old TV reruns. Desperate for original programming, Turner tried something truly original: he offered the Atlanta Braves, losers of 94 games the previous season, $3 million for the rights to air 60 Braves games a year for five seasons.

"We weren't even sure people could get WTCG on their TV sets," said Bob Hope, who'd become the PR director of the Braves once Ted bought them on January 6, 1976. This, after Turner's mid-December announcement that he was putting up the WTCG signal for satellite distribution. The first four markets: Grand Island, Nebraska; Newport News, Virginia; Troy, Alabama; and Newton, Kansas. Huh? Say what?

Soon 24 states across the South became part of Ted's regional network for bad Braves baseball. He didn't stop there. He bought the club for $11 million. And then he went full-bore into cable television. As Turner's TV advertising campaign later famously proclaimed: "I was cable before cable was cool."

From his humble UHF TV beginnings, Turner built a television empire and a fortune. And WTBS, "the SuperStation," turned the Braves into "America's Team."

Even when the Braves stunk in the '70s, finishing that decade with 92, 101, 93, and 94 defeats, from 1976 through '79, people across the country tuned in. They loved the broadcast team: "Uncle Ernie" Johnson, and Skip and Pete—the sarcastic, hilarious Skip Caray, and the "Professor," a baseball historian and pure professional named Pete Van Wieren.

The TV critics raved. "Is there a better broadcast team than Skip, Pete, and Ernie?" asked Ray Kenney of the *Milwaukee Journal*. "I haven't been exposed to it." Howard Rosenberg of the *Los Angeles Times* would write, "The best TV broadcast crew in any sport may be working on cable TV at WTBS. Ernie, Skip, and Pete blend so well alternating on TV and radio that you hardly notice when one is replaced by another."

To Jack Bogaczyk, then of the Roanoke, Virginia, *Times & News World*, "America's team is really Skip and Ernie and Pete."

Mostly, people everywhere just liked watching baseball on TV every night. By 1982, as the Braves were building toward an NL West title, their popularity had skyrocketed. Even in Storm Lake, Iowa, one of several towns *Sports Illustrated* featured in an August article entitled, "The U.S.A. is the Home of the Braves."

"They fill a void, because we're so far away from anything, there's nothing to relate to," said Steve Getty, news director of KAYL Radio (part of the St. Louis Cardinals radio network). "Five years ago, you'd mention the name Biff Pocoroba to anyone around here, and they'd go, 'Who?'"

By '82, the backup Braves catcher was a minor celebrity at Puffs White Cap Inn in Storm Lake. In Valdez, Alaska, dozens of oil town regulars hit the Totem Inn most afternoons to watch the Braves play night games on live TV several time zones to the east. As Totem Inn bartender Louie Steamer told SI, WTBS had provided the first live television in town. Now there was something to actually watch and root for. In Reno, Nevada, reportedly, the working girls at one local brothel hung a Braves team photo in one room. Everyone thought the Braves hung the moon.

WTBS was now shown on 4,152 cable TV systems in all 50 states. As Bill Taafe of *Sports Illustrated* wrote, "Incredible as it seems, 21.2 million Americans can now watch Rufino Linares' every move."

Nine years later, in the worst-to-first miracle season of 1991, many millions more were still watching Ted Turner's Atlanta Braves on television.

27 The One That Got Away

For all their greatness and success throughout the 1990s and midway through the next decade, the Atlanta Braves suffered real heartbreak, too. They played in five World Series in the '90s, finally winning one—and only one—in 1995. Of their four defeats in the Fall Classic, only one was no contest. In 1999 the New York Yankees affirmed that they were the team of the '90s—or at least the second half of the decade—with a four-game sweep.

In the epic 1991 World Series, the Braves could well have won the World Championship in Game 6 in Minnesota…and again in Game 7 in the Metrodome. Each time, they lost in excruciating fashion—in extra innings by a run. In 1992, after the miraculous "Braves Win! Braves Win!" Game 7 in the NLCS, the Toronto Blue Jays were the better team in that World Series.

The one that got away? The one they really should've won? The 1996 World Series. Ask any Brave. They all agree.

Had the Braves defeated the Yankees, they would have silenced the critics once and for all. All that talk about a record 14 consecutive division titles but just one world championship? A second World Series trophy would've put a stop to that. How many World Series did Cincinnati's Big Red Machine win anyway? That's right, two.

In 1996, as in 1995, the Braves were the best team in baseball. They looked it in the first two games of the World Series. In the Bronx, they crushed the Yankees 12–1 in the opener on two home runs by teenaged Andruw Jones. Greg Maddux then shut out the Yanks 4–0, 21 of the 24 outs he recorded in eight innings coming via 21 ground balls. Afterward, Yankees owner George Steinbrenner was livid and embarrassed as the teams flew to Atlanta.

New York's 5–2 win in Game 3 seemed a minor speed bump, especially when the Braves roared to a 6–0 lead in Game 4. Denny Neagle was throwing a two-hit shutout through five innings. Derek Jeter's single started a three-run Yankee sixth that included a key single by Cecil Fielder. Neagle was lifted. Come the eighth, the Braves still led 6–3.

For the first time all season, Bobby Cox brought in closer Mark Wohlers in the eighth inning. He gave up two singles. When shortstop Rafael Belliard misplayed a grounder and got one out instead of a double play, Jim Leyritz came to the plate with two runners on.

More than a decade later, sitting in a booth at an Atlanta institution named Manuel's Tavern, Cecil Fielder recalled it all: how Leyritz had trouble getting around on Wohlers' fastball that sometimes hit 100 mph on the radar gun. How Leyritz kept fouling off pitches, some directly toward the owner's box, where Jimmy Carter and Henry Aaron sat with Ted Turner and his wife, Jane Fonda. Fielder remembered fearing for the safety of the ex-president and the all-time home run king, as Leyritz swung late and fouled off six pitches.

When Wohlers finally threw a hanging slider, Fielder couldn't believe his eyes. Neither could a capacity crowd of 51,881 as Leyritz jumped on the pitch and hit a three-run homer for a 6–6 tie. The crowd was stunned, the stadium virtually hushed.

When the Yankees scored twice in the 10th to win 8–6, the Series was tied at two games apiece. But the tide was irrevocably turned.

Bobby Cox knew that. When he finished answering questions in a postgame press conference, the stunned manager walked into the Braves clubhouse and then through his open office door. All of us within earshot heard him scream: "Bleep!" Cox knew. Everyone knew. The Series that once clearly belonged to the Braves was now even at best, New York's at worst.

In the quiet of a shell-shocked clubhouse, Wohlers gave the classiest, most stand-up postgame performance by an athlete this author has ever seen in nearly four decades of sportswriting. He answered question after question about the fateful at-bat to wave after wave of writers from across the country, from all four time zones on varying deadlines. Wohlers was as professional as his team was soon doomed.

In Game 5, in the last game in Atlanta-Fulton County Stadium history, Andy Pettitte beat Smoltz in a 1–0 pitchers' duel. The only run came in the fourth inning, when Fielder doubled home Charlie Hayes. Hayes had reached base when Marquis Grissom, Atlanta's Gold Glove center fielder, dropped Hayes' fly ball in right-center after nearly colliding with Jermaine Dye.

The rookie Dye appeared to have cut in front of Grissom just before the ball glanced off Grissom's glove. But Grissom, another stand-up Brave, refused to blame Dye. It was his fault, his error.

Back in New York, the Yankees quickly jumped on Maddux for three runs and won 3–2 for their first World Series championship since 1978. A world championship that every Brave will tell you should have belonged to them. The one that really got away.

28 Hello, World...Series

That's essentially what Andruw Jones did in October 1996. Before uttering a word, he introduced himself to the world at the World Series. As introductions go, this one was going, going, gone…and then again a short while later.

A night after Game 1 of the Fall Classic was postponed by rain, the precocious Jones made an immediate impression. In his first at-bat in his first World Series, the teenager from Curacao hit a two-out, 3–2 fastball from Andy Pettitte and launched it into the 10th row of the left-field bleachers at Yankee Stadium. The 388-foot blast made it 2–0 Atlanta.

It also made Jones the youngest player ever to hit a homer in World Series history. At the age of 19 years, 180 days, he broke Mickey Mantle's record of 20 years, 362 days. Due to the previous evening's rainout, Jones made history on what would have been the late Mantle's 65th birthday.

And he was merely beginning. Autumn in New York? Try awesome in New York.

In his next at-bat in the third inning, Jones technically became the second-youngest player to homer in a World Series, as well. Against Yankees reliever Brian Boehringer, Jones' three-run home run made it 8–0. He joined Gene Tenace of the 1972 Oakland A's as the only players ever to homer in their first two World Series at-bats. Yet Tenace never had the kind of power the kid Jones possessed.

"I really don't lift weights. I think God gave me this power," he said after the Braves crushed the Yankees 12–1. It was the Yanks' worst World Series loss in their long Series history. The previous nadir? A 13–5 beating by the Milwaukee Braves in Game 2 of the 1958 World Series.

"He's just a great, great player," Braves manager Bobby Cox said of Jones afterward. "He's not your normal 19-year-old."

It's abnormal for a kid to start the season in lower Class A ball and end up making history in the Bronx cathedral of baseball. Following Jones' second homer, Braves broadcaster Pete Van Wieren told his radio audience, "After his meteoric rise through our farm system, from Macon to Durham to Greenville to Richmond, does Andruw realize there's no higher league he can go to?"

"At the beginning of the year, I never thought that it could happen this fast," said Jones, a late-season call-up who'd had just 106 big-league at-bats before his historic two-homer night. "But it's great fun to have made it to the World Series. Now that I'm here, I just want to have fun."

The evening was no fun for New Yorkers, especially the ones wearing pinstriped uniforms. "We just flat-out got beat up," said Yankees right fielder Paul O'Neill. Speaking of Jones and his two-homer, five-RBI night, the Yankees' Mariano Duncan said, "I think he's the one who killed our club tonight." You think?

Andruw Jones watches his home run soar into the left-field bleachers at Yankee Stadium during the second inning of the 1996 World Series. This was Jones' first at-bat in his first World Series.

"He makes it look easy," said Atlanta's Chipper Jones. "Even at 19, he looks like he should be here. Even when he was 16, he looked like he belonged here."

Going back to the sixth inning of Game 7 of that year's NLCS, and including his homer in that 15–0 clincher over St. Louis, Jones had homered in his last three official at-bats. For the 1996 World Series, he hit .400. But after Greg Maddux shut out the Yankees 4–0 in Game 2, the Yanks won four games in a row to dethrone Atlanta. Playing in all six games, Jones didn't homer again in the Series but hit .400 (8-for-20) with six RBIs and six walks.

29 Mad Dog: A Three-Part Appreciation

The résumé is remarkable, the first-ballot cakewalk into Cooperstown a given. Indeed, Greg Maddux may well receive the highest percentage of votes for Baseball's Hall of Fame. And why shouldn't he? Considering:

- his four consecutive Cy Young Awards (1992 through 1995), the first of only two pitchers to do so
- the 75–29 record and 1.98 ERA during that stretch, while allowing an average of less than a runner per inning
- the 355 career victories, eighth on the all-time list, second most in baseball's live ball era (post-1920) and topped only by another Braves pitcher, Warren Spahn (363, the most wins of any lefty ever)
- a record 17 straight seasons with at least 15 wins, one of just 10 pitchers to record 300 wins and 3,000 strikeouts (3,371 to be exact)
- his 18 Gold Gloves

Who knows? The man they called "Mad Dog" might even be the first unanimous choice for the Hall. In 1995, the year Atlanta finally won the World Series, all Maddux did was go 19–2 with an earned-run average of 1.63, ballooning up from the previous year's 1.56—the second-lowest in baseball since Bob Gibson's 1.12 ERA in 1968 resulted in the lowering of the pitcher's mound.

I was privileged to witness most of that Maddux excellence. I covered the Braves for part of the 1990s, writing regularly about them into the first half of the next decade. He remains the most remarkable pitcher I've ever seen. All those numbers don't even begin to do his mastery justice.

So instead of more statistics, I offer three of my favorite anecdotes about Doggie, as the Braves called him. They are telling, about the pitcher and the man.

July 2, 1997. A Wednesday afternoon getaway game in Yankee Stadium where, the previous October, Maddux lost the decisive Game 6 of the World Series 3–2. Back in the Bronx, he was vintage Mad Dog with a three-hit, no-walk, eight-strikeout, 2–0 shutout of the world champion Yanks. Maddux needed just 84 pitches that day, 61 of which were strikes. His was a matinee idyll.

He faced just 28 batters, the Braves turning one double play, and Maddux promptly picking off Mark Whiten after he'd singled and reached second on a teammate's groundout. Derek Jeter struck out twice, the first time looking at a classic called-third strike on the outside corner. This was the first season of interleague play, and John Hirschbeck, an American League umpire who'd never worked behind the plate with Maddux pitching, was later asked about his first up-close look. "As advertised," the ump said admiringly.

What I also admired was the economy with which Maddux pitched. The game lasted only two hours, nine minutes. Getting to LaGuardia Airport from Yankee Stadium can take an eternity, especially in rush-hour traffic. That day, the cab ride was a breeze. After filing my story, I easily made my flight home to Atlanta. Thanks, Doggie.

The following Tuesday, a few hours before Maddux would pitch in the All-Star Game in Cleveland, his father was arrested and accused of fondling a housekeeper at a downtown hotel. Dave Maddux was charged with third-degree sexual imposition, a misdemeanor that carried a $500 fine and, if convicted, up to 60 days in jail.

Greg Maddux throws during first-inning action against the Cincinnati Reds in Game 3 of the 1995 NLCS in Atlanta. That year Maddux went 19–2 with an ERA of 1.63 and helped his team to a World Series victory.

Maddux said he didn't know any of this until after the game, in which he pitched two innings and gave up a solo homer in the National League's 3–1 loss. The following day, when the arrest story broke, an editor in the sports department where I worked told me to call Maddux and get a comment. When his wife, Kathy, answered the phone, I identified myself, apologized for bothering her, and explained I was ordered to call Greg and ask him about his father's arrest.

Kathy was not pleased and let me know in so many words, including, "Don't you ever call us at home again." I apologized once more, and she hung up.

The next afternoon in the clubhouse, before the Braves resumed their season that evening, Maddux approached me and asked, "Did you call my house yesterday?" Yes, I said, explaining that an editor had assigned me to. When I began to apologize, Maddux cut me off. "You call my house any time you need to," he said. He meant it, too. That's a pro. That's Maddux.

A few years later I was working on a story about athletes who'd had Lasik eye surgery. Maddux had undergone the procedure and raved about it, urging me to have it done, as well. He agreed to talk to me on a Thursday morning, when the clubhouse opened at 10:00 before that afternoon's game. I arrived, sat in a chair beside his locker, and waited as Maddux walked into the player's lounge to get another cup of coffee and something to eat.

Moments later he came storming back into the clubhouse in a mock rage. "Can you believe this?!" he shouted to the few people already there, including teammate Wally Joyner. Behind Maddux came a chagrined clubby, a relatively new clubhouse kid who'd committed a mortal sin. Sent out to pick up doughnuts, the kid came back with Dunkin' Donuts, not Krispy Kremes.

"How do they expect us to play like champions," Maddux shouted, "when they don't *feed us* like champions?!"

"No problem," said Joyner, who'd grown up in the Atlanta suburb of Stone Mountain and knew the drill. He left the clubhouse and came back about 25 minutes later with two or three large boxes of hot, glazed Krispy Kremes.

"Which one did you go to?" I asked. "The one on Ponce de Leon, of course," Joyner said. "Of course," I said agreeing, knowing the place well. "The Vatican."

With that, Maddux sat down, ate a doughnut, and told me about his Lasik surgery.

Thanks again, Doggie.

30 Those '69 Braves...and Mets

By 1969, the first-year euphoria of '66 was long gone. After three straight indifferent seasons, the novelty of Braves baseball had worn off. In 1968 attendance had plunged by more than 400,000 from the initial peak of 1,539,801. But in baseball, as throughout society, 1969 was a landmark year.

Man walked on the Moon. More than 400,000 people walked all over Woodstock. In October a half-million Vietnam War protestors came to the Washington Mall and asked the U.S. government to give peace a chance. This, a week after the Atlanta Braves' first postseason sojourn was abruptly cut short by…the New York Mets.

The Age of Aquarius was also the advent of divisional play in the major leagues. Baseball not only expanded from 20 to 24 teams in '69, but from two leagues to four divisions. For that, Atlanta was grateful, as well as one of six clubs in the new NL West. The city turned out, too, to support the Braves under new manager Luman Harris.

The longtime luminaries were still in place: Henry Aaron, who'd hit 44 homers and drove in 97 runs; Phil Niekro, who won 23 games, including the division clincher with help from another knuckleballer, Hoyt Wilhelm, picked up on waivers in September; and, of course, the "Beeg Boy," Rico Carty, one of the finest pure hitters in franchise history. Which was more impressive: that Carty hit .342 that year, or that he'd spent all of 1968 fighting tuberculosis?

The Dominican spent nearly five months in a sanitorium before being released. The illness did not affect his batting eye. Beginning in 1964, he hit .330, .310, and .326. Carty would later win the NL batting title in 1970 with a .366 average, the highest in the majors since Ted Williams' .388 in 1957. Carty also set a team record by hitting safely in 31 consecutive games, and the club won 27 of its last 38 games to take the first NL West title. Yet neither the Beeg Boy nor any of his teammates could do anything against the '69 Miracle Mets, who'd compiled the first winning season in club history since the original 120-loss misfits of '62.

"Seven hundred losses later, here we are," Ed Kranepool, an original Met, smiled and said to himself as Niekro walked to the mound for Game 1. It was no contest. Beat the Mets? Not a chance in a best-of-five NLCS.

New York took a 2–0 lead in the second inning. The second run scored on a passed ball by catcher Bob Didier.

Aaron would double in a run and later homer off Tom Seaver for a 5–4 lead. But Braves' fielding blunders allowed the Mets to tie it, retake the lead on an Orlando Cepeda throwing error, and finally win 9–5.

"It seems things go that way when we play the Mets," said Cepeda. "They don't do anything wrong."

In Game 2 the Mets jumped all over 18-game winner Ron Reed. He lasted 1⅔ innings and was gone after Tommie Agee's two-run homer. The Mets shelled three Atlanta relievers, and it was 8–0 after 3½ innings. Not even an Aaron three-run homer could prevent an 11–6 defeat.

In the frenzy of Shea Stadium, Atlanta instantly took a 2–0 lead in Game 3. In the third, with Braves on second and third and a 1–2 count on Carty, Mets manager Gil Hodges suddenly yanked Gary Gentry in the middle of the at-bat. Needing a strikeout, he called on a young kid from Texas.

Nolan Ryan would later become baseball's all-time strikeout king. That afternoon, all of 22, he was the Prince of the City of New York. He struck out Carty swinging on a fastball. After walking Cepeda to load the bases, Ryan struck out Clete Boyer. When Didier flied out, the Atlanta threat was over. So were the Braves. The Mets teed off on Pat Jarvis, winning 7–4.

"The Mets beat the hell out of us," Luman Harris said. The Mets also partied on the field at game's end like it was, well, 1969. They went on to stun the favored Baltimore Orioles in a five-game World Series. Atlanta wouldn't sniff the postseason again for another 13 years.

31 The Game at Shea after 9/11

For all the memorable games the Braves played in Shea Stadium—the good and the bad, the triumphant and terrible—the most memorable moment came on Friday night, September 21, 2001. Those of us who were there will never, ever forget it.

It was the first major professional sporting event in New York City following 9/11. Ten days after the terrorists attacked and the Twin Towers fell, baseball returned to the city and to Shea. And that was a fine thing.

The night before, the Braves had concluded a series in Philadelphia. Following the opening game of that four-game set, Phillies broadcaster Harry Kalas had asked everybody in the stadium press lounge to stand, hold hands, and join him in singing "God Bless America." Now, that series finally over, a limousine driving north on the New Jersey Turnpike was taking the Braves' broadcast crew to Manhattan. As usual, they talked baseball over drinks.

The talking and sipping abruptly stopped as the limo neared the city. Pete Van Wieren saw the shafts of light from Ground Zero and thought, *My God, this is where it happened.* The rest of the trip was in silence.

The next morning, about 20 Braves players, broadcasters, and club officials left the Grand Hyatt Hotel and rode a downtown subway from Grand Central Station to near where the World Trade Center once stood. They saw the ruins, the twisted shards of steel. Dust was everywhere, a strange odor in the air.

Back at Grand Central, there were hundreds, thousands of missing-person photos. The city was so, so quiet. The 7 train subway line to Shea Stadium, though, was packed later that afternoon. People were relatively subdued, but it was time to play baseball again. It would prove cathartic for a city in mourning, and make the evening unforgettable.

The pregame ceremonies included police and fire personnel from each of the five boroughs. Pipes were played by the bagpipers who traditionally play at all fire and police funerals in New York City. As usual, numerous city and state officials were on hand, including Mayor Rudy Giuliani.

And there were the teams. All the Braves lined up along the third-base line for the pregame ceremonies. The Mets aligned themselves up the first-base line, in front of their dugout. Marc Anthony sang a stirring rendition of the National Anthem. There was a 21-gun salute, and players from both teams later picked up the shells in the outfield as keepsakes.

Most memorably, after the pregame ceremonies concluded, players from both sides walked toward each other and then embraced. By then, TV had gone to a commercial. Back on the air, Van Wieren recalled his broadcast partner Don Sutton was emotionally overcome. "The players are hugging each other," Sutton said, choking up. "I've never seen that before."

During the game, the Mets wore caps representing the New York City police and fire departments, EMTs, and the Port Authority. Jason Marquis, the Braves' starting pitcher, had grown up on Staten Island. He was thinking of Michael Cammarata, a childhood friend and Little League teammate who'd become a New York firefighter and was killed in one of the towers.

With a 1–1 tie in the seventh inning, Liza Minnelli performed a rousing rendition of "New York, New York." The crowd of 41,235 sang along, then roared. They roared even louder in the bottom of the eighth. After Atlanta took a 2–1 lead, Mike Piazza came to bat with a runner on. Facing Braves reliever Steve Karsay, who'd grown up in Flushing just a few miles from Shea, Piazza hit a game-winning, two-run homer.

As Tom Glavine said afterward, "There was a higher power at work here tonight."

In September 2010, when Bobby Cox made his last trip to Flushing at Citi Field, where the Mets now play, he recalled that post-9/11 game. "Piazza hit a home run to win it," he said, "and it didn't bother me. Generally, you get beat, you want to beat your head against the wall. I mean, I didn't want to lose that game, but it was a New York thing that night."

32 "The Last Great Pennant Race"

Or was it "The Last Pure Pennant Race?" Or simply "The Last Great Race?" By any name, the Braves-Giants race of 1993 was simply the best, better than all the rest, and the perfect way to climax the last regular season before the advent of the wild-card.

"Confidence," Greg Maddux said on the final day of that regular season. "Even when we were seven or eight games behind, these guys were surprised they weren't in first place."

In the off-season Maddux had signed a five-year, $28 million free agent contract with Atlanta. But even after adding Mad Dog to a rotation of Glavine, Smoltz, and Avery, even with the July 20 acquisition of Fred McGriff, the two-time reigning National League–champion Braves found themselves 10 games behind San Francisco in the NL West on July 22.

That was two nights after the infamous press-box fire in Atlanta-Fulton County Stadium on the day the Crime Dog arrived from San Diego. He homered, and the Braves rallied to win. He kept homering—five in the next seven games—and the Braves kept winning (eight of nine to finish July). Before a three-game series in San Francisco on August 23, with his team still 7½ games behind, Terry Pendleton said, "We know what we have to do. We have to sweep."

Done. After Avery and Glavine outdueled the opposition, Atlanta belted six homers—two each by David Justice and McGriff—and roughed up Bill Swift in a 9–1 rout.

"That," Maddux later said, "is where it all started."

The Braves won 19 of 26 games in August. They'd routed Swift again in a rematch in Atlanta. After winning eight of their first 10 games in September, the Braves found themselves tied with the Giants for first—but not for long. Follow the bouncing pennant race: the Giants inexplicably lost eight straight in Candlestick Park, and Atlanta took a four-game lead. Now the Giants rallied, winning 11 of 12, and then 14 of 16 to get right back in it.

When Barry Bonds hit four homers in three games, and Atlanta lost 5–2 to the Astros in the 157th game of the season, the Giants and Braves were tied atop the division, each with 100 victories.

"I think I know how Lazarus felt," said Giants manager Dusty Baker.

Entering the season's final weekend, the Braves faced the Rockies while the Giants opened a four-game series in Los Angeles against their hated rivals, the Dodgers. Both teams won on Friday—the Braves behind Steve Avery's 18th win and Pendleton's five RBIs, the Giants on Barry Bonds' two homers and decisive double—to remain tied. "That right there is what MVPs are all about," Baker said presciently. Bonds would win the NL MVP Award at season's end. It would have to serve as his only solace that winter.

A continent away, Pendleton—the '91 NL MVP—helped batter the Rockies 10–1 the next day, only to have the Giants hold serve with a 5–3 win. On October 3 each team had 103 victories. "We've got to throw a win up there early so they see it," McGriff said in Atlanta, three hours ahead of the Pacific time zone.

"Let's break their hearts this time," said Dodgers manager Tommy Lasorda, whose club got knocked out by the Giants on the last day in '91 to give Atlanta the division.

In the bottom of the seventh in Georgia, Justice hit his 40th homer, driving in his 120th run, and Atlanta won 5–3. Justice joined Henry Aaron, Jeff Burroughs, and Dale Murphy as the only Braves to go 40–100 in a season. Then Justice joined his teammates in front of the TV. In Los Angeles Mike Piazza homered twice, his three-run shot in the eighth making it 10–1. "It's over," Justice declared in Atlanta. "Bonds can't hit an eight-run homer."

Despite winning 14 of their final 17 games, the Giants lost the Last Great Pennant Race by one game. "Only good thing about it is, I didn't have to see them on the field," Bonds said of the Braves. "Didn't have to see them parade around like the last two years." As a Pirate, Bonds had lost the previous two NLCS titles in excruciating fashion.

Drained by the long, exhausting pennant race, the Braves were beaten by Philadelphia 4–2 in the NLCS. The Phillies went on to lose to Toronto in the World Series. The Braves went home, winners of 104 games in the regular season but still seeking their first world championship. "It was like we had to play perfect baseball all the time," John Smoltz said in a quiet clubhouse. "It's going to be a frustrating off-season."

33 Lou or Lew?

That was the question. Everyone knew how to pronounce Selva Lewis Burdette's nickname. Spelling it was another matter. So, was it Lew or Lou?

"I write it however it's spelled on my checks," Burdette once said. Well then, in lieu of a definitive answer, let's move on to the other burning question about Burdette.

What on earth was he throwing in the 1957 World Series against the mighty New York Yankees? What was the pitch that so befuddled the Bronx Bombers? "My psychological pitch," Burdette slyly called it back then with a grin. A "sinkerball specialist," he labeled himself. Opponents called his secret weapon a spitter, Jackie Robinson going so far as to virtually call Burdette a cheater.

"No man can make a ball sink like that," said Robinson, the man who broke baseball's color barrier. "If it's a sinker, it's the best in the business."

Whatever it was, the pitch enabled Burdette to beat the Yankees three times that classic fall, including the 5–0 Game 7 shutout to give Milwaukee its only World Series title. That season the Yankees of Mantle and Berra, Bauer and Skowron won a league-high 98 games while being shut out just twice in that 154-game season. Burdette beat them three times in nine days, shutting them out twice in the last 72 hours of the series.

In Game 2, after giving up single runs in the second and third innings, Burdette blanked the Yanks the rest of the way in a 4–2 victory. Thus began his string of 24 consecutive scoreless innings. Burdette bested Yankees ace Whitey Ford in a magnificent Game 5 pitching duel, winning 1–0 with the aid of Wes Covington's sensational catch to rob Gil McDougald of a homer and Joe Adcock's sixth-inning RBI single.

Warren Spahn, the incomparable left-hander who led the National League that season with 21 wins, was the scheduled Game 7 starter. But he'd been sick with the flu for three days, so manager Fred Haney turned again to Lew, or Lou, working on two days' rest. The rest was easy after Milwaukee's four-run third inning gave Burdette the cushiest of cushions.

He baffled the Yankees again and beat them 5–0. He allowed seven hits (six singles), finished with a World Series ERA of 0.67, and threw his third complete game. He was easily voted the series' Most Valuable Player. It was a nice payback for Burdette, who briefly broke in as a Yankees rookie in 1950 before being traded to the then-Boston Braves for veteran pitcher Johnny Sain.

But Burdette's motivation wasn't revenge, and his genius wasn't just his "psychological pitch" itself but the gyrations he went through before throwing it.

"I wouldn't know how to throw a spitter even if I wanted to," said the man nicknamed "Nitro" for his hometown in West Virginia. "But if the hitters have that in their minds that I'm throwing one, then all it does is give them something else to think about."

Opponents thought about it whenever they faced "Fidgety," another of Burdette's nicknames. Dodgers manager Walter Alston told his players to step out of the box and let the ball dry if they thought Burdette was throwing a spitter. Reds manager Birdie Tebbetts, through general manager Gabe Paul, asked National League president Warren Giles to reprimand Burdette. Giles wrote back, "Nothing in the rules prohibits a pitcher from moistening his fingers if he doesn't apply moisture to the ball. We have watched Burdette warm up, and we are satisfied up to now he has not violated rule 8.02."

Lew Burdette throws the final pitch of the 1957 World Series at Yankee Stadium. Yankees first baseman Bill Skowron hit the ball to Braves third baseman Eddie Mathews to end the game and give Milwaukee its only Series title.

Burdette's explanation? "I'm nervous on the mound," he said. "I touch my cap, I tug at my pants. I pull my sleeve loose. I wipe the sweat off my eyebrows. The sweat comes off my forehead into these bushy things [his eyebrows] and then drips into my eyes. I got a right to see, don't I? I wouldn't have taken off my pants if Birdie wanted me to. He just wanted to get my goat."

No one ever did. Beginning with his 15–5 breakthrough season of 1953 through '62, Burdette won 167 games in that 10-year span. He went 20–10 in '58, for a league-high .667 winning percentage. He led the NL with 21 victories in '59, including his 1–0, 13-inning complete-game win over Pittsburgh's Harvey Haddix, who lost a perfect game in that fateful 13th. That off-season, Burdette asked for a then-astronomical $10,000 raise.

"I'm the greatest pitcher that ever lived," he said. "The greatest game that was ever pitched in baseball wasn't good enough to beat me, so I've got to be the greatest." His hypothesis was as convoluted as his mannerisms on the mound. The club disagreed.

Traded to St. Louis in 1963, Burdette retired in 1967 with a career record of 203–144. A masterful control pitcher, he was 179–120 as a Brave, inducted into the Braves Hall of Fame in 2001, and died in 2007. One of his 179 wins came in Milwaukee on August 18, 1960. The game he became "No-No" Burdette, no-hitting Philadelphia and scoring the lone run in that 1–0 victory.

The only Phillie who reached base was Tony Gonzalez, hit by a pitch in the fifth inning. Once Gonzalez was promptly erased on a double play, Burdette finished by facing the minimum of 27 batters. That game, as opponents often found when facing him, Burdette was a real Lew-Lou.

34 The Night Ted Managed

He was cable before cable was cool. He built TBS, won the America's Cup, bought the Braves, married Jane Fonda, bought half of Montana, built a personal fortune worth nearly $3 billion, and made CNN the world's TV channel of choice. And then there's Ted Turner's most memorable role: manager of the Atlanta Braves.

On May 10, 1977, in his second season of ownership, Turner's ballclub was in a funk. The Braves had just lost their 16th consecutive game. What's an owner to do? Why, get rid of the manager. Not permanently, just for a brief sabbatical.

That was the gist of the phone call Pete Van Wieren got that morning at the team hotel in Pittsburgh. The Braves broadcaster, who also doubled as the club's traveling secretary, knew manager Dave Bristol was upset as soon as he answered the phone. Bristol wasn't being fired, but he was being sent on a leave of absence. His replacement? His boss. Turner was flying in from Atlanta that day to assess the situation.

Van Wieren easily got Bristol a plane ticket back to Atlanta. Getting him out of town was another matter. The manager was extremely embarrassed and didn't want to be seen leaving the William Penn Hotel. Bristol waited down on the loading dock, where Van Wieren brought his luggage and then tried to hail a cab. He managed to avoid Braves second baseman Rod Gilbreath and sportswriter Frank Hyland, who were walking down the sidewalk, and finally flagged down a taxi. The cabbie refused to drive down the ramp. So Van Wieren carried Bristol's luggage up to the street level, put it in the trunk, got Bristol in the cab, and sent him to the airport.

The fun was just beginning.

When the Braves got to Three Rivers Stadium that afternoon, there was a huge media contingent. There, too, was Ted Turner, sitting behind the desk in the visiting manager's office, dressed in a full road uniform. He had a wad of chewing tobacco in his cheek. By then, Turner had already run wind sprints in the outfield to get into the spirit of things. He was excited at the prospect of managing. He was also clueless.

Turner met with his coaching staff to delegate responsibilities. Third-base coach Vern Benson would handle game strategy. Pitching coach Johnny Sain would make all of the pitching moves. Chris Cannizzaro, the bullpen coach, would sit next to Turner in the dugout and tell him what the hell was going on.

"Any questions?" Turner asked. One coach raised his hand.

Owner Ted Turner put on a uniform and took over as manager, replacing Dave Bristol for a May 1977 game against the Pirates. Turner's efforts extended the team's losing streak to 17 games.

"Where's Dave?" Johnny Sain asked meekly, likely the only guy in town who didn't know about Bristol.

The Braves lost, naturally, 2–1, but not before Turner had Darrell Chaney make a rare pinch-hitting appearance with a runner on first. Chaney doubled; if the ball hadn't bounced over the outfield wall for a ground-rule double, Pat Rockett would've tied the score. Instead, it was loss No. 17.

Afterward, Turner wanted to go out and get something to eat and drink. This was long before the revitalization of downtown Pittsburgh, and most of the city had already shut down for the night. Van Wieren was part of a small entourage that accompanied Turner, who was merely looking for a good slice of pizza and a glass of red wine.

They finally found a pizza parlor, a little hole-in-the-wall joint. Perfect. Turner ordered his slice and a glass of red.

"When the order arrived," Van Wieren recalled, "Ted looked at it in disbelief. Instead of a triangular slice, the pizza was served as a small rectangular square. The wine came in a small juice glass."

The neophyte manager was not amused. "What is this?!" Turner asked the waitress. "We didn't come here for communion! Bring me some pizza and wine!"

The next day brought an end to Turner's brief managerial career. Chub Feeney, the National League president, invoked Rule 20, Section A, which prohibits a player or manager from owning stock in a team. Ted Turner would be no modern-day Connie Mack. He retired 0–1 as a manager. Back in Atlanta, Dave Bristol resumed managing. He was fired at season's end.

35 Be Seated by Walter Banks

Ted's usher. That's how he came to be known back in the halcyon '90s. Yet to call Walter Banks simply an usher is like calling Sinatra just a saloon singer.

On most nights, Banks is the most dignified person in Turner Field. He's a gentleman and a gentle man. He's almost courtly, even in his khaki pants and high-top, white canvas Converse All-Stars. Walter's not merely a numbers man but a numerical savant. In a sense, he's even something of a sage for a franchise that moved to Atlanta in 1966.

"We grew up together," Banks, one of the Braves' few remaining original employees, told Atlanta writer Bill Banks (no relation) during the 2010 season. "It's like how the largest oak tree in the forest began as an acorn. The Braves and me, we both started as acorns."

From that little acorn came a rather remarkable man. Banks has ushered more than 3,600 Braves games…and counting. That includes regular season games, the postseason, and two All-Star Games. He's worked nearly every home game in Atlanta Braves history, the vast majority as caretaker of the owner's box—first in Atlanta-Fulton County Stadium and, since 1997, in Turner Field.

At the Ted, he's the soul of section 107, where the rich and famous and connected often sit. Banks handles them all with an easy smile and the ease of a seasoned maître d'—the politicos and poseurs, the celebrities and sportsmen, and especially the longtime season-ticket holders. The regulars. The real fans.

People like the Carlins, Michael and Jan, season-ticket holders since 1982. As Banks told Bill Banks, '82 was not only the season the Braves won the National League West, but the summer the Carlins started taking their kids to ballgames. Now Banks ushers in Grandma and Grandpa Carlin right beside their grandchildren.

In the 2003 season a Braves intern named Bret Kovacs and his fiancée, Sarah Shils, were married in a club-level suite one Sunday morning before a ballgame. After the wedding, which was performed by Skip Caray—who'd somehow been Internet "ordained" to legally marry them—Sarah told her father, Jonathan, "I want to tell Mr. Banks what we did."

For years, while returning from his regular mid-game food runs to the media dining room, Banks always brought Sarah a cup of ice cream on his way back to section 107. That Sunday, before going to the 755 Club for a celebratory Bloody Mary, then returning to her father's regular seats for wedding day hot dogs, Sarah gave Mr. Banks her big news before anyone else.

On a summer night in 2010 the Grillo family—Jerry, Jane, and their son Joey—came to the ballpark. It was Joey's ninth birthday and his first Braves game. Joey has cerebral palsy and is confined to a wheelchair. Before the first pitch, Walter Banks stopped by section 201, posed for photos with the Grillos, and made a little boy's night a little brighter.

But that's just Walter being Walter. He's 71, a native Atlantan, old Howard High Class of '57. He's a Summerhill baby, raised in the neighborhood where Atlanta-Fulton County Stadium once stood and Turner Field now stands.

He worked at Rich's department store, and later Macy's, for a half-century. When the Braves set up shop in Atlanta in 1965, a year before the team moved South, Banks applied for a job, persisted, and was hired in '66. He's been with them ever since. At 6′½″ and 145 pounds, he moves with the grace, measured speed, and savvy of a veteran shortstop who can still turn a double play.

Banks has been to former Braves owner Ted Turner's ranches three times—twice in Montana, once in New Mexico. Ted's indoor suite beneath the stands in section 107 and behind the home dugout was named the Walter Banks Suite.

Banks was in the original owner's box, in the old ballpark, on the night of April 8, 1974. He was sitting with Jimmy Carter, then governor of Georgia, and an Alabama couple named Herbert and Stella Aaron, whose son Henry hit his historic 715th home run that night. As he has so often since 1966, Walter Banks was a witness to history.

Once Jimmy Carter became the 39th president and later jumped aboard the Braves worst-to-first bandwagon in 1991 and for much of the next decade, Banks was always prepared. "He doesn't eat much when he's here," Banks told Bill Banks. "He wants to focus on the game. But I always make sure I have his peanuts waiting."

The former peanut farmer from Plains always appreciates that. And like everyone else, Carter is astounded by Banks' recall of numbers and games. A self-described "storyteller with numbers," Walter's amazing.

As Bill Banks reported, a glance at the stadium clock reading 7:14 prompted this: "Babe Ruth hit 714 home runs, which you probably knew. But did you know that Jack Webb's badge number on *Dragnet* was 714? Matter of fact, Tim Hudson was born on 7/14." He paused. "Hank Aaron and Eddie Mathews both hit their 500th home runs on 7/14, although one year apart. Both against the Giants, incidentally, Mathews on 7/14/67, Aaron on 7/14/68."

Banks doesn't claim a photographic memory. Rather, he's always been an avid reader and associated people he read about with certain numbers. Like Aaron's 715th: "Interesting fact is when Hank hit it, Darrell Evans was on first, and he wore No. 11. Dusty [Baker] was on deck and had No. 12, and Dodgers catcher Joe Ferguson had 13. Go ahead and look it up."

I did. They did.

Banks worked the Braves' first postseason game in Atlanta in 1969, when Tom Seaver beat Phil Niekro. And Atlanta's first World Series game in 1991. And the Braves' night of nights, October 28, 1995, when Tom Glavine's pitching and a David Justice home run beat Cleveland 1–0 for Atlanta's only World Series title.

"Dave Justice, you might recall, wore No. 23," Walter Banks told Bill Banks. "The first modern-style baseball stadium, Yankee Stadium, was built in 1923. Two Chicago players, Hall of Famers in different sports, wore 23: Ryne Sandberg of the Cubs and Michael Jordan. Maine is the 23rd state admitted to the union. It's the first state that sees the sun in the morning and, I heard, the only state that doesn't have poisonous snakes."

But Georgia, not Maine, is the only state that has Walter Banks. Who knows when he'll retire? So come 2011, make it a point to meet the man, and let him still seat you while he can.

36 Stand in Walter's Well...

Better yet, shoot a photo from the Walter Victor Camera Well in Turner Field. Take your camera along when you take a guided tour of the Ted and, on the stop at Walter's Well, take your best shot. Walter Victor did so for four decades.

From 1966 until midway through the first decade of the 21st century, Walter Victor took more photographs of the Atlanta Braves than anyone else. He shot candid photos of ballplayers and visiting celebrities, folks who threw out the first pitch, those who sang our national anthem. Victor captured game action with a click, and also the most distinctive photo in club history:

Teammates Jeff Blauser and Mark Lemke, standing near home plate, arms around each other's shoulder, with the flames from the 1993 press box fire raging high above them.

It's Victor's favorite photograph, and one of his 12 on display in the Baseball Hall of Fame in Cooperstown. For nearly 40 years, he was the Braves team photographer. Well, eventually he was.

"He was never really hired as the team photographer," Lee Walburn, the Atlanta Braves' first PR director, once told Atlanta writer Scott Freeman. "He just showed up one day. We threw him out, and there he was again the next day."

To the persistent Victor went the job. Bill Lucas, the club's VP of player personnel, hired him as the team photographer. For years, he captured most of Atlanta's baseball heroics. Few fans knew that Victor himself was usually the most heroic man on the field. A highly decorated World War II veteran who, well, let's let Furman Bisher, the legendary *Atlanta Journal-Constitution* columnist, capture Victor—something the Germans could do only briefly.

"My God, how he survived it all makes Private Ryan look like a tourist," Bisher wrote in the introduction to *Brave at Heart*, Victor's life story. Published in 2007, it includes hundreds of photos and details his military exploits.

"Walter did it all in the style of GI Joe, living in foxhole to foxhole," Bisher wrote. "Walter campaigned through North Africa, Sicily, landed on the beach at Normandy, and spent eight months sloughing through the hedgerows of France into Germany, and survived the vicious scrimmage for the bridge at Remagen and the Battle of the Bulge. He can tell you what it was like to be talking one minute to a buddy sharing a foxhole, and then suddenly the buddy was gone. Shot dead by a sniper's bullet.... He could tell you what it was like to hear General Patton in a rage. He can confirm that war is hell, and he has four Bronze Stars and eight Combat Ribbons to back him up."

The son of Polish immigrants, Victor was one of eight children who grew up in Dupont, Pennsylvania, near Scranton. His father, Frank, a coal miner, was killed in a mining accident in 1919 when a tunnel collapsed. His mother, Agnes, a devout Catholic, taught her children about resilience and determination.

"She made whiskey in our basement," Victor, who learned how to distill spirits, told biographers Anne B. and Sidney R. Jones about his moonshining mom.

At 17, Victor dropped out of high school to help support the family. He went down into a coal mine, quit after a dynamite blast nearly killed him, hitchhiked to New York City, and found work in a factory, then later in a steel mill. At 22, he was drafted and stationed at Fort Bragg, North Carolina.

In the summer of '42 Victor was shipped overseas, landing in North Africa just a month after he'd married a pretty southern girl named Ruth Martin. Victor and the rest of the 9th Infantry Division served in Algeria, French Morocco, and Tunisia, and later Sicily. The "Old Reliables," as the 9th Infantry was known, later took part in the decisive event of World War II: the D-Day invasion of Normandy, landing at Utah Beach.

"Machine guns were waiting for us and killed our men left and right," Victor recalled. "The ocean ran red with blood. We were instructed not to help anyone because if we were distracted, the invasion would fail. We were terrified and held our rifles over our heads as we moved toward shore."

Victor was trained as a gunsmith and sharpshooter, skills that served him well as the 9th moved from northern France through the Ardennes, Belgium, and on into Germany. He was captured once and taken to a prisoner-of-war camp. "I wasn't there long," Victor said, "because I slipped out through a tunnel."

He returned to his unit, often repairing soldier's guns on the front line as battles raged. Later, while checking empty houses for provisions, Victor found a camera. He kept it in his gas mask carrier, taking photos wherever he went. When the 9th captured a Leica factory that made cameras and film, he learned how to develop photographs.

The 9th Infantry fought in two of the fiercest battles of WWII: the Battle of the Bulge, Germany's last major offensive, and the fight for Remagen Bridge, a key railroad bridge over the Rhine connecting France and Germany. Two decades later Victor would befriend another veteran of those conflicts: Braves pitcher Warren Spahn, the greatest left-hander in baseball history.

Back home after the war ended, Walter and Ruth moved to Georgia, settling in Dawsonville, north of Atlanta. They still live there. Victor worked as a civilian at Fort Gillem for 33 years. In 1966 he also began putting his camera to good use at the ballpark. Victor's favorite Braves? Phil Niekro and Dale Murphy.

On May 19, 2004, the Braves unveiled a plaque in the camera well beside the home dugout: "Walter Victor Camera Well." He was also presented with a framed Braves jersey. VICTOR is the name on the back. His number: 9.

"I have no idea if Victor is his real name, or a translation, or an adaptation," Furman Bisher wrote. "All I can say is, it couldn't have been more appropriately applied to any human being, one of the Greatest Generation."

37 On the Move...

The distinction comes with a caveat, of course. To be the only franchise in baseball history to win the World Series while based in three different cities, a ballclub must also move twice. Franchise relocations are never made because business is too good, profits too lucrative. Exhibit A? The Boston Braves.

"I have a difficult announcement to make," Braves owner Lou Perini said on March 14, 1953. "We are moving the Braves to Milwaukee."

Say it ain't true, Lou. That's what many Bostonians said that day. Many, but not nearly enough. In the wake of the '48 World Series, a veteran Braves ballclub chafed under the increasingly dictatorial style of manager Billy Southworth. A spring training boot camp? Midnight curfew checks on the road during the season? A slew of injuries in '49? A clubhouse mutiny? By August, Southworth temporarily left the team for health reasons.

The Braves fell to a fourth-place finish, their first of three such seasons in succession. Needing cash, Perini traded away Eddie Stanky and Alvin Dark. Southworth returned to manage in 1950, and the pitching improved markedly. Warren Spahn won 21 games, Johnny Sain—healthy again—20, and Vern Bickford 19. The Braves went 83–71, still only good enough for fourth place. Attendance fell below 1,000,000 for the first time since '46. It would only get worse.

Southworth, once more citing health reasons, resigned for good less than halfway through the 1951 season, although he still had a year and a half left on his contract. Perini had made improvements to Braves Field, sprucing up the old park for the fans' benefit. He also broadcast all Braves games—home and away—on the radio, anything to boost business.

Nothing worked. The bottom line was Boston was clearly a Red Sox town, hardly a two-team city. In 1951 the Braves finished 76–78, again in fourth place, but this time 20½ games behind the Giants. The attendance decline was undeniable: after peaking at 1,455,439 in the 1948 World Series season, it fell to 944,391 in 1950, nearly half that (487,475) in '51.

The franchise was on financial life support. Perini had lost nearly $700,000 in 1950 and '51. The huge profits from the years 1947 through 1949? Nearly all depleted. A stumbling 13–22 start didn't help matters. This came under manager Tommy Holmes, the popular veteran outfielder who'd taken over for Southworth midway through the previous season. One shining light? Rookie Eddie Mathews, a sweet-swinging third baseman who hit 25 homers. That wasn't nearly enough.

The Braves staggered home 64–89, 32 games out of first place. Worse, they drew a paltry 281,278 fans and lost nearly $600,000. Boston papers ran rampant with rumors of the club leaving the Hub.

Publicly, Perini played his PR cards close to the vest. He made a few trades that winter. He said, "We'll give Boston fans two more years to support the Braves." By March, the ballclub was down in spring training, seemingly readying for Opening Day at Braves Field.

Then Lou Perini played his version of '52 pickup. Yes, the previous season had been the Braves' last in Boston. The club was moving to Milwaukee, the *Sporting News* reported. It was the obvious move.

Milwaukee had already built a brand-new stadium, seemingly for the minor league Brewers (the Braves' Triple A affiliate), but actually a magnet for a major league team on the move. Perini had blocked

St. Louis Browns owner Bill Veeck from moving his floundering franchise to Milwaukee, claiming territorial rights. He'd also agreed never to stand in Milwaukee's way of acquiring a big-league franchise. Initially, Perini wouldn't deny or confirm the Braves' move to the Midwest. The day after the *Sporting News* report, Perini announced the Braves were leaving the Olde Towne for Beer Town. Milwaukee.

Perini was properly apologetic to all. "Maybe I'll be back in Boston," he said. "Maybe someday Tom Yawkey will sell the Red Sox and I'll buy them."

The Braves wouldn't return to Boston until 1997, the first season of interleague play. They would move to Milwaukee where, for the rest of the decade, they'd find baseball bliss…at least before moving once more.

38 Toasts of the Town

"This is only the beginning of good times for Milwaukee." So said baseball commissioner Ford Frick in 1953, and throughout the decade he proved prophetic. Milwaukee embraced its new Braves with unbridled fervor. On March 15, a cold midwestern day, the Ides of March was festive in Sudsville. Nearly 10,000 people flocked to the unveiling of brand-new County Stadium, three weeks before the team would even hit town.

When the Braves' train from spring training finally pulled in on April 8, more than 12,000 fans cheered them at the depot. The parade through downtown drew more than 60,000 people. Merchants lavished the Braves with freebies and complimentary services. A rain-shortened, two-inning exhibition game against the once-rival Boston Red Sox still attracted more than 10,000 fans. Better times had instantly come for the Braves in Milwaukee.

Lou Perini, president of the Milwaukee Braves, wears an Indian headdress in Milwaukee as members of the National League club arrive from spring training and exhibition games in April 1953.

Following a season-opening 2–0 win in Cincinnati, the home opener was box-office boffo: a sellout crowd of 34,357 roared as Warren Spahn took a no-hitter into the fifth inning against St. Louis. Tied 1–1 in the eighth, Spahn got a reprieve when rookie Billy Bruton, the Braves' stylish center fielder, raced down Stan Musial's liner and timed his leap perfectly. Bruton promptly tripled and scored the go-ahead run, only to see the Cards tie it in the ninth. But in the bottom of the 10th, having hit just five homers as a minor league Brewer in '52, Bruton's blast into a strong wind hit off Enos Slaughter's glove and over the wall for a walk-off homer. County Stadium erupted and continued to do so for many summers.

The Braves went 92–62, a 28-win improvement over the '52 finish, and wound up second to Brooklyn. By May 20, in just their 13th home date, the Braves surpassed the previous season's total attendance of 281,278. They drew an NL record 1,826,397. Eddie Mathews led the majors with 47 homers. Spahn went 23–7, with a 2.10 ERA. The love affair between town and team was in full bloom.

"There's a skinny kid in the clubhouse carrying a duffel bag," said Braves equipment man Joe Taylor to manager Charlie Grimm in spring training of '54. The kid was Henry Aaron, fresh out of Class A ball. But the future, like the kid, was a sure thing. Aaron had remarkably strong, quick wrists, and won the left fielder's job after Bobby Thomson broke his ankle that spring.

The Braves drew 2,131,388 fans in going 89–65, the first of four straight years they'd top the 2-million mark. A 20–2 late surge nearly caught the Giants, but now this time it was Aaron who broke his ankle in early September. Two straight second-place finishes followed, with Grimm losing his job early in the 1956 season. It was a heartbreaking ending for the Braves of '56. In St. Louis, just a game behind Brooklyn with two left to play, a bad-hop bouncer off Mathews' knee in the bottom of the 12th turned a sure DP into a Cards' victory. Spahn, who'd pitched all 12 innings, was in tears afterward and flung his glove at a photographer trying to snap his picture.

The Dodgers clinched the next day to the delight of the borough of Brooklyn if nowhere else. "The whole country is going to be sore at us for spoiling it for the Braves," said Cardinals outfielder Hank Sauer. "Everybody wanted them to win." Heaven, and Milwaukee, could wait one more year. Gladly.

39 Stopping Pete's Streak

In June 1978 Gene Garber was aghast. He'd just been traded from the perennial first-place Phillies to the dead-last Braves. Garber was so shocked and traumatized, he asked Braves' general manager Bill Lucas for a few days off to come to terms with his predicament before resuming relieving.

"Gene, that's a great idea," said Lucas, the first black GM in major league history. On August 1, Lucas was rewarded for his compassion.

The previous evening Cincinnati, its 1975–1976 two-time world-champion Big Red Machine still largely intact, came to Atlanta and beat the Braves. A media mob accompanied the Reds, chronicling Pete Rose's hitting streak. The first night, Rose went 1-for-4 to tie Wee Willie Keeler's National League 44-game record set in 1897. His next mission was to break it, then pursue Joe DiMaggio's record 56-game hitting streak.

"You can't ask for anything more than to pitch in meaningful games," Garber told me. In that 69–93 season of despair, facing Rose was as meaningful as it got.

"You know what, Karen? I feel I'm going to be the one to stop the streak," Garber told his wife then. "If Pete doesn't have a hit, we'll probably have the lead and I'd be pitching."

In his second at-bat that August night, Rose was robbed of a hit by Braves rookie starter Larry McWilliams, who somehow made a behind-the-back stab of a liner. In the seventh inning, another Rose line drive—this one off Garber—turned into a double play. When two big innings gave Atlanta a 16–4 lead entering the ninth, manager Bobby Cox told Garber he was taking him out.

"No, you can't," Garber said. "Bobby, I'm gonna end this streak. I will start and go nine innings for you tomorrow night, but I'm staying in."

"Go get 'em, Geno," Cox replied.

Garber retired the first two Reds in the ninth. Rose came to the plate. Suddenly, Garber thought, "If I walk him here, I'll be as low as you can get! I'll never live it down." For the only time in his career, Garber was afraid of walking a batter.

That fear increased when he fell behind in the count 2–1. Garber threw his best pitch, his change-up, and Rose fouled it off. Then Garber threw the change again and cringed. "It came right down the middle, screaming, 'Hit me! Hit me!'" he said. "And Pete swung right through it." Strike three. Game, and 44-game hitting streak, over. Garber leaped, raising his arms triumphantly. The fun was just beginning.

TBS stayed on the air to televise the postgame Rose news conference live from a room in the bowels of the stadium. He didn't know it was a live feed. First question: "How do you feel now that it's over?" Rose's reply: "Well, one good thing, I won't have to talk to you assholes every day."

Rose dropped a few more bleeps and blips during the interview. The TBS switchboard lit up with complaints. At one point, McWilliams sat beside Rose. Charlie Hustle had no idea who the kid was. Garber, meanwhile, was in the players lounge in the Braves clubhouse, drinking a Coke and watching Rose on TV.

"He said, 'I can't believe, with a 16–4 lead, Garber's pitching to me like it's the ninth inning of the World Series,'" Garber said. "I said, 'Thank you, Pete. That's the best compliment I'll ever get.'"

When reporters asked Garber about Rose's World Series ninth-inning jab, he said, "I have a feeling that's exactly the way Pete hit for, what, 14,000 at-bats? That's why he was probably the best hitter in the game."

The next night, after collecting four hits, including a home run, Rose still griped that Garber had pitched him so carefully and craftily, working the corners instead of attacking him. "I honestly think," Rose said, "that in that last at-bat, Garber didn't throw me a single strike."

40 14 in a Row

For the longest time, the question lingered: how best to assess Atlanta's unparalleled excellence? How to convey the sheer magnitude of what the Braves accomplished from 1991 through 2005? In what context does one put 14 consecutive division championships?

And then came the morning of September 28, 2010, and news accounts of another Philadelphia title. The night before, the Phillies had done it again. The National League's finest team—indeed, baseball's best ballclub—had proven its pedigree once more. In Washington, D.C., battling the Nats and the gnats, the Phightin' Phils prevailed 8–0.

The 2008 World Series champions, the reigning three-time National League pennant winners, had won the NL East Division title again.

For the fourth straight season.

Congrats, boys.

Only 10 more and you catch the Braves.

"An insane number," Ruben Amaro Jr., the Phillies' general manager, admiringly called Atlanta's run of 14 completed seasons with a division title.

Rich Hofman, the *Philadelphia Daily News* columnist, wrote, "Almost no one survives the injuries and the ennui and the relentlessness of the thing for this long." The thing. The season. "This is the flag that is taken again with six months of perspiration, not with October serendipity—and that is true even if a lot of people these days see it as only a box to be ticked off on the ultimate baseball journey. Division title, check."

Check these out:

When the Phillies won the division in 2007, it ended their 14-year postseason drought.

For Roy Halladay, the clincher in D.C. was not only the pitcher's 21st victory of the season, it was also the first time he'd ever punched his postseason ticket, after 12 empty Octobers with Toronto.

The first major league team to lose 10,000 games, the Phillies are the very same franchise that suffered the greatest collapse in baseball history, blowing a 6½ game lead with 12 to play in 1964. The Phils lost the NL pennant by a game to St. Louis, which then beat the New York Yankees in the World Series.

For first-year Phillie Mike Sweeney, 37, this was his first postseason in a 20-year career. As Paul Hagen of the *Philadelphia Daily News* reported, Sweeney hadn't won a championship of any sort since his Ontario, California, high school team won the California Interscholastic Federation 3-A title. To celebrate, the kids drank apple cider. In D.C. Sweeney celebrated with champagne, having played in 1,451 major league games without a taste of the postseason.

"Next time, I'd better go get some goggles," said Sweeney, whose eyes stung from the bubbly. "Because as good as it feels…whoo."

In returning to the postseason the Phillies joined some very select company. They're now tied with the New York Giants of 1921 through 1924 with four consecutive postseason appearances, second-most in National League annals. A mere 10 behind the Atlanta Braves' 14.

Fourteen. Think about that for a moment. Fourteen straight seasons. The Braves won in different ways, in the '90s usually with pitching. They won their first by playing worst-to-first baseball in 1991 to edge the Dodgers by a game. In '93, the final season before the wild-card was introduced, Atlanta won a stirring pennant race with the Giants. Another one-game margin climaxed what came to be known as the Last Great Pennant Race.

Yes, the Braves were in second place, six games behind Montreal, when the players' strike of 1994 ended that season after Atlanta had played 114 games. But the next season the Braves ran away from everyone, won the division by a staggering 21 games, and, ultimately, Atlanta's first World Series championship. They set the franchise record with 106 victories in '98, winning by 18 games.

From 2000 to 2005, the last six years of its dominance, Atlanta won by a game in 2000 and twice by two—including 2005, the last year of the run. The Braves won by 19 games with a team earned run average of 3.13 in 2002. In '03 they hit a franchise-record 235 homers—71 more than in '02—to win No. 12 in a row. They won their 14 straight titles by an aggregate 116½ games. They had six 100-win seasons.

And yet many criticized the Braves. The nerve of them, winning just that one World Series in 1995. Some critics labeled them "the Buffalo Bills of baseball," for the NFL team that lost four straight Super Bowls. That kind of talk incensed Braves broadcaster Pete Van Wieren.

Certainly, he knew the Braves could've won the World Series in 1991 and 1996. In fact, they should have won in '96. "But you can't take away winning that 162-game, regular season grind 14 straight times," Van Wieren said. "The day I start believing that isn't a remarkable achievement will be the day somebody else does it."

41 The Dibble Homer

On the night of October 1, 1991, there was trouble in worst-to-first paradise. Potentially big, bubble-bursting trouble.

With only five games remaining in the season, the Braves had fallen a game behind the Los Angeles Dodgers in the National League West. Even worse, in Cincinnati that evening the Reds had struck for six runs in the bottom of the first at Riverfront Stadium. No, the outlook wasn't brilliant for the visiting nine that night, especially with hard-throwing Jose Rijo on the mound for the Reds.

But slowly, slowly, the Braves demonstrated the resilience they'd displayed all season. They nibbled off Rijo and somehow got back in the game. By the ninth inning, Atlanta had drawn within 6–5, and Rijo was gone.

Now pitching for the Reds? Rob Dibble, the fire-balling closer with a temperament to match. Now batting for the Braves? David Justice, who'd grown up in the Cincinnati area as a rabid fan of the Reds' vaunted Big Red Machine teams of the 1970s and early '80s.

And then it happened. With a runner on, Justice turned on a Dibble fastball and crushed it. The two-run homer gave the Braves a 7–6 lead. They held on in the bottom half to win, cutting the Dodgers' lead to a half-game.

In Greenville, South Carolina, then home to the Braves Double A farm club, a veterinarian named Ed Moseley was watching all this rather intently. When Justice launched his game-winner in the ninth, Moseley, watching downstairs in the den, jumped up and began screaming, "Get out! Get out!"

Naturally, that awakened Moseley's wife, Kathleen, who'd been fast asleep upstairs. Just as naturally, Mrs. Moseley immediately dialed 9-1-1. Having heard her husband's screams, she thought an intruder had broken into their home. A few minutes later, a police car, its blue lights flashing, pulled into the Moseleys' driveway. Ed explained to the officer that he'd been yelling at the TV about a homer, not a burglar.

Back in Atlanta, a man who'd been watching the game in some discomfort got excited about the Justice homer, too. He slowly got off the couch, walked to the foot of the stairs, and called up to his wife, the big Braves fan, "Are you watching this? You'd better get down here."

Down she came. Down went the Reds. Up went a roar. Then the man said, "Of course, you know what we have to do now." Pause. "We have to go watch the Dodgers-Padres game at Manuel's."

There was no *Baseball Tonight* back in those days. ESPN wasn't airing baseball games regularly each night. There was no such thing as the MLB Network. But with the great local fervor over the pennant race, the L.A.–San Diego game was being carried in Atlanta.

Off the couple went to Manuel's Tavern, where they'd met and wooed and had their wedding reception in the back room. Their first dance? "Take Me Out to the Ballgame," recorded at a waltz tempo. As his wife parked the car and raced inside, the man eased out slowly. Very slowly. He'd had a vasectomy that afternoon. No matter. You've gotta watch hurt. The Dodgers-Padres game was on.

So he sat there, with his legs stretched out and feet up on a wooden chair, an ice pack in his lap. Sitting with the happy couple was her ex-husband, a good guy and great Braves fan. In between pulling for the Padres and against the Dodgers, he busted the man's, uh, ice pack. Resisting the urge to yell "Get out!" himself, the man raised a glass when the Padres won, and the three of them toasted the Braves.

42 "We're Losing Our Vin Scullys"

The 2003 season will be remembered as the year the TV suits messed up, Bobby Cox spoke up, Braves fans rose up, and Pete Van Wieren and Skip Caray realized just how much they meant to their audience. Despite another quick postseason exit after another divisional title, 2003 was a big year for the little guy.

Hoping to jump-start the team's television ratings in an increasingly over-saturated TV market and seeking to attract a younger viewership/demographic and make Braves' broadcasts less local and more national, Turner Sports, well, shook things up. How bad? Think New Coke.

Returning from spring training, Van Wieren and Caray were blindsided by new executive producer Mike Pearl. "We have decided to make a change in the broadcast pairings." Translation: old broadcast partners Skip and Pete were back together again, but now doing just 36 TV games on SportSouth, Turner Sports' regional network. Don Sutton and Joe Simpson would work the 90 televised games on TBS, while Pete and Skip would call those games on the radio.

Van Wieren and Caray were shocked. "MLB on TBS." That's what the telecasts would now be called.

"But these are all Braves telecasts, are they not?" Van Wieren asked. "Yes, it's the same schedule," Pearl said, "but we are going to try this approach."

Elaine Van Wieren is a very smart woman. When her visibly upset husband came home and delivered the news, Elaine said, "That'll never work. The fans are going to be very upset."

When Caray called that night, he, too, told Van Wieren, "It's not going to work…but in the meantime, I'll see you on the radio."

When the news broke, Braves president Stan Kasten quickly called Van Wieren and said, "I just want you to know that we [the Braves] had nothing to do with this." Van Wieren knew that. This came from the TV side.

When Bobby Cox found out about the changes before an exhibition game in Florida, the manager told Dave O'Brien of the *Atlanta Journal-Constitution*, "That's ridiculous. I'm completely shocked! We're losing our Vin Scullys."

Cox later confided to Van Wieren that he'd been reprimanded by club officials for his candor. "This is a television issue," Cox was told. "Stay out of it."

The fans quickly had their say, loud and clearly furious. In an AJC.com on-line poll that asked, "Do you like the Braves' juggling of their TV announcers," the first night alone produced more than 11,000 responses. The results—no, it's horrible: 9,902 (89 percent); yes, it's great: 1,245 (11 percent).

Once the season began, the outcry got louder. On March 30 sportswriter Mike Tierney wrote that of the now more than 20,000 poll respondents, 92 percent went with "horrible." Online petitions sought to "Bring back Skip and Pete." Paper petitions circulated through the crowd at Turner Field. Meanwhile, Turner executives said things like, "We need to maintain a vibrancy to the telecast," and, "We've been squeezing this same orange for an awfully long time."

Scott Zucker of *USA Today Baseball Weekly* wrote: "A 63-year-old man [Caray] is being pushed aside after decades of loyal service.... But the real victim here is Van Wieren, who has long been the best and most professional part of the Braves' broadcast."

The MLB on TBS ratings plunged 29 percent. Three Turner execs resigned, including Pearl. On July 7, with the Braves in New York to play the Mets, Caray and Van Wieren were summoned to a meeting at the office of David Levy, the new president of Turner Sports. After the All-Star break, the broadcasters would return to their usual four-man rotation between TV and radio. No apologies were issued.

When the meeting ended, Van Wieren and Caray walked back to the team hotel. En route, Caray stopped and said, "You know, I don't even care about being back on TV—I like radio so much better. But you know what I do care about?"

"What's that?" Van Wieren asked.

"We beat the bastards!" Caray shouted, high-fiving Van Wieren. Both were humbled by—and appreciative of—the fans' response.

In a front-page story in the next day's *Atlanta Journal-Constitution*, Levy said, "Ultimately, the fans have spoken, and we have listened."

43 40-40-40

As in, Davey, Darrell, Henry. As in, the long-ball firm of Johnson, Evans & Aaron. As in, 40 homers apiece. Yes.

In 1973 Henry Aaron, Darrell Evans, and newly acquired Davey Johnson each reached the 40–home run pinnacle. It was the first time one team has had three players hit 40 or more homers in a single season. Colorado did it twice, in 1996 and '97.

40-40-40. Yes, yes, yes.

That Aaron hit 40—and he did, precisely—was no surprise, even given his age (39) and the season-long pressure and looming presence of another number: 714. Babe Ruth's career home run total, the most sacred number in baseball and the one Aaron had squarely in his crosshairs.

The last of the Hammer's 40 homers that year came in the penultimate game of the season. On September 28 he took Houston's Jerry Reuss deep. It not only gave Aaron his eighth and final 40-homer season, it was 713. More than 41,000 fans flocked to the ballpark in rainy Atlanta the next day, hoping to see history. But after singling in each of his first three times up, Aaron popped up in his last at-bat of the season.

That Evans hit 40—actually, 41—was no surprise either. In his second full big-league season, the slugging third baseman who would belt 414 career homers had come under the tutelage of Eddie Mathews. Then the Braves manager, Mathews—a Hall of Famer with 512 home runs himself—encouraged Evans. But he did his best work with his new second baseman.

That Johnson hit 40—actually, 43—was astonishing. In his first seven full seasons with Baltimore, he never hit more than 18 in a single year. The previous season he'd hit five. But in 1973, 42 of his 43 came as a second baseman, tying Rogers Hornsby's 1922 season record for homers by a second baseman. One of Johnson's blasts was a pinch-hit homer.

Nearly all 43—at least most of his 26 hit at home—came with Mathews' advice in his ear. He taught him, urged him, to pull the ball. To take advantage of the shorter left-field porch, and the way the ball flew out of the stadium known as the Launching Pad.

Ironically, Johnson, part of a six-player, off-season trade between Atlanta and Baltimore, was known for his defense. That, the Braves hoped, along with the addition of O's pitchers Pat Dobson and Roric Harrison, would help an awful Braves pitching staff. Instead, Atlanta allowed an NL-worst 774 runs with a staff ERA of 4.25. And instead, Johnson, Evans, and Aaron ignited the offense.

At times, Johnson was on the defensive about his offensive surge. He bristled at questions concerning the Launching Pad. "I hit 18 [actually 17] of my home runs on the road," he said, "and the rest were real home runs. None of them were cheap."

Two other factors worked in Johnson's favor. There was no pressure whatsoever. The Braves went 76–85, finishing fifth in the NL West, 22½ games out. Also, Aaron's pursuit of Ruth's home run record completely overshadowed the 40-40-40 trifecta. All Johnson and Evans had to do was go out and swing, often for the fences.

The only major leaguer to homer more often than Johnson in '73? Pops. Pittsburgh's Willie Stargell, who popped 44.

In his first seven full seasons with Baltimore, Johnson had 66 home runs. After '73, he never hit more than 15 homers in a single year. Nearly a third of his 136 career homers came in that magical summer.

Johnson hit .270 that season with a career-high 99 RBIs. His .546 slugging percentage was third-best in the league and easily his highest in any full season. He was fourth in total bases (305).

The *Sporting News* honored Johnson as its NL Comeback Player of the Year. In 118 games in 1972 he'd hit just five homers with 32 RBIs and a career-low .221 average.

On April 8, 1974, Aaron broke Babe Ruth's record with his 715th homer; he finished with 20 that year. That season, Evans hit 25. Johnson ended the year with .251, 15 homers, and 62 RBIs.

From 40-40-40 to 25-20-15.

44 Glav

He was the next in line, the clear heir in the Braves' royal line of succession. The new face of the Atlanta franchise, Tom Glavine would follow in the footsteps of Henry Aaron, who begat Phil Niekro, who begat the sainted Dale Murphy and finally gave us Glavine himself.

On the night Turner Field officially opened, Friday, April 4, 1997, Denny Neagle threw the first pitch. But not before a moving pregame ceremony in which Glavine, appearing through the foggy mist in an opening in the outfield wall, in his very own *Field of Dreams* dream sequence, carried the old home plate from Atlanta-Fulton County Stadium. As Glavine walked through center field toward home, the great Aaron came out to greet him. Then the two men walked homeward, carrying the old plate like a relic.

The next year, Glavine won his second NL Cy Young Award. Two years earlier, of course, he'd pitched the greatest game in franchise history, stifling the potent Cleveland Indians 1–0 on one hit in Game 6 of the 1995 World Series. Glavine was named the World Series MVP, having given Atlanta its only World Series championship.

That happened a year after the players strike cut short the '94 season. Glavine was the strike's most visible face. He was smart, articulate, and was only doing his job for his union. Years later, in retrospect, Glavine said if he'd had it to do all over again, he might not have been so out front, so outspoken. After he left the Braves in free agency due to contentious negotiations with the ballclub,

Hank Aaron looks on as pitcher Tom Glavine sets the home plate from Atlanta-Fulton County Stadium in place at Turner Field before the Braves opened their new home against the Chicago Cubs on April 4, 1997.

Glavine was vilified every time he came home to Atlanta as a New York Met.

The venom in the stands was as vile and profane as it was wrong. Glavine's family, his wife, Chris, and their children, faced the brunt of it. It was hateful and disgraceful. Glavine returned to the Braves in 2008 as a 300-game winner and a Cooperstown shoo-in. Of his 305 career wins, 244 came as a Brave. But his return in '08 was cut short by injury. After Glavine's rehab assignments, the Braves released him in early 2009, just before a $1 million clause in his contract was to kick in.

Team president John Schuerholz saw the error in all this and signed Glavine as his special assistant for 2010. For Glavine, the most meaningful moment came on August 6, when he was inducted into the Braves Hall of Fame. That night, his No. 47 was retired.

As Carroll Rogers of the *Atlanta Journal-Constitution* put it so perfectly in her story, "For the master of the change-of-pace, Tom Glavine got one of his own Friday night. With the unveiling of his No. 47 on the left-field upper-deck façade at Turner Field...Glavine heard nary a boo from 42,178 Braves fans.

"Braves fans showered him with admiration, and Glavine responded with rare emotion for a pitcher who had hidden behind a stony-faced exterior on the mound for so many years."

Glavine's eyes grew moist when his No. 47 was unveiled up on the façade. He's the seventh Brave to have his number retired, and the second-winningest left-hander in franchise history behind Warren Spahn.

"I'm in awe. I'm stunned. I really am," he told the crowd. "There are not many moments when I've been this emotional and this speechless, but this is one of them." He thanked his parents, his siblings, his wife and children, his manager and teammates, and then the fans.

"I hope at the end of the day, whether you watched the game here at the stadium or on TV, when you saw No. 47 walk to the mound, you knew I was going to give you everything I had," he said. The crowd roared its approval.

Earlier, at a luncheon at the Omni Hotel, Glavine was inducted into the Braves Hall of Fame. "This is the right place for me to be," he told the 830 fans, now seated, who'd given him a standing ovation. "This is the way this thing should have all ended."

For that, give Schuerholz his due. Glavine, too. "Obviously, me and the organization have had our rifts over the years, unfortunately," Glavine said. "But that's a part of the business. I'm just thankful that when all was said and done, we were all able to be big boys and put our differences aside and get things back to where they belong."

That place, Glavine knows, is back with the Braves. Back at Turner Field. Not just for his sake, but his family's, too.

"I want my kids to be Braves fans," Glavine said. "I want my kids to want to go down to the ballpark. And for a little while there, that wasn't happening. Now it is. You feel like you've come full circle."

45 Spahn and Sain...

Poetically, the Bambino of baseball poems is "Casey at the Bat." Batting second? "Tinker to Evers to Chance," that ode to the Chicago Cubs' early 20th-century double play wizardry of shortstop Joe Tinker, second baseman Johnny Evers, and first baseman Frank Chance.

And in the three hole? "Spahn and Sain, then pray for rain."

That's the epigram, the condensed version of a poem that appeared in the *Boston Post* on September 14, 1948. It was composed by Gerald V. Hern, the *Post*'s sports editor, to herald the essentially two-man pitching rotation keeping the Boston Braves afloat in the National League pennant race: Warren Spahn, who'd become the winningest left-handed pitcher in baseball history with 363 victories—all but seven with the Braves. And his right-hand man, Johnny Sain, the NL's finest pitcher in '48, Boston's best season since those Miracle Braves of 1914.

First we'll use Spahn, then we'll use Sain,
Then an off day, followed by rain.
Back will come Spahn, followed by Sain,
And followed, we hope, by two days of rain.

The Braves fans' mantra came to be known as either "Spahn and Sain, then pray for rain," or, "Spahn and Sain, and pray for rain."

Warren Spahn, left, and Johnny Sain, the pitching mainstays of the Boston Braves, pose during a workout in preparation for the 1948 World Series against the Cleveland Indians.

Either way, eat your heart out, Dylan Thomas.

Hern was inspired by Spahn's and Sain's actual heroics earlier that month. The Braves had swept a Labor Day doubleheader from the Brooklyn Dodgers, with Spahn pitching a 14-inning complete game for a 2–1 win in the opener. In the nightcap, called after seven innings, Sain threw a 4–0 shutout.

Following two off days on the schedule, it actually did rain. Spahn and Sain then won a doubleheader on the 11th. Three days later Sain won yet again, as did Spahn the following day. After one more off day, Sain and Spahn did it again, sweeping a two-game series in Pittsburgh. In 13 days, they'd gone 8–0.

Beginning September 3, Spahn and Sain started 16 of Boston's next 26 games. In nine starts Sain went 8–1 with a 2.19 ERA. Spahn won four times in 13 days, compiling an ERA of 1.22 during that stretch. Yet it was Vern Bickford, under clear skies on

September 26, who pitched the pennant clincher. Bob Elliott's three-run homer in that first inning was all Bickford needed in a 3–2 win over the Giants.

That season was hardly an anomaly, at least not for Spahn and Sain. From 1947 to 1950, they combined to win 153 games, fully 46 percent of Boston's victories during that period. In '48 Sain was simply sensational. He went 24–15 (one of his four 20-win seasons, and third in a row), with a 2.60 earned run average. Sain led the league in victories, starts (39), complete games (28), and innings pitched (314⅔). The *Sporting News* named him the NL Pitcher of the Year.

Sain even finished second in the National League Most Valuable Player voting ahead of his teammate, shortstop Alvin Dark, and behind only Stan Musial of the Cardinals, who'd won two legs of the Triple Crown.

Spahn went 15–12, a relatively humdrum year for him, with a 3.71 ERA. He did pitch 16 complete games, however. In the club's first World Series in 34 years, Spahn and Sain gave the Braves their only two victories over Cleveland. If only it had rained more that October.

In Game 1 in Boston, the Braves managed just two hits off Cleveland's Bob Feller but beat the Indians 1–0 on Sain's four-hit shutout. Spahn lost 4–1 to the Indians' Bob Lemon in Game 2, then Sain suffered a 2–1 loss in Game 4 despite allowing just five hits, and Cleveland led the series 3–1. But Spahn, making a rare relief appearance, worked 5⅔ innings in relief of Nels Potter and got the win in an 11–5 Game 5 rout of Feller to keep Boston's hopes alive. Spahn allowed just one hit and one walk while striking out seven.

That sent the series back to Boston, but to no avail. Again, Spahn worked in relief, this time going the last two innings. But Braves starter Bill Voiselle was charged with a run in the eighth inning that gave the Indians a 4–3 victory and made them the world champions.

There would be one more 20-victory season for Sain, who won 100 games for the Braves from 1946 to 1951. He was traded late in the '51 season to the New York Yankees for young right-hander Lew Burdette and $50,000. Sain, meanwhile, won three World Series with the Yankees from 1951 to 1953 before turning to relief in 1954. He finished his career with 139 victories and then became a pitching coach, one of the most acclaimed in the game.

Sain worked with six different teams, including the Yankees and Atlanta, once the Braves moved south from Milwaukee. He became the pitching guru to Leo Mazzone, the Braves' pitching coach during their playoff run from 1991 through 2005. But Jim Bouton of *Ball Four* fame was perhaps Sain's most devoted acolyte.

"Johnny Sain is the greatest pitching coach—ever," said Bouton. "He taught me everything I know, how to put on sanitary socks, how to negotiate a contract. I admire him more than any man I've ever met. All players like him: white, black, conservatives, liberals, loud, quiet, they all do. Johnny Sain gets a pitcher's allegiance before any manager."

And as for that Burdette kid who was traded for Sain? He and Spahn combined to return the Braves to the World Series in 1957, again in '58. Burdette beat the imperial Yankees three times in '57 when the Braves finally became world champions once again. Spahn, of course, went on to pitch two no-hitters, compile a left-handed résumé that will never be approached, and was a first-ballot inductee into the Baseball Hall of Fame in 1973.

But no one wrote poems about Spahn and Burdette. And that is the truth one should never forget.

46 Lonnie

In the "woe is me" world of what-if, one name always came to mind. Lonnie. No last name necessary. If you said, "Lonnie," someone replied, "Why?" As in, "Why, oh why did he hesitate? Why, oh why didn't he keep running?"

Along with Johnny Pesky holding the ball and Bill Buckner letting that roller slip slowly between his legs, Lonnie Smith's World Series base-running misadventure is a Fall Classic perennial. Just let someone screw up in a World Series, and there's "Skates" again on TV.

That was Smith's nickname. Never renowned for his fielding, he sometimes appeared to be ice skating in the outfield while chasing down a batted ball. But this gaffe is the one that always guarantees Smith some late-October TV time. "That's definitely the one associated with me," he told me, "the one they remember and show."

Remember? How can you ever forget? In Game 7 of the 1991 World Series, the greatest ever played, Smith walked to the plate and shook hands with Twins catcher Brian Harper. How appropriate. How classy. How in the hell then did the eighth inning go so awry?

"The mistake I made was I didn't take a peek in," Smith said. "I didn't know where the ball was. If anybody wants to blame me for anything, blame me for not looking at the batter."

In the eighth inning of that scoreless, decisive game, he singled to lead off the inning. In the indoor maelstrom of the Metrodome, with Terry Pendleton at bat, Smith attempted a delayed steal. The noise was deafening, the dome a virtual white-out with Twins fans waving white towels. As Smith took off for second, he never picked up the ball off Pendleton's bat. No, he wasn't deked by Twins second baseman Chuck Knoblauch. Looking out toward the outfield, Smith saw Kirby Puckett and Dan Gladden converging in left-center field.

Until much later, Smith didn't realize that he'd virtually stopped at second base. He had. When he saw the ball hit the wall, he raced toward third, where coach Jimy Williams held him up. If only he'd picked up Williams in his vision sooner.

"Why he stopped, I just don't know," Braves manager Bobby Cox said afterward.

"We should have won the game," said general manager John Schuerholz, "and we should be world champions."

Instead, Smith stood on third base. Indeed, the Braves had runners at second and third with nobody out. "Nobody pays attention to that," Smith later pointed out.

What's remembered is Ron Gant's weak groundout, forcing Smith to hold at third. David Justice was intentionally walked to load the bases, and Sid Bream bounced into a 3-2-3 double play to end the inning and the threat. The Twins won it in the bottom of the 10th, their 1–0 win breaking Atlanta's communal heart.

"If I'd known we wouldn't score, I'd have tried to steal home," Smith joked years later. "Not that I'd have made it. I guess people all think I should have scored on Terry's double. [But] if you don't know where the ball is at, you can't be running blindly."

Not that Pendleton ever blamed Smith. Never. "We still had three opportunities [to score]," Pendleton said of that fateful 10th. "Lonnie Smith didn't lose that for us. We wouldn't have been there if not for Lonnie Smith."

He had homered in Games 3, 4, and 5 back in Atlanta. Those home runs were critical in the first two of those games, both one-run affairs. When Smith went deep in the 14–5 Game 5 laugher, he became the first National Leaguer in World Series play to homer in three consecutive games.

Indeed, without Skates, the Braves might not have even been in Minneapolis, playing Game 7 at all.

47 30-30

Hank. Murph. Gant, and Gant again. That's it. That's the extent of the Braves' 30-30 club, that highly exclusive fraternity of major leaguers who've hit at least 30 home runs and stolen 30 bases in a single season. The Braves are blessed to have three such men who, between them, have accumulated four 30-30 seasons.

As usual, there's Henry Aaron, from whom almost all good things emanate when it comes to the franchise record book for batters. In 1963, while the club was still based in Milwaukee, Aaron became the third player to reach the 30-30 level in home runs and stolen bases. Like his other 30-30 brethren, Aaron was that rare blend of power and speed. In '63 he belted 44 home runs and stole 31 bases, joining Ken Williams of the old St. Louis Browns and the great Willie Mays of the San Francisco Giants as the only 30-30 men on the planet.

It's a testament to Aaron's talents, and to Dale Murphy and Ron Gant, too, that they qualified for this most exclusive of clubs. Those three measured up. Few others did. It's illustrative to note that when Ken Williams, an outfielder for the Browns, went 30-30 in 1922 with 39 homers and 37 steals, it was another 34 years before Willie Mays turned the trick. And then repeated it in 1957. Mays put together consecutive 30-30 seasons with 36 homers and 40 steals in 1956 and 35 and 38, respectively, in '57 before he and the Giants bade New York City good-bye. The Say Hey Kid gave New York fans something to really remember him by.

In 1983, the second of his two consecutive National League MVP seasons, Murphy belted 36 homers and stole precisely 30 bases to qualify for 30-30 status. Seven years later, it was Gant in 1990, after several disappointing seasons at the plate, who put together the magic 30-30. He became just the 13th 30-30 man in major league history, with 32 home runs and 33 stolen bases. By then an outfielder, Gant went 30-30 again in '91, hitting 32 more homers and stealing another 34 bases. He joined Mays and Bobby Bonds as the only players at that time to record consecutive 30-30 seasons.

Gant also led the majors with 21 game-winning hits that season, many of which helped escalate the Braves' miraculous worst-to-first pennant push. Gant finished sixth in the National League Most Valuable Player balloting and won a Silver Slugger as one of the league's top three offensive outfielders. In the National League Championship Series, Gant set an NLCS record with seven steals.

He also established one of the most eye-popping moments in postseason annals. In the '91 World Series, with Lonnie Smith on first, Gant singled in the third inning of Game 2 at the Metrodome. Rounding first base hard, Gant pulled up and got back to first base in time. Or so he thought.

The throw reached first just after Gant did. Then Kent Hrbek, the Twins' first baseman and a big World Wrestling Federation fan, demonstrated what he'd learned from watching those WWF telecasts. "The hefty tag," it was called in print that night.

"When I hit the bag," Gant said, "Hrbek caught the ball and hooked my right leg with his glove and kind of pulled my leg off the bag." Gant was livid. He was also out. "The umpire called me out," he said the next morning, "and I went ballistic."

Gant would lose the argument. The Braves would lose the World Series in seven magnificent games. It would be no consolation, not even to a 30-30 guy.

48 The '96 Comeback

With all the magical moments that occurred throughout the '90s, one historic accomplishment remains underappreciated, long overlooked, and now almost forgotten amidst that decade-long string of superlatives.

The 1996 National League Championship Series.

Although it lasted seven games, that series may have been an even more impressive performance than the Braves' sweep of

Cincinnati in the 1995 NLCS—the first four-game sweep in NLCS history. Atlanta had to rally to win the first two games in Cincinnati in extra innings, scoring the winning runs in the last inning each time.

After scoring in the ninth inning of Game 1 to tie it 1–1, Atlanta won 2–1 in the 11th on Mike Devereaux's game-winning single. The next night, the Braves went to extra innings again. This time, a three-run homer in the 10th by catcher Javy Lopez beat the Reds 6–2.

Back home in Atlanta, Greg Maddux beat Cincinnati 5–2. In Game 4, Steve Avery became the first pitcher to start three shutouts in the NLCS (two in the '91 NLCS) and got the win in a 6–0 rout. Five of those runs came in the seventh inning, three on a homer by Devereaux, a late-season acquisition from the White Sox who was named the Most Valuable Player of the NLCS.

From there, the best team in baseball in '95 beat Cleveland in six games to win Atlanta's only World Series title.

The 1996 NLCS was another animal altogether. When John Smoltz, who won a league-leading 24 games that season en route to winning the NL Cy Young Award, won Game 1 4–2 on Javy Lopez's two-run single in the eighth inning and Greg Maddux (who'd captured the four previous NL Cy Youngs) took the mound against the Cardinals in Atlanta for Game 2, Braves fans were confident. Supremely so. Not so much, however, after Gary Gaetti's grand slam off Maddux punctuated a five-run Cards' seventh in their 8–3 victory.

This was the second time the Braves and Cardinals had met in the NLCS. In 1982, in Atlanta's first postseason appearance in 13 years, the clearly superior Cards swept the Braves in three games. This time, Atlanta was the overwhelming favorite. But in Busch Stadium, ex-Brave Ron Gant homered twice off Tom Glavine, driving in all three runs in a 3–2 win.

In Game 4 Atlanta took a 3–0 lead into the seventh, only to see St. Louis score thrice to tie it. In the eighth outfielder Brian

Jordan—who'd later play for the Braves—homered off Greg McMichael. For the second straight game, Cards' closer Dennis Eckersley closed out the Braves. As St. Louis broadcaster Joe Buck called the final out: "A ball and two strikes on Grissom...ballgame!"

The Braves were seemingly in grave trouble, and Cards fans rejoiced. Even many Cardinals players were celebrating, almost as if the outcome were inevitable. Joe Buck again: "The month of September showed the Atlanta Braves may have feet of clay. That clay now may be starting to crack."

For the Braves, the only crack was the crack of the bat. They scored five runs in the first inning off Todd Stottlemyre, the big hits a Chipper Jones double and Jeff Blauser's triple. They added two more runs in the second, three in the fourth. Smoltz was spotless again, and Atlanta won 14–0. The Braves pounded out an LCS-record 22 hits. Lopez went 4-for-5 with a homer. Lemke had four more hits himself, and his on-the-road golfing buddy Fred McGriff homered.

Back in Atlanta-Fulton County Stadium, which was scheduled for demolition at season's end, Maddux more than atoned for Game 2. He threw seven shutout innings, aided by a spectacular catch by Grissom. An eighth-inning wild pitch by closer Mark Wohlers gave the Cardinals their only run. But he closed out Atlanta's 3–1 win that forced a decisive Game 7.

Has there ever been an easier Game 7 for the victors? Joe Buck, are you there? "Into left field...Gant can't get it, that will empty the bases! Six to nothing, Atlanta!"

That was after Glavine's two-out, three-run triple climaxed Atlanta's six-run first inning off Donovan Osborne. Lopez belted a two-run homer in the four-run fourth. McGriff homered again, and so did the precocious young outfielder Andruw Jones, a preview of his impending coming-out party in the Bronx. Glavine threw seven shutout innings and, behind 17 more hits, was the easy winner in Atlanta's overwhelming 15–0 victory—an LCS record for runs scored in a game.

Javy Lopez was named the MVP after batting .542 (13-for-24) with five doubles, two homers, and six RBIs.

"Here comes Atlanta, New York!" Joe Buck advised Yankees fans.

The Braves became just the eighth team in baseball history to win a postseason series after trailing 3–1, and the first to do so in NLCS annals. They outscored the Cards 32–1 in the last three games, 44–18 overall, and out-hit St. Louis 77–45. Manager Bobby Cox also became the first manager to be on both ends of such a comeback. His 1985 Toronto Blue Jays blew a 3–1 lead against Kansas City in the ALCS.

All in all, it was an astounding accomplishment for the Braves. If only they hadn't had to play that World Series and those damn Yankees.

Leo

When it came to Leo Mazzone, there were two prevailing pitching schools of thought. One is best characterized by Roger Kahn, the renowned baseball author whose *The Boys of Summer* immortalized those Brooklyn Dodgers of yore. Kahn wrote many more books, including *The Head Game*, his 2000 treatise on the art of pitching. In it, he anointed Mazzone the "Pope of Pitching" and compared Leo's chronic bench-rocking in the dugout to "Orthodox Jews praying at the Western Wall in Jerusalem."

Well now. The second school of thought regarding Rockin' Leo is best expressed by an Atlanta baseball man who shall remain anonymous. With apologies to Lou Gehrig, it goes like this: "Every morning, when Leo's shaving, he should look in the mirror and say, 'Today-ay-ay, as in every day-ay-ay, I consider myself-elf-elf, the luckiest man-an-an on the face of the earth-earth-earth…'"

Translation: how tough is it to be the pitching coach on a club where you can routinely trot out Maddux, Glavine and Smoltz, followed by, say, an Avery or a Neagle, and maybe Millwood or Burkett as your fifth starter?

"I can't say enough about the work Leo did for us," then–general manager John Schuerholz said that October day in 2005 when Mazzone left the Braves to join his old buddy Sam Perlozzo, the new Orioles manager, as his pitching coach. "He's been part of one of the great pitching legacies in baseball."

In June 1990 Mazzone was called up from the minors to replace fired pitching coach Bruce Dal Canton. That season the Braves finished with the highest ERA in baseball. Never again.

Over the next 15 years, Mazzone's staffs led the majors nine times in lowest ERA. Three others finished second. Under his guidance and regimen, Braves pitchers posted nine 20-win seasons, and 18 18-victory campaigns. They won six Cy Young Awards in the 1990s: three straight by Greg Maddux (1993 through 1995), two by Tom Glavine (1991 and 1998), and one by John Smoltz in 1996. How'd Leo do it?

"What makes for a great pitching staff is great pitchers," Mazzone once said. "And what makes for a good pitching coach is not messing up great pitchers."

There's much to be said for not screwing things up, especially with platinum pitchers like the Braves' Big Three. Mazzone was an acolyte of Johnny Sain, the great old Boston Braves pitcher turned pitching coach and guru. Sain believed in starters throwing twice, not once, between starts. Mazzone preached that, along with the gospel of pounding the down-and-away strike, attacking with a fastball with movement, changing speeds, never giving in.

That philosophy served Mazzone and most of his pitchers exceedingly well. He was demanding, particularly with younger pitchers or newly acquired reclamation projects from other clubs, with whom Leo did some of his best work. Youngsters Jason Schmidt and Odalis Perez chafed under his tutelage before finding success elsewhere. But Mazzone did some fine retooling with guys like Juan "Señor Smoke" Berenguer, Rudy Seanez, Mike Remlinger (who admittedly had his battles with his coach), and Chris Hammond.

His greatest reclamation, though, may have been John Burkett, a 22-game winner with San Francisco in 1993 but on the junk heap, not the mound, when he came to Atlanta in 2000 after being released by Tampa Bay in spring training. Burkett was 35 and, after going 27–33 the previous three years, likely done.

As Burkett told Tom Stinson of the *Atlanta Journal-Constitution* in 2005, "I think the best thing about Leo is, he has this sternness and his belief in what he's doing. He's very convincing, and he has the track record to back it up.

"When you look at some of the guys who were washed up when they came over—me being one of them, because I was done—maybe I was even starting to believe it at that time," Burkett continued. "But I remember throwing on the side one time when I first got over there, and Leo told me, 'You have the best control I've ever seen on the side, besides Greg Maddux.'

"And then he said, 'And your slider [stinks]. When you get behind in the count, quit throwing that thing. Throw your fastball down and away.' And I did that. I mean, there were times when I was thinking, *Man, I can't throw this guy a fastball down and away. He's going to kill it.* And I'd throw one and he'd take it for a strike.... That went a long way for me. I kind of took off after that."

Burkett was the fourth starter that year, going 10–6. He was an NL All-Star in '01, his ERA of 3.04 the lowest of his career. Once on the verge of quitting, Burkett instead went 47–35 over four years before retiring in 2003.

So, Leo. Pope Leo? The Pope of Pitching? "One of my greatest compliments ever," Mazzone told me after Kahn's book came out. "To be in the same company with the other people in that book is one of the greatest compliments I could ever receive."

From 1992 to 2002, Atlanta's staff finished first or second in ERA in the majors. "It's the greatest run in the history of the game," Mazzone said. "No question about it."

Mazzone's Maryland homecoming didn't pan out. The O's were awful, and he and Perlozzo were gone after two seasons. Mazzone, who'd signed a three-year contract at $500,000 annually, is now a radio sportscaster in Atlanta.

50 The Lemmer

In baseball's rich pantheon of unexpected postseason heroes, few were more unlikely—or heroic—than a little switch-hitting, slick-fielding second baseman who answered to a variety of names. Lemmer. Scoots. Or the compliment Bobby Cox paid him in that seminal season of '91.

"The original dirt player." That's how the Braves manager characterized Mark Lemke, capturing him perfectly. A gamer, a guy who wasn't afraid to get his hands down and his face dirty. A guy who'd do whatever he could, whatever was needed to help the ballclub win. A guy who, much like Pigpen of *Peanuts* cartoon fame, scooted around in a perpetual cloud of dust.

In October 1991 Lemmer's dust was stardust.

Just a month earlier, the notion that a 5′9″, 167-pound backup second baseman might not only help the Atlanta Braves reach the World Series but bring them to the cusp of a world championship would've seemed ludicrous. Until Jeff Treadway was injured in mid-September, Lemke was his understudy. By late October, though, Lemke looked like "Mister October"—or perhaps, given his youthful appearance, "Master October."

Indeed, if not for the pitching heroics of Minnesota's Jack Morris in Game 7 of the World Series, if Atlanta hadn't blown several scoring chances in that 1–0 heartbreak, if the Braves had won, Lemmer would've been the World Series MVP. The *Atlanta Journal-Constitution* issued a commemorative coffee mug from that postseason, featuring some of the paper's memorable headlines. Including this one: "ReMARKable!" That he was.

Lemke had batted just .234 during the regular season, getting only 136 at-bats. His October heroics began in Game 2 of the NLCS. He doubled in the only run in Atlanta's 1–0 victory in Pittsburgh, his sixth inning, topspin chopper bouncing over Pirates third baseman Steve Buechele and scoring David Justice. "One of the stranger hits I've ever gotten," said Lemke, who also made a diving stop of Jay Bell's grounder up the middle in the eighth inning. He'd kept the ball in the infield and the tying run from scoring.

"In '91 I don't think you can ever duplicate that outpouring of affection," Lemke said. "I mean, everybody was into it. We'd go to the airport, and the [prison] chain gang dropped their tools and did the Tomahawk Chop when our buses drove by. They're probably ticked off at the world, and they turn and give you the Chop."

But it was in the World Series, after Atlanta upset the Pirates in the NLCS, where Lemmer truly made his mark. On the flight from Pittsburgh to Minneapolis, Lemke and Ron Gant kept telling each other, "We're not going home! We're going to Minnesota! We're going to the World Series!"

In the opener, Treadway, not Lemke, started at second base, Cox going with the veteran. "Maybe Bobby was taking my heartbeat," Lemke said. "It was going so fast, to the point where it gives you amnesia. There's only a couple of things I remember."

One thing was very memorable: the enthusiasm of the home crowd back in Atlanta. "You really loved it," Lemke said. "In basketball, they call it the sixth man. In football, Texas A&M has the

12th man. In baseball, that's what fans were like to me. It meant a lot to have a full stadium. The first game when I broke in [as a 1988 call-up], 3,500 people were in the stands."

After the Braves lost the first two games in Minneapolis, Lemke was the catalyst in their three straight wins in Atlanta-Fulton County Stadium. In Game 3 he singled in the game-winning run in the bottom of the 12th inning of that 5–4 thriller. A sliding Justice barely beat Dan Gladden's throw to the plate for the first Atlanta win in World Series history, a four-hour, four-minute marathon.

After that, "Then it was into La-La Land," Lemke said. "I went into an unconscious state of mind. I was in a zone. It was, like, *Wow!*"

In Game 4 he tripled and scored the winning run in the bottom of the ninth, tagging up on pinch-hitter Jerry Willard's fly ball and barely sliding home safely for a 3–2 victory.

Lemke tripled twice more to fuel the 14–5 Game 5 rout and batted .417 in the World Series, the highest average on either team. His slugging percentage was .708. His three triples tied a World Series record.

After establishing himself as the starting second baseman, Lemke later hit a career-best .294 in the strike-shortened 1994 season. He committed just three errors that season to set a franchise record for second baseman with a .994 fielding percentage. The old mark had stood for 32 years.

When Turner Field opened in 1997, Lemke began having vision problems—"Little spots in my right eye"—that eventually ended his career in '99. This, after joining the Boston Red Sox that season and suffering a severe concussion during a game. He's now a member of the Braves broadcast crew, doing pre- and postgame work, and still lives in Atlanta.

Like all his teammates, Lemke treasures his memories of the 1995 World Series champions, if other memories more. "As a player, you always play to win," Lemke said. "So '95 will always go down as No. 1. But it will never compare to '91. Never."

51 On the Move...Again

In the afterglow of Milwaukee's 1957 World Series title, everything changed. Dramatically so for National League baseball, when Walter O'Malley abandoned Brooklyn and moved his beloved Dodgers to Los Angeles. Along for the West Coast ride was Giants owner Horace Stoneham, taking his club to San Francisco. In Milwaukee the change was more subtle.

"I didn't realize it at the time," Henry Aaron said in 1958, "but after we won the seventh game of the World Series in 1957, everything started to go downhill."

Yes, the Braves would win another pennant and return to the World Series. No, Lew Burdette couldn't recreate his Fall Classic magic. He won Game 2 to give Milwaukee a quick 2–0 advantage. When Warren Spahn shut out the Yankees 3–0 in Game 4, the Braves needed just one more win for a second title.

Instead, the Yankees became the second team to overcome a 3–1 deficit and win the World Series. Burdette lost both Games 5 and 7 to "Bullet Bob" Turley. The Braves were dethroned after losing the last two games at home, and Milwaukee's civic love affair was already losing some of its luster.

Despite winning the 1957 Series, the Braves' attendance declined in '58 by more than 250,000. That July, manager Fred Haney was hanged in effigy from a construction crane in downtown Milwaukee. Some fans didn't like his conservative strategy. Others seemed spoiled by success. Popular shortstop Johnny Logan was unintentionally prophetic in saying, "We're a tiresome team."

The Braves' decline and their fans' indifference continued in 1959. The outcries against Haney, too. The team finished in a tie with Los Angeles, although Logan said, "We should have won [the pennant] by 10 games." When L.A. took the first two games in the best-of-three playoff, Haney resigned. The good times were gone for good in Sudsville.

The club finished second again in 1960, going 88–66. In their 13 years in Milwaukee the Braves never had a losing season. But from 1961 on they never finished higher than fourth. Whether it was fan indifference, TV's influence, or Vince Lombardi's dynastic Green Bay Packers, attendance plunged. Just 555,584 turned out in '65 to say their good-byes.

Rumors of a move first surfaced in 1963, when the team's new ownership, based in Chicago, took control. Bill Bartholomay, the chairman of the board, said, "We didn't buy the Milwaukee franchise to move it to Atlanta. How do these things get started?" By season's end, team president John McHale said, "The Braves will be in Milwaukee today, tomorrow, next year, and as long as we are welcome."

By 1964, ownership's intentions were clear, the city-team relationship contentious. Lawsuits were filed, congressional action considered. Milwaukee County chairman Eugene Grobschmidt even accused the Braves of playing lousy ball, so they wouldn't flee the city after winning a pennant. McHale threatened a slander suit. Fans were either disgusted or indifferent.

That off-season, the Braves were ready to move. The county, however, filed suit, alleging antitrust violations. The ballclub countered with a harassment suit. The team offered Milwaukee County a $500,000 settlement to move immediately, but the county board refused in a 24–0 vote.

The insults, threats, and legalese continued. On the final weekend before Opening Day in 1965 the Braves played three exhibition games in Atlanta's brand-new Fulton County Stadium. They drew more than 106,000 fans and two more huge crowds in June for off-day charity games against the White Sox and Twins.

Ownership gleefully announced that those five dates outdrew the first 28 home games in Milwaukee.

The sad end to a once-wonderful relationship came on September 22, 1965. Just 12,577 fans bid the Braves farewell. A bugler in the crowd played "Taps." The Braves lost to the Dodgers 7–6 in 11 innings and finished the season 86–76, 11 games behind L.A. On April 12, 1966, the Atlanta Braves debuted at home, with the National League's blessing. But not before a circuit court judge in Milwaukee had ruled that the NL had violated Wisconsin's antitrust laws. The NL was ordered to find Milwaukee another baseball team by 1967 or else return the Braves to Wisconsin. The league appealed in state court and won. The state asked the U.S. Supreme Court to hear the case, but by a 4–3 vote, the high court declined. The Atlanta Braves could play ball.

52 Fun at the Ol' Ballpark

Ted Turner took that baseball bromide to heart. After buying the Atlanta Braves in January 1976, the new owner knew this: he didn't know much about baseball. That, and the fact that his team was terrible. As if anyone cared.

The '75 Braves lost 94 games and finished 40½ games out of first. They drew just 534,672 fans, down nearly a million from the '69 playoff team. How to put fannies in the seats? Promotions. And you thought Bill Veeck was a showman.

Turner's first attraction? Himself. On Opening Day he introduced himself to a capacity crowd. Once Ken Henderson homered in the bottom of the second, Turner hopped out of his field-level box and ran to the plate to shake Henderson's hand. The crowd roared. The looniness started soon after.

Turner's promo man was a creative young guy named Bob Hope. Ted told him, "I want this team to be like McDonald's. I want an atmosphere that will make kids come to the ballpark." The traditional baseball promotions didn't appeal to Turner—forget Fan Appreciation Day, Old-Timers' Day, Bat Day. On the first Sunday of the '76 season Hope hyped one of the world's largest Easter egg hunts right on the field. Hippity, hoppity, Turner's on his way.

On July 6 fans were served postgame watermelon, but Hope also staged a frog-jumping contest. Worried about a lack of frogs, Hope's media blitz urged fans to "bring your own frog." Frogs hopped all over the infield and made national news.

Almost anyone could sing the national anthem, and did. Just ask. Later that season, while the Summer Olympics were being held in Montreal, the club staged a pregame Braves Olympics with the Phillies. Some players tossed basketballs from home plate into a barrel at second base. Others flung a football into a peach basket. Only two men entered the Great Baseball Nose Push: Tug McGraw, the Phils' enlightened reliever, and Ted Turner. The owner got down on all fours and furiously pushed a baseball with his nose from first to home, beating McGraw and bloodying his face in the process. The crowd went nuts as Ted held the ball aloft.

Ah, the Great Ostrich Race. The jockeys: Ted, broadcasters Ernie Johnson, Pete Van Wieren, and Skip Caray, sportswriter Frank Hyland, and radio deejay Skinny Bobby Harper. They wore racing silks, with nicknames on the back ("Poison Pen" for Hyland). They rode their trusty fowl in heats. Turner accused Caray of cheating, and Skip replied, "How can I cheat? It's a freakin' ostrich!" Hyland's mount, the best behaved, won.

There was the Cash Scramble, with $25,000 in $1 bills scattered on the infield and five contestants given 90 seconds to scoop 'em up. On Wishbone Salad Dressing Night fans scrambled through a gigantic salad bowl at the plate in search of the keys to a new car.

Who can forget Headlock and Wedlock Night, originally planned as Wedlock Night? The 34 couples who responded were to be married at home plate—groomsmen, bridesmaids, attendants, and all. Each couple walked beneath an arch of bats held aloft by Braves and Mets players. But there was one problem: Turner had also promised a Headlock Night, a ballpark wrestling event, to his pal Jim Barnett, the owner of Georgia Championship Wrestling. The only available date was July 11. Wedlock Night.

As Ernie Banks would say, "Let's play two!" After the nuptials and the ballgame, the newlyweds and others circled the wrestling ring set up on the field and enjoyed some pre-honeymoon rasslin'.

Later that summer, Hope invited Karl Wallenda, the legendary patriarch of the Flying Wallendas, to strut his stuff in the park. A 300-foot wire was strung on the stadium's rim, stretching from way beyond first base to third. Between games of a double-header, Wallenda, 70, worked without a net and despite a fierce wind. Turner told Hope to cancel on the grounds that it was "too risky." Wallenda refused. He walked the walk. It took 12 minutes, taking everyone's breath away, Ted's included.

More madness followed. Bathtub races. Wet T-shirt contests. A hybrid that was ridiculous even by Hope-Turner standards—a mattress-stacking contest meets 25¢ beer night. College fraternities and sororities throughout the Southeast descended on the stadium, trying to make the Guinness Book of World Records. The goal being to stack as many people as possible on a mattress in a minute. The frat brothers of Emory University's Sigma Chi recruited Mr. Ted Turner as a ringer. And there was Ted, going to the mattress, on the bottom of a pile. The bodies piled up above him, and Turner's face turned beet-red. Gasping for breath afterward, beaten and bowed, Turner vowed, "I've got to stop. I'll kill myself, and I've never been to a World Series."

That wouldn't come until 1991. All this lunacy was in the first season alone.

53 Visit the Braves Museum and Hall of Fame

The Ivan Allen Jr. Braves Museum and Hall of Fame is named for the late, great Atlanta mayor who helped bring big-league baseball to town. The museum covers it all, not just Atlanta, but also Milwaukee and Boston, the team's previous homes before heading south in 1966.

As Carolyn Serra, the museum and hall's director, said, "We always try to do stuff including Boston, Milwaukee, and Atlanta."

This is the longest continuously operating franchise in Major League Baseball, in business since 1871. And the rich history of those Boston Beaneaters-turned-Braves, of Milwaukee's '57 world champion Braves, and especially of the Atlanta Braves from Aaron's 715th to 14 consecutive division titles, is all on display.

For that, great credit goes to Serra. She's not just the director but also a rabid baseball fan, an encyclopedic Braves historian, and a museum-quality curator.

Her baseball *Mona Lisa*? "The grand one, right there," she said, pointing to a glass-enclosed case. "Our biggest one." Actually, two—the historic 715th home run ball and the bat Henry Aaron used to hit it and break Babe Ruth's record on April 8, 1974.

"It should be here [and not in Cooperstown], because this is where it happened," Serra said. "It still says, 'Baseball's Home Run King,' but he'll always be Atlanta's Home Run King."

The museum is divided into three major areas and exhibits.

Atlanta (1966–present)

Start with a 17-minute video of Atlanta Braves highlights since Opening Night in '66. There's the original dugout bench from

Atlanta-Fulton County Stadium, the 1995 World Series trophy and replica rings, and Dale Murphy's 1982 and '83 MVP Awards. You'll also find a franchise record leaderboard (Chipper's everywhere) for franchise and Atlanta hitting and pitching leaders that is updated daily during the season.

"We just got all of this this year," Serra said, pointing to another glass-enclosed treasure trove from the 1970s, one of four such decade displays. "Dale Murphy sent all his stuff to us," including his old spikes, glove, and baby-blue road uniform.

"A lot of players are keeping their stuff at home now, building their own museums," Serra said. "It's too bad, 'cause only their families and close friends get to see it."

Here's where you'll see the Channel 17 jersey Ted Turner had Andy Messersmith wear once before MLB yanked the blatant ad. "Clever, though," Serra said, smiling. "It's very Ted."

There's Phil Niekro's 2,000th strikeout ball, his Braves contract in 1967, when he signed for $12,000, and a 1975 press release when he became the first $100,000 pitcher.

The 1980s display includes the Pascual Perez "I-285" blue jacket, given to the pitcher after he got lost on his way to the ballpark and kept circling 285, the perimeter highway. Bob Horner's bat and a ball from his four-homer game in '86 are there, along with more than 200 items in "14 Straight," a new exhibit highlighting Atlanta's 14 consecutive division titles from 1991 to 2005.

"This is very popular," Serra said. "It's also where you realize how old you are, when you have a kid standing in front of one and saying, 'I was born in this year!'"

Milwaukee (1953–1965)

The Milwaukee section of the museum sports a superb selection of old Milwaukee memorabilia, including Warren Spahn's glove he used while winning his 300th game and throwing two no-hitters and his 1957 Cy Young Award. Ernie Johnson's '57 warm-up jacket and a copy of the first issue of *Sports Illustrated*, from August 16, 1954, with Eddie Mathews at-bat before a full house at County Stadium, are here, too.

This section also holds a fan favorite—a 26-foot cross section of an original Baltimore & Ohio Railroad car, the "Bobolink," with a refurbished interior and artifacts from that era. You can look into a few sleeping compartments and listen to audio of Bad Henry and Uncle Ernie describing the Braves' experiences riding the rails.

Boston (1871–1952)

This area is truly fascinating, with all the old Boston nicknames—Rustlers, Doves, Bees—on and alongside paraphernalia from the ages: an 1876 Spalding & Bros. mushroom bat, old catcher's masks, a crudely-stitched ball. You'll find a copy of Babe Ruth's 1935 contract with Boston and Sibby Sisti's 1946 satin uniform—the club felt those shiny unies would show up better on TV night games. Bad idea.

There's truly heroic WWII history here, too, including Warren Spahn's Purple Heart and Ernie Johnson's Marine Corps winter overcoat.

Want more from the museum in general? Sid Bream's knee brace from his slide home to win the 1992 NLCS, the lineup card from the last game at Atlanta-Fulton County Stadium, and the one from the first game at Turner Field can be found here. A moving display from the post-9/11 game, when the Braves played the Mets in Shea Stadium after the terrorist attacks, should not be missed, including a No. 38 uniform worn by Jason Marquis. The Braves' starting pitcher that night, he grew up on Staten Island and mourned a childhood friend, Michael Cammarata, a Little League teammate-turned-NYC firefighter, who died in the towers' collapse. And there's also a piece of limestone from the attack on the Pentagon.

It goes on and on. You just have to see it yourself.

54 Joltin' Joe

No, not DiMaggio. Adcock. Joe Adcock, the slugging first baseman for the Milwaukee Braves from 1953 to 1962. One of the game's most dangerous home run hitters during that decade, Adcock—batting behind Eddie Mathews and Hank Aaron—helped make middle-of-the-lineup misery for pitchers throughout the National League.

He also made some significant baseball history himself in 1954. And in 1959 Adcock helped ruin the near-perfection of Pittsburgh's Harvey Haddix.

On April 29, 1953, in his first month with Milwaukee after being traded by Cincinnati, Adcock launched a mammoth home run. The 6′4″, 220-pound Louisiana farm boy became the first player to hit a ball into the center field bleachers at the Polo Grounds in New York since 1923, when the distance from home plate to those bleachers was lengthened to 483 feet.

On July 31, 1954, Adcock continued his Homeric odyssey. In Ebbets Field he homered off four different Brooklyn pitchers, becoming just the seventh player in major league history to hit four homers in a game. Adcock also doubled to set a big-league record with 18 total bases.

He did all that with a bat he'd borrowed from teammate Charlie White, after breaking his own the previous evening. That night Adcock had merely singled, doubled, and hit just one homer in the Brooklyn bandbox he made his own playground. Coming into the July 31 game, Adcock was hitting .442 for the season against the Dodgers, .467 in Ebbets.

He led off the second inning with a homer to left field off Don Newcombe. In the third Adcock doubled off reliever Erv Palica.

When he faced Palica again in the fifth, Adcock crushed a three-run homer into the upper deck in left-center. It was 9–1 Milwaukee, and Adcock was merely warming up.

Come the seventh, he hit a two-run homer to left off Pete Wojey, the third straight Brooklyn right-hander he faced. Adcock punctuated the night in the ninth with his historic fourth home run, this one to left-center off lefty Johnny Podres to make it 13–6. Final score: 15–7.

At the time, Adcock was one of just five players to hit four homers in a nine-inning game. He saw just seven pitches in his five at-bats, homering on four of them. He had seven RBIs and scored five times. At 26, anything seemed possible for him.

The next day Adcock doubled his second time up after a knockdown pitch by Russ Meyer. In his next at-bat Adcock was beaned by Brooklyn's Clem Labine and was carried off the field.

On June 17, 1956, he hit another majestic home run, this time off Brooklyn's Ed Roebuck, to become the only man to hit a ball out of Ebbets Field in left field. It cleared the 83-foot-high roof, just to the left of the left-field light tower and high above the 348-foot sign on the outfield wall. That was one of Adcock's 13 homers against Brooklyn that season, an NL record against one team.

He hit a career-best 38 in all to go along with his .291 average and 103 RBIs. Add Aaron's totals—a league-leading .328 average, 26 homers, and 92 RBIs—and Mathews' line of .272, 37 home runs, and 95 RBIs. That's 101 homers and 290 RBIs in all.

On May 26, 1959, Adcock broke up the best-pitched game in baseball history. In Milwaukee County Stadium, Harvey Haddix, Pittsburgh's 5′9″ left-hander nicknamed "the Kitten," was the big cat this night. Against the two-time NL champions lineup, Haddix was perfect through 12 innings, retiring the first 36 batters he faced. No one in modern National League history had ever pitched a nine-inning perfect game, much less 12.

As first baseman for the Milwaukee Braves from 1953 to 1962, Joe Adcock hit 239 home runs, four of which came in a single game against Brooklyn in July 1954.

Finally, in the bottom of the 13th leadoff man Felix Mantilla reached first on a throwing error by Pirates third baseman Don Hoak. After Eddie Mathews sacrificed Mantilla to second, Haddix intentionally walked Henry Aaron, setting up a double play. Instead, Adcock belted a ball over the right-center-field fence. Many fans left, assuming a 3–0 Braves' win.

Once Mantilla crossed home plate, Aaron, unaware the ball had left the yard, touched second base, turned and trotted toward the dugout. Adcock, meanwhile, circled the bases, passing Aaron on his way to third. Umpire Frank Dascoli called Adcock out for passing Aaron; the crew chief ruled that hit a double, not a homer, and that

Aaron's run counted because he'd left the basepath voluntarily. Apparently, it was a 2–0 Braves win.

The next day NL president Warren Giles ruled that because Adcock's "homer" was ruled a double, Aaron could not have advanced beyond third. Thus, it was a 1–0 Braves win, finally, despite Haddix's one-hit, near-miss at perfection. The winning pitcher? Lew Burdette, who pitched all 13 innings, allowing 12 hits.

After the 1962 season—in which he'd homered in his final at-bat as a Brave—Adcock was traded to Cleveland and then played three years for the Angels before retiring. In 17 big-league seasons he hit 336 home runs—then 20th on the all-time homer list and seventh among right-handed batters. Joe Adcock died at age 71 from Alzheimer's disease.

55 It's a No-No-No!

In baseball jargon, it's a no-no. Shorthand for a no-hitter. But what to call what transpired one Atlanta evening nearly two decades ago? Let's call it a no-no-no. A no-hitter by committee. A three-pitcher no-hitter. One strong left arm, two rights—one young, one not so young—all three combining to make history and win a crucial game in a most unlikely pennant race.

But not without some controversy.

On Wednesday, September 11, 1991, Kent Mercker, Mark Wohlers, and Alejandro Pena teamed up to throw the 13th no-hitter in Braves franchise history. Three seasons later Mercker would author a no-no all his own. But on this night, before an apprecia-tive crowd of 20,477 in Atlanta-Fulton County Stadium, the trio held San Diego hitless in a 1–0 victory.

It was the first combined no-hitter in National League history, Atlanta's first since Phil Niekro no-hit the Padres on August 5, 1973. And it kept the surprising Braves in the thick of the NL West race with the Dodgers.

It was also one of the most unique, quirkiest, and controversial no-hitters ever.

As Bob Nightengale, the longtime, esteemed baseball writer who was then covering the Padres for the *Los Angeles Times*, wrote that night, "It came compliments of what must be considered a generous decision by official scorer Mark Frederickson on Darrin Jackson's ground ball in the ninth inning."

For the first six innings, Mercker—making just his third career start—was merely untouchable. The young left-hander faced just 20 batters, walking two and striking out six with fastball after fastball. But in the seventh inning Braves manager Bobby Cox pulled Mercker. He needed a victory, not history. When rookie right-hander Mark Wohlers came on for the seventh, trotting in from the bullpen, Braves fans expressed their displeasure with Cox.

"When the fans started booing," Wohlers said afterward, "I was the one who felt like the bad guy."

Wohlers worked two scoreless innings. The only threat to the no-hitter? Fred McGriff's 401-foot fly ball in the seventh, which Ron Gant caught a foot in front of the 402 sign on the center-field wall.

In the ninth enter Alejandro Pena, the veteran right-handed closer the Braves had acquired two weeks earlier from the Mets. Pena retired the first two batters. On an 0–2 fastball, Jackson hit a high chop to the left side, toward shortstop Rafael Belliard. Terry Pendleton, the third baseman, stepped in front of him, ready to field the chopper. But he lost the ball in the lights. The ball glanced off the tip of Belliard's glove and bounced away. The crowd moaned, then suddenly roared. "E-5" had flashed up on the scoreboard. Error, third baseman.

When Tony Gwynn flied out to Otis Nixon, the rare no-hitter was complete. Or was it?

As Nixon ran in from left field with the ball, he jogged toward the dugout, looked at the spectators, and tossed the ball into the stands. The Braves were aghast. Nixon shrugged. In exchange for some Braves bats and balls, the fan who'd caught the last ball used in the no-hitter returned it to Pena.

In the clubhouse, Pena placed the ball on the top shelf of his locker. He'd inscribed it with the single-minded mentality of a closer. It read:

> 9-11-91
> ATL-1
> SD-0
> Save 8

Afterward, Pendleton insisted it was his miscue, not a hit. "It was an error, all the way," he said. "E-5, baby." He then giggled, and asked Frederickson if the call would stand, if it wouldn't be changed to a single. Yes, it would stay an error. And a no-hitter.

"I just missed it," Pendleton said then. "I lost it in the lights. I reached for it and just lost it."

Nightengale wrote: "He looked at Frederickson, shrugged his shoulders, and said, 'Sorry. Just telling the truth.'"

According to Nightengale, when Jackson heard about Pendleton's admission, he replied, "That's not good. He [the scorer] heard it and still didn't change it. Hey, when you have guys making up their own rules, there's not much you can say."

Frederickson had immediately made his decision, calling the play an error without looking at a TV replay of it. His explanation of the call: "Pendleton could have had the ball. He let it go by. Pendleton committed on the ball, and if he would have gone ahead and made the play, he would have thrown him out."

Tony Gwynn said this: "Really, it's simple. It's an error when there are two outs in the ninth inning."

No, it's not, or at least it shouldn't be, even that close to a no-hitter. That's a baseball no-no. Yet, perhaps, not in this case of a no-no-no.

56 The Catch

Even on the other side of the pond, it made an enormous splash. Even in Barcelona, in the International Press Center at the 1992 Summer Olympics, talk among American journalists—especially those from Atlanta—quickly turned from the Games to The Catch.

July 25, 1992. The night Otis Nixon gave new meaning to the term Otis Elevator. Actually, it was already the 26th in Spain when the wayward Atlanta Braves center fielder made the most sensational catch in franchise history. A decade later, Andruw Jones had assembled a portfolio of impossible catches. But Nixon's the one, The Catch above all others.

It wasn't just the play itself but also its import and, especially, the opposition and victim. The Atlanta Braves, in the midst of another pennant race, had won 12 games in a row and were leading the National League West. On this night they'd managed one hit but led Pittsburgh 1–0 in the top of the ninth inning. The Pirates' Jay Bell was on first base, having singled. Alejandro Pena, the Atlanta closer, checked the runner, then delivered the pitch. And Andy Van Slyke, the Bucs' terrific center fielder, swung.

Take it away, Skip Caray: "There's a drive, deep right-center field. Nixon goes as far as he can go…" There's a five-second pause here, the only sounds the screams and shrieks of a full house in Atlanta-Fulton County Stadium. Then Skip again: "He caught the ball! He caught the ball! I can't believe it! What a catch by Otis Nixon!"

Another pause, short. Then Caray's broadcast partner Joe Simpson: "There's nothing I can say to add anything to this. Just watch."

The replay rolled: Nixon sprinting toward the wall in right-center, racing at top speed, leaping, with his left foot digging into the padded wall, then pushing off on it and up, up, reaching with his glove on his left hand, a good foot over the yellow line atop the outfield wall...and making the catch, pulling the ball back over the wall and landing safely on the warning track, sticking a two-footed dismount like an Olympic gold medal gymnast.

In Barcelona, we watched the replay many times. Thank goodness for Ted Turner and CNN. "It was gone," Skip Caray cried. "He stole a home run from Andy Van Slyke."

That Otis did. Jay Bell hustled safely back to first. Left-hander Kent Mercker relieved Pena and got Barry Bonds to ground out to end the game. It was just the first of two heartbreaks Van Slyke would suffer that season in Atlanta. The second, and most devastating would be Francisco Cabrera's two-out, two-run single in the bottom of the ninth in Game 7 of the NLCS to stun Pittsburgh 3–2 and clinch Atlanta's second straight pennant.

But Nixon's catch was remarkable nonetheless. It was quintessential Otis, who was blindingly fast on the field, too often troubled off it. He stole an MLB-record six bases in one game in '91, a Braves-record 72 steals that season. In 17 big-league seasons Nixon played for nine different teams. He was arrested on cocaine charges with Cleveland in 1987. On September 16, 1991, Nixon was suspended 60 days for substance abuse.

In 1992 the switch-hitting Nixon was the Braves' leadoff hitter in Game 6 of that World Series against Toronto. In the bottom of the 11th he unsuccessfully tried to reach on a two-out drag bunt. That made the Blue Jays world champions.

Nixon ended his career in 1999 with the Braves, his speed helping them defeat the New York Mets in Game 6 of the NLCS and return to the World Series. He finished his career with 620 stolen bases—and also, for always, The Catch.

57 Tony C...as in Cloninger

For openers, Tony Cloninger could have used a closer. A late-inning reliever, even in the midst of a tied, extra-inning ballgame. Someone to hand the ball to before heading to the clubhouse to ice his weary right arm. Not on Opening Night, though.

On April 12, 1966, before a near-capacity crowd of 50,671 in the newly relocated Braves' first regular season game in Atlanta Stadium, Atlanta mayor Ivan Allen Jr. threw out the ceremonial first pitch. Then Tony Lee Cloninger tossed the first official pitch in Atlanta team history. Thirteen innings later, he was still chuckin' it. Somehow, his arm hadn't fallen off.

Pitching philosophy was different back then. The manager gave the ball to his starter and let him go as long as he could, as long as he was effective. That night, Cloninger was very effective, at least until the very last. Pitch counts? What's that?

Hadn't Cloninger made 38 starts (including 16 complete games) the season before, the Braves' last in Milwaukee? Hadn't he led the staff with 24 victories, a Milwaukee record? And on Opening Night in Atlanta hadn't Cloninger shut out the Pittsburgh Pirates through seven innings? Why would manager Bobby Bragan make a call to the bullpen?

Even when the Pirates' Jim Pagliaroni homered in the eighth to tie it 1–1, Cloninger kept firing his fastball. On into the top of the 13th, when Willie Stargell popped a two-run home run. Although

Cloninger's battery mate, catcher Joe Torre, hit his second solo homer in the bottom half, the Braves lost 3–2. Despite striking out 12 batters, walking just three, scattering 10 hits, and pitching 11 scoreless innings out of 13, Cloninger took the loss.

Bragan took the heat for allowing Cloninger to throw 13 innings so early in the season. The manager didn't survive. The Braves, who hadn't had a losing season since leaving Boston after the '52 season, fired Bragan on August 9 with a 52–59 record. His Opening Night pitcher was never the same again.

Cloninger went 14–11 that season, completing 11 of 38 starts and pitching 257⅔ innings (this, after 242 and 279 innings, respectively, in the two previous years under Bragan). In his last six seasons Cloninger reached double figures in victories once, winning 11 but losing 17 for Cincinnati in 1969. His combined record after his 1966: 32–45.

Later in that inaugural season, though, Cloninger made real history with his bat. On June 16 he homered twice against the New York Mets. On July 3, in Candlestick Park in San Francisco, he launched some pre-Fourth of July fireworks of his own. He became the first player in National League history—and, for nearly another 33 seasons, the only—to hit two grand slams in the same game.

A career .192 hitter, Cloninger saw his buddy Torre belt a three-run homer in the top of the first that July 3. Not to be outdone, Cloninger hit a grand slam off Bob Priddy to trump Torre. In the fourth Cloninger did it again, this slam coming against Ray Sadecki. He became the first National League player ever to hit two grand slams in one game, and remains the only pitcher in either league to do so.

It would be 33 years before the Cardinals' Fernando Tatis duplicated Cloninger's feat—but he did so in the same inning in Los Angeles on April 23, 1999. Tatis is the only man with two slams in the same inning. Washington's Josh Willingham joined the NL slam-fest with his two-fer in 2009.

Before he was finished that day in Candlestick Park, Cloninger singled in a run in the Braves' 17–3 rout. That gave him nine RBIs, still a one-game record for pitchers. From 1992 through 2001, Cloninger was the bullpen coach for the New York Yankees. From 1996 through 2000, he helped them—and manager Joe Torre—win four World Series.

58 ROYs...and Wally

Six Braves have won the Rookie of the Year Award. It was originally presented by the Chicago chapter of the Baseball Writers Association of America (BBWAA) before going national in 1947. Initially, only one rookie was chosen for the ROY. In 1947 the full BBWAA membership voted for the top rookie in the major leagues: Jackie Robinson.

The Brooklyn Dodgers first baseman batted .297, scored 125 runs, and stole 29 bases. More important, Jack Roosevelt Robinson conquered an Everest of a barrier: he broke baseball's color line to become the first black player in major league history. The next Rookie of the Year? Boston Braves shortstop Alvin Dark. He was the last winner before the ROY was given to the top rookie in each league, starting in 1949.

In 1987, on the 40th anniversary of Robinson's integration of the game and his selection as baseball's best rookie, the Rookie of the Year Award was renamed the Jackie Robinson Award. Of the six Braves who've won it, two played in Boston: Dark, and outfielder and racial pioneer Sam Jethroe (1950). Interestingly, none won while the club was based in Milwaukee. Four played in Atlanta: catcher Earl Williams (1971), third baseman Bob Horner (1978), outfielder David Justice (1990), and shortstop Rafael Furcal (2000).

Five More Braves Rookies of the Year

1948: Alvin Dark, shortstop. Hit .322, 3 HR, 48 RBIs. Won two World Series, as a player with the Giants in their 1954 sweep of Cleveland and as Oakland A's manager in 1974.

1971: Earl Williams, catcher. Hit .260, 33 HR, 87 RBIs. First Atlanta Brave to win the award.

1978: Bob Horner, third baseman. Hit .266, 23 HR, 63 RBIs. Had 218 homers, all but three with Atlanta in 10 injury-plagued seasons.

1991: David Justice, outfielder. Hit .282, 28 HR, 78 RBIs. Hit game-winning homer in 1–0 win in Game 6 of 1995 World Series for Atlanta's only world title.

2000: Rafael Furcal, shortstop. Hit. 295, 40 stolen bases, 87 runs. Swift, with a powerful throwing arm.

There might well have been a seventh, if only the award had existed back in 1930 when Wally Berger broke in with a bang: a then–club record 38 homers.

Berger's homers also set a National League mark for a rookie. He batted .310 and established a new rookie mark with 119 RBIs. Young Wally loved the long ball and almost always aimed for the fences. Yet his batting eye was keen: in 555 at-bats in 1930, he struck out just 69 times. The next two seasons, he had just 70 Ks in 617 at-bats in 1931, 66 in 602 at-bats in '32. He was the Boston Braves' best rookie since the 1911 and 1912 seasons, when catcher Hank Gowdy and Rabbit Maranville joined the club, respectively.

In 1935 Berger would lead the NL in homers (34) and RBIs (130). But his finest and most valuable season may well have been 1933. For the first time since '21, the Braves finished in the top half of the eight-team league, nine games out but still in fourth place. Their improvement and 83–71 record resulted in a then-franchise attendance record of 517,803, the third straight year topping the 500,000 mark.

At August's end the Braves even dreamed of catching the lordly Giants, six games ahead of Boston, with the teams beginning a rare six-game series. In the opener Berger's 25th homer helped the Braves win 7–3. The following day more than 50,000 fans filled Braves Field for a doubleheader. The great Carl Hubbell won the first game of that sweep. The Giants took the fourth and fifth games of the series, too. Had the sixth game not been stopped because of darkness with the score 4–4, New York may well have won a fifth straight.

Ill with the flu for the season's last two weeks, Berger managed one last home run. His 27th, a grand slam, not only gave Boston a win in its season finale, but a fourth-place finish. Finishing in the first division earned each player an extra $242 bonus. When Berger crossed the plate after his slam, Maranville kissed him on each cheek.

Traded in mid-1937, Berger ended his 11-year career in 1940 with a .300 average and 242 home runs. And he might well have been the Braves first Rookie of the Year had the award existed when he broke in.

"Jet." That was Sam Jethroe's nickname as well as his playing style. The outfielder could fly, certainly as a younger man when he played for the Cincinnati and Cleveland Buckeyes in the Negro Leagues and later as a Boston Brave. In 1950 Jethroe became the first black player in franchise history and was voted the National League Rookie of the Year.

At age 33, Jet was—and remains—the oldest Rookie of the Year in baseball history. In 1950 Jethroe was one year older than the 2000 AL Rookie of the Year, Seattle reliever Kazuhiro Sasaki.

In the Negro Leagues, Jethroe had been a swift, star outfielder who'd won a pair of batting titles, helping the Buckeyes win two pennants and the 1945 Negro League World Series. He'd done so after receiving a military deferment from serving in World War II.

On April 16, 1945, after pressure from a Boston city councilman, Jethroe was one of three African American players invited to try out for the Red Sox on a recommendation from black sportswriter

Wendell Smith. The other two? Marvin Williams and Jackie Robinson. Two Sox coaches—including Hugh Duffy, he of the .438 average in 1894—watched the workout. None of the players made the team. No way were the Red Sox ready to integrate.

Once Robinson broke the color line in 1947, Jethroe played from 1948 through 1949 for the Montreal Royals, Brooklyn's Triple A affiliate in the International League for whom Robinson had played. After he led the International League with 89 steals in '49 and scored 154 runs, the Braves traded three players for Jethroe and Bob Addis, starting the switch-hitter in center field during spring training.

On April 18, 1950, Jethroe became the first black player in Boston Braves history. The switch-hitter was quickly a hit in Boston, and literally a steal. He had two hits in his first game, including a homer. Jethroe went on to lead the National League with 35 stolen bases (the most by a Brave since Hap Myers' 57 in 1913), and did so again in '51 with 35 more. Jethroe batted .273 with 18 homers and 58 RBIs, scoring 100 runs. And he was voted the NL's Rookie of the Year, the second successive year a black man had won the award (Dodgers pitcher Don Newcombe won in '49).

Jethroe's totals were nearly identical in 1951: a .280 average, 101 runs, 65 RBIs, 160 hits, 18 homers, and 35 stolen bases. He would slump badly in 1952, however, hitting just .232. Reportedly, he had vision problems. And there were questions about his actual age. The East St. Louis, Illinois, native was originally believed to have been born in 1922. In actuality, he was born on January 23, 1917.

Jethroe led all National League outfielders in errors in each of his three full seasons. He was among the top four in strikeouts each year, too (93, 88, and 112, respectively). On June 8, 1952, Jethroe hit the last grand slam in Boston Braves annals before the franchise moved to Milwaukee.

Switch-hitter Sam Jethroe became the first black player in Braves history, debuting for the Boston team in April 1950. At 32, he was the oldest player to earn Rookie of the Year honors.

Traded to Pittsburgh in '54, he played just two more major league games, finishing out six Triple A seasons before retiring. Jethroe moved to Erie, Pennsylvania, found factory work, and then opened a bar. The 1950 NL Rookie of the Year, and the first black player in Braves history, died in 2001. He was 84.

59 Skip's Longest Day

"The Family Business." That's what the Carays called it. The business of broadcasting baseball, reverently passed down from generation to generation. In the name of the father, and of the son, and of the "Holy Cow!" ghost of a grandfather. Amen. That's how it unfolded one sunny Friday afternoon in the Friendly Confines. With Harry, alas, in heavenly absentia. Which was not the plan at all.

In a perfect world, Harry, Skip, and Chip, three generations of Carays, would've worked alongside each other in the Wrigley Field broadcast booth that Friday, May 29, 1998. But that, and other plans, were dashed when Harry died of a heart attack in February. His funeral mass was televised live on WGN from Holy Name Cathedral in downtown Chicago. Chip, the new TV play-by-play man on the Cubs' WGN broadcasts, wouldn't break in beside his grandfather after all.

"It'll be like walking into the house for the first time [after Harry's death]," Skip had said back in Atlanta. "If Dad and Chip could've worked together, it would've been so great. But Chip wound up with a helluva job, through no fault of his own. It's almost like Dad said, 'What the hell, let the kid do it.'"

Skip dreaded returning to Wrigley for the first time without Harry. In fact, he nearly chickened out. "But I wanted to see my boy," he said. "And I thought, *The hell with it. Let's face up to it and get it over.*"

Skip couldn't watch the Cubs' April 3 home opener on TV. Too emotional. There were too many memories. Good times in Chicago between a father and son, catching up on lost time. In St. Louis Harry had been the Cardinals' big voice and bon vivant around town, when Skip just wanted to spend time with his dad. Once Harry became a Cubs Fan and a Bud Man, the most famous beer drinker in America, Skip came to town with the Braves, and the two went out on the town after games. Most nights ended in the wee small hours of the morning, sharing one last cocktail.

Entering the broadcast booth, however, with Chip but without Harry, would be tough. "All right, I'm ready for this thing to start, and for it to be over," Skip said, writing the lineups in his scorebook two hours before the first pitch. At 2:00, after posing with Chip for a *Chicago Tribune* photographer, Skip said, "I'm doing okay. Not as okay as I look, but okay."

At 2:22, after his broadcast partner Pete Van Wieren tossed it to him, Skip said, "Okay, Pete, thank you very much. Hello again, everybody. Kerry Wood completes his warmup tosses, and Walt Weiss leads it off for Atlanta."

The toughest part, Skip knew, would be the seventh-inning stretch, when Harry always led the crowd in singing "Take Me Out to the Ballgame." He'd become an institution. Now guest conductors did the honors, and Skip planned to leave the booth for the bathroom. He did, but returned just in time for one of the all-time worst renditions of that classic. Sweetness? How could you butcher that baseball anthem, Walter Payton?

"Well," Skip said, back on the air, "they finally found someone who could sing it worse than my father." That was the only reference to Harry during the broadcast.

"I started to wimp out," Skip later admitted, "but I felt, *What the hell, I'm not gonna let 'em run me off.* So I just listened and shuddered." He smiled. When Brant Brown homered off John Rocker to beat Atlanta 5–3, Skip did the *10th Inning Show*, climbed down from the booth, walked outside through Gate D, and headed toward the corner of Addison and Sheffield.

A convertible drove by. In the front passenger's seat was a man in a black jacket with an enormous cartoon head, a shock of white hair, and an oversized pair of black-framed glasses. Yes, it was a Harry Caray-cature.

"Look at that!" Skip said, grinning and raising a fisted salute to his Dad's image. He then turned to a friend and said, "Yeah, I'll have a beer with you."

He sat at a table, sipping and chatting with fans. Many put it perfectly: "We loved your Dad, and Chip is doing a great job." Skip autographed anything, signing one Cubs cap "Chip Caray's Dad."

"Oh, man, that's a little rough," he said to a man in a T-shirt bearing several autographs, including, "Holy Cow! Harry Caray." Skip signed beneath it.

"People tell me they loved Dad so much," Skip said in the early-evening sun. "But if they only knew that it's a millimeter of how much I loved him."

60 The Chop and the Chant

It began, as many things do in the deep-fried, football-frenzied South, with a pigskin connection. It began with Deion being cut.

When the New York Yankees released Deion Sanders in September 1990, the sports world shrugged. Sanders, after all, was a football player, once a quicksilver cornerback and kick returner at

Florida State, now an Atlanta Falcon, always better at returning a punt than hitting a curveball. When the Atlanta Braves signed Neon Deion, he was a curiosity, a two-sport wannabe.

Yet by the summer of 1991, he'd inadvertently helped inspire Atlanta's baseball rallying cry: the Tomahawk Chop and Chant. The months of September and, especially, October would become the Chop's prime time.

Just stick out your arm, bend your elbow, and, with an open hand, start chopping up and down as if using a tomahawk. FSU football fans had done it for years, chanting a Seminoles war cry. When some attended Braves exhibition games, they chopped for each Deion at-bat. When he made the club and came north with the Braves, Atlanta slowly started chopping, too.

And when the Braves' stunning about-face unexpectedly put them in a pennant race with the Dodgers, Atlantans started chopping themselves silly. The Tomahawk Chop proved as unifying and inspiring as it was politically incorrect.

Many fans fashioned their own homemade tomahawks and brought them to the ballpark. Braves general manager John Schuerholz encouraged stadium organist Carolyn King to play the Chop when Sanders batted and at other appropriate times. Atlanta-Fulton County Stadium suddenly had a new name: the Chop Shop. A few over-exuberant fans were even in danger of suffering chop elbow.

An Atlanta businessman named Paul Braddy hoped to cash in on the craze. He manufactured a few thousand foam-rubber tomahawks that were on sale at stadium concession stands. Business wasn't brisk, at least not until the September 14 nationally televised Saturday matinee against the Dodgers.

The Braves were just a half-game behind L.A. A local sponsor, UNOCAL gasoline, supplied a free foam-rubber tomahawk to each of the 44,773 fans in the sellout crowd. In the bottom of the ninth inning, with Braves on first and second and the score tied 2–2,

David Justice walked to the plate. The fans needed no prompting from Carolyn King.

A spontaneous chant, an a cappella Tomahawk Chop, erupted in the ballpark and beyond. It was heard more than a mile away at a Morehouse College football game, a Gregorian baseball chant. It so startled Justice, he had to step out of the batter's box and take it all in: the deafening sound and the sight of 40,000 orange tomahawks (UNOCAL's color) chopping in time.

In the radio booth Pete Van Wieren and Don Sutton stared at each other, stunned, and got goosebumps. Van Wieren later described the wave of sound like "the Mormon Tabernacle Choir times 10."

Although Justice struck out, it hardly mattered. The Braves won 3–2 in 11 innings and took over first place. A new Braves tradition was born. And Justice got to savor, as he put it, "one of the most memorable moments of my career."

"That was really the birth of the chant being our war cry," Van Wieren said. "Over the next couple of weeks, we were inundated with hundreds of homemade tomahawks that we received in the mail. Wooden tomahawks. Knit tomahawks. Even an electric neon tomahawk. The phenomenon attracted network television news coverage across the country."

At home, Braves fans began dressing as Indians, beating drums. Even on the road, large crowds of Braves fans chopped and chanted in unison. As unifying as the Tomahawk Chop was for Atlanta fans, it could also disconcert opponents.

When the 1991 National League Championship Series moved from Pittsburgh to Atlanta for Game 3, Pirates center fielder Andy Van Slyke predicted, "The fans will be coming at us like it's Custer's last stand."

During the postseason, Native American protestors outside the ballpark demonstrated against the Chop, the Chant, and the Braves' nickname—particularly during the four World Series games in Minneapolis. But during Game 3 of the NLCS, thousands upon thousands of Braves fans waved souvenir red foam tomahawks, even owner Ted Turner and his wife, actress Jane Fonda. They all chanted so boisterously, they momentarily drowned out Carolyn King on the organ.

Even former President Jimmy Carter, sitting in Turner's box, not only chopped enthusiastically but heartily defended it, too.

"With the Braves on top, we have a brave, successful, and courageous team," Carter said. "And I think we can look on the American Indians as brave, successful, and attractive."

61 Bill Lucas

As visionary as Ted Turner was, he never planned on becoming a Civil Rights pioneer or social activist. Especially not in the context of baseball. Yet that's precisely what happened on September 17, 1976, the day Turner promoted Bill Lucas and made him the first African American general manager in Major League Baseball history.

Technically, Lucas' official title was vice president of player personnel. He'd been named the director of the Braves' farm system in 1972, then elevated to VP of player personnel. If Lucas was a general manager without portfolio, without that official GM title, it didn't matter. He was a wise baseball man and a warm, "What can I do for you to help you do your job?" human being.

A former infield prospect in the Braves' minor league system, Lucas was widely respected and universally well-liked. Such prospects as Dale Murphy and Brett Butler had developed nicely under his care, and Lucas was duly credited. When Turner had a GM opening in '76, he knew where to turn.

"I don't care what color he is," Turner said. "Bill Lucas is the best man to help me run the Braves."

He was 40, and he had Braves in his blood. Lucas was a native of Jacksonville, Florida, where the Braves had long had a minor league affiliate. A graduate of Florida A&M and a U.S. Army officer, Lucas signed with the Milwaukee Braves in 1957 and spent six years as an infield prospect before injuring his knee in 1964. He was also the brother-in-law of Henry Aaron.

In 1965 Lucas was the public relations director for the minor league Atlanta Crackers. He was then part of the Braves' transition team in their move from Milwaukee to Atlanta, working in the sales and promotion department. Lucas had originally turned down the Braves' offer to work in the front office, concerned that he was simply a token hire. Assured that wasn't the case, Lucas went to work in sales and promotions; he made sure to hire one black stadium worker for every white, promoting harmony between the races in quest of a common goal.

Lucas rose quickly through the PR department in 1966 and became assistant farm director in '67. After becoming the farm director in 1972, he attained GM status by '76, but not before a telling moment at the 1972 All-Star Game in Atlanta.

For decades baseball's off-the-field All-Star festivities were stag affairs, men only. As Lucas was entering the pregame gala, he saw Susan Hope, the wife of Braves PR man Bob Hope, denied entrance. "Let's go have a drink," Lucas said, taking her by the arm. Susan Hope said she wasn't allowed into the party. Lucas replied, "Look, my people weren't allowed to enter nice places for years, either. Come on, someone's got to be the first woman to integrate baseball." They entered together.

As the GM, and once young Bobby Cox took over as the manager in 1978, Lucas had the Braves developing nicely. On May 1, 1979, in Pittsburgh, Phil Niekro won his 200th game. Back in

Atlanta Lucas called Cox afterward, saying, "Tell Phil congratulations. And tell him to go out and celebrate and send the bill to me."

That was Lucas, as considerate and popular as he was smart. At the hotel, the entire team was invited to a party for Niekro in one of the team's suites. It was a long, wonderful evening. Niekro's mother was there, in from Ohio. At 6:30 the next morning, word came that Lucas had suffered a massive cerebral hemorrhage after calling Cox and was on life-support in an Atlanta hospital. The team was distraught.

Lucas' blueprint to turn the team around was taking shape. He was rebuilding from within. The Braves would finally win the NL West again in 1982, but Lucas never witnessed it. He died on May 5, 1979. He was just 43.

62 The Unlikeliest Walk of All

As walks go, this was the most improbable one of all, particularly given the batter, the situation, and the stakes. Which was more unlikely: a man walking on the moon in 1969 or, 30 years later, a notorious free-swinger drawing a walk to win the pennant? That's one small step for man, one giant leap for Andruw Jones.

A walk-off walk to advance to another World Series? Even Braves manager Bobby Cox scarcely believed it. Hey, Bob, take a walk on the wild side. Any walk, by anyone. Even Andruw.

In Game 6 of the 1999 NLCS, in the bottom of the 11th inning, Jones patiently, uncharacteristically worked the count and drew a bases-loaded walk off Kenny Rogers. That gave Atlanta another NL pennant and, after a two-year absence, a fifth trip to the World Series that decade. It also gave Bobby Valentine a severe and very public case of agita. He, not Kenny Rogers, was the gambler in this scenario.

It was Valentine, the ever-cocksure manager of the New York Mets, who'd loaded the bases in the fateful 11th. After Rogers—normally a left-handed starter but now pitching in relief—allowed a leadoff double by Gerald Williams, and once Williams was sacrificed to third base, Valentine ordered Rogers to intentionally walk Chipper Jones and Brian Jordan. That loaded the bases with one out and Jones coming to the plate to face Rogers—not, as many expected, rookie reliever Octavio Dotel.

Valentine was a particularly prickly thorn in Bobby Cox's side back then and remained so. To say Bobby V was confident was to put it mildly. A year earlier, when the Mets were in Atlanta, falling apart and seemingly out of playoff contention, Tom "Blumpy" Keegan, then of the *New York Post*, wrote after one nightmarish Friday night debacle, "If Bobby Valentine had known the Mets would butcher baseball as they did here last night, he would have never invented the game in the first place."

Now, with the pennant on the line, Valentine went with Rogers, not the rookie Dotel, and had him load the bases. He bypassed Chipper Jones—the National League MVP that year—and the veteran Jordan. Surely, Rogers would fare better against Andruw Jones, and perhaps outfox him, get him to chase a pitch out of the zone and go down swinging.

In 1998 Jones' second season as a regular, he'd drawn just 40 walks in 582 at-bats, 631 plate appearances. In '99 his batting eye and selectivity improved under new Braves hitting coach Don Baylor. He walked 76 times in 592 at-bats, 679 plate appearances. But still, Andruw struck out a lot and walked little.

The 1999 NLCS turned out to be a remarkable, memorable milepost during the Braves' 14-season playoff parade. They won the first two games at home, 4–2 and 4–3, getting power from an unexpected source: Eddie Perez. The light-hitting catcher homered in each game. In Game 2 Perez promptly followed Jordan's two-run homer in the sixth inning with one of his own. It came off…Kenny Rogers, and it gave the Braves a commanding 2–0 lead in the series.

When the series moved to Shea and Atlanta won Game 3 1–0 on a first-inning, unearned run and seven shutout innings by Tom Glavine, the Braves were thinking sweep. John Olerud's two-run single in the eighth inning off Shea villain John Rocker gave the Mets a 3–2 win and life. It also set the stage for an unforgettable Game 5 and a memorable Game 6.

Fifteen innings. That's how long it took the Mets to remain on life-support in an epic Game 5, a 15-inning marathon that lasted five hours, 46 minutes. At the time, it was the longest game in terms of time in postseason history. The Braves took a 3–2 lead on Keith Lockhart's triple in the top of the 15th, only to see the Mets answer with a bases-loaded walk by Todd Pratt and then Robin Ventura's swing of a lifetime. Hobbling on an injured leg, Ventura launched a drive through the rain. It cleared the right-field wall, kept the Mets alive, and became a rarity: a grand slam single. Ventura was mobbed by his teammates after rounding first, and they rushed him off the base paths. He ended up with a one-run single and another flight to Atlanta.

When the Braves scored five times in the first inning of Game 6, it was seemingly over. It was still 7–3 when the Mets scored four times to tie it. They took one-run leads in both the eighth and the 10th, and each time Atlanta tied it. In the fateful 11th, with the bases loaded, Andruw Jones came to bat. And the occasional walking man walked, driving in the pennant-winning run and setting off a mosh-pit celebration at the plate.

And in the visitors' dugout? The enduring image of Valentine, pounding on the railing and screaming, "No! No! NO!" as Rogers walked in the winning run.

63 The Unlikeliest Homer

The lead went something like this:

O' somewhere in this land of ours, the sun is shining bright.
Somewhere birds are singing, and somewhere hearts are light.
But here at Shea in Flushing, grown men and children weep,
For there is no joy in Metville, mighty Raffy has gone deep.

At blessed last.

Atlanta newspaper subscribers awoke to that poetry one Saturday, and some promptly lost their breakfast. It wasn't just my typing. It was the gist of that little ditty. The previous evening, September 27, 1997, Rafael Belliard, the diminutive Dominican shortstop of the Atlanta Braves had gone yard for the first time in a long while.

In the seventh inning at Shea Stadium, Raffy launched a home run off left-handed Mets reliever Brian Bohanon. It traveled 388 feet and more than a decade. It was mighty Raffy's second career homer, a mere 10 years, 4 months, and 21 days after his first dinger. After 1,869 at-bats between homers, Raffy—the 5′6″, 160-pounder whose other nickname was Pac-Man for the way he gobbled up ground balls—was the bomb.

"I've been looking for that for 10 years," Belliard said, beaming. "Finally, I get it tonight. It's unbelievable. I'm dreaming."

"Bo definitely didn't know about his power," Mets manager Bobby Valentine deadpanned.

On May 5, 1987, as a young Pittsburgh Pirate, Belliard hit his first home run off Eric Show of San Diego. Surely, the second would be just a matter of time. But a decade came and went, and still Belliard had but one. In a big-league career that spanned 17 seasons, no one ever raved about Raffy's bat. He hit just .221 for his career. Indeed, his bio could've read "Throws: Right. Bats: Wrong."

Two days before coming to Shea, however, Belliard got his 500th career hit. After that, he thought, "Now I've got to go for the big one." When it happened, "It felt so nice when I hit it," Raffy said that night in Flushing. "I watched it all the way. It's a great feeling. The whole game I'm thinking about my home run."

Belliard's homer tied the game at 6–6. The Braves won it in the 11th on Danny Bautista's run-scoring single. It was Atlanta's 101st victory, but it was Raffy's night. When he returned to the clubhouse after the game, he walked beneath a canopy of bats held aloft by his teammates. They chanted his name: "Raf-FY! Raf-FY!" One shouted, "Presidente!" A placard at his locker read "HR" and beneath it "II" in Roman numerals. Three celebratory bottles of chilled champagne were popped.

"I thought we'd see Tommy [Glavine] winning his 15th and Greg [Maddux] winning his 20th," manager Bobby Cox said of that road trip. "But I didn't think we'd see Raffy hit a home run."

No one did. They expected the defensive save Belliard made in the 10th inning, fielding an infield hit and keeping it from going into the outfield and the Mets from scoring.

As interminable as Belliard's homer drought seemed, it didn't begin to approach the major league record for home run futility. In 1926 Tommy Thevenow of the old St. Louis Browns hit two homers that season but never hit a third. When his career ended in 1938, Thevenow had gone 3,347 at-bats without another homer.

Of Raffy's second round-tripper, Braves shortstop Jeff Blauser cracked, "That will be a special memory for everyone who was here to see it. It just goes to prove his first one wasn't a fluke."

Not that Raffy thought so. "All my friends told me before the game that I was going to hit it tonight," he said afterward. "My wife had a dream that I'm going to hit another one. Maybe now we have to wait 10 more years."

Raffy retired in 1998 with his two homers in 2,301 at-bats (2,524 plate appearances). He still holds the major league record for the most at-bats between homers, with 1,869.

64 The Unlikeliest Win

By 1994, Bedrock's career was nearly over. Steve Bedrosian, once a hard-throwing, right-handed reliever who'd debuted with the Atlanta Braves in 1981, was still winding up yet winding down a fine career.

He'd been a valuable reliever on Atlanta's 1982 NL West champions. His lone season as a starter? Not so good; but then, going 7–15 in 37 starts for the hapless, 96-loss '85 Braves was no crime. Traded to Philadelphia, Bedrosian became, uh, the bedrock of the 1987 Phillies' bullpen. He was 5–3 in 65 appearances, with a 2.83 ERA for a bad ballclub. He led the National League with 40 saves. He even won the NL Cy Young Award as a real rarity: a reliever on a losing team.

"I knew there had only been a handful who'd preceded me," Bedrosian said after becoming the sixth reliever to win a Cy Young. He gave much credit to set-up man Kent Tekulve, who invariably turned over a ninth-inning lead to Bedrosian. "I was blessed."

Fortunate, too, that there was no dominant starting pitcher in the league that year. "I just kept saving games," Bedrosian recalled, "and people said, 'Hey, you've got a chance.'

"I don't want to say I backed into it," he said. "But the numbers, well, that's what the [BBWAA] writers thought and how they voted. The voting was close, probably the closest ever."

Bedrosian won with 57 points. The Cubs' Rick Sutcliffe, who led the NL with 18 wins, was second (55), Rick Reuschel (54) third.

Fast forward to 1994. By then, Bedrosian had been traded to the Giants and, in 1991, pitched for the Minnesota Twins who beat the Braves in that worst-to-first World Series. In May 1994, back in Atlanta, Bedrosian was a year away from retirement but had far graver concerns than making a mid-life transition from baseball. Cody, his son, was sick again.

Cody was three when he was first diagnosed with leukemia in 1990. The cancer went into remission but returned in '93. Bedrosian was back with the Braves by then and, in May 1994, back on the mound the night his family and team paid tribute to six-year-old Cody.

About 25 Bedrosian family members and friends, including Steve's wife, Tammy, were sitting in section 101 in Atlanta-Fulton County Stadium. They all stood and cheered when Cody and his older brother Kyle walked out to the mound to throw out the ceremonial first pitch.

Cody went first, throwing a strike to his father and doffing his Braves cap. The crowd roared, then roared again when Kyle mimicked his little brother. Bedrosian signed the balls for both his boys, then all three posed for a photo.

"It's funny," Bedrosian told me years later. "I thought everything was going to go great that night. I was going to get in the game and do great. It didn't. I got shelled."

Bedrosian's teammates had dedicated that game to Cody and Steve. Some wore their game pants knee-high, or their sock stirrups high, both a la Bedrock. But in the seventh inning, when Steve relieved Mark Wohlers, all hope sagged.

"Incaviglia crushed it," said Bedrosian. Pete Incaviglia's grand slam flew 481 feet. It was 8–1 Philadelphia. In despair, Kyle held his left hand to his head.

In the bottom of the ninth, Cody and his grandfather stood and headed up the aisle. The boy ran back down to retrieve the ball he'd thrown out for the first pitch. Then Cody and his grandpa made their way down to the Braves clubhouse to see Steve.

"I'd felt so dejected," Bedrosian said. "I felt like I'd let Cody down, my teammates down. But my teammates picked me up. It was almost like it was a storybook ending."

The Braves singled and singled and singled. Mike Mordecai hit his first major league homer. Javy Lopez drove in the tying run. It was 8–8. Bedrock was, well, relieved. Cody and his grandfather watched on the clubhouse TV through the 10th inning. And the 11th, and on and on until, with two out in the bottom of the 15th, reliever Mike Stanton bunted home Deion Sanders with the winning run.

"I stood in my locker," Bedrosian said, "and watched everyone congratulate and hug Cody."

"Before it even started, this game was for Cody," Stanton said that night. "Having him in here, going through what he's gone through, a comeback victory like that makes this victory even more special for us. You look what he's gone through, you notice baseball isn't important. You see all the fight in his eyes and all the love in Steve's eyes, and baseball isn't important.

"If baseball gives Cody happiness, it probably means more than anything tonight."

Cody got healthy again. He played baseball again but, "He hung up his spikes at 12," Bedrosian said. "He said, 'Dad, I really don't want to play anymore.' I said, 'That's fine with me.'"

Cody graduated from the Art Institute of Atlanta. He has his own career now, as well as the memory of the unlikeliest, and sweetest, Braves win imaginable.

65 Cyclin'

It is one of baseball's least appreciated and most overlooked accomplishments. Statistically, it's even rarer than throwing a no-hitter, yet it carries nowhere near the cachet. It's called going for the cycle. It's something Lance Armstrong could never even conceive of doing.

But Albert Hall did it.

"Count me in," Hall said excitedly on the night of September 23, 1987. In the last week of an otherwise abysmal season, Hall provided one shining moment for a sparse Atlanta-Fulton County Stadium crowd and secured a little piece of franchise history for himself. In Atlanta's 5–4 victory over Houston, Hall hit for the cycle. He hit a single, a double, a triple, and a home run all in the same game. It had been more than three-quarters of a century since the last Braves cycle, when the club was based in Boston and the ball was dead.

"It was exciting," Hall said afterward, "especially because it was in the major leagues."

Five years earlier, while playing the outfield for Atlanta's Triple A affiliate in Richmond, Hall had also hit for the cycle. But that was the minor leagues. This was big, literally. Not merely the big leagues, but a significant achievement in Braves history. Hall's cycle was not just the fifth in franchise history, but the first in 77 years.

A Boston Braves rookie named Bill Collins, like Hall a little-known outfielder, hit for the cycle in 1910. His was the fourth in club annals, following Herman Long (1896), Duff Cooley (1904), and John Bates (1907). Then Hall, a swift, switch-hitting center fielder, joined their exclusive fraternity in the Braves' franchise record book.

And now we know how many hits it takes to fill the Albert Hall scrapbook of big-league highlights: four, one of each kind.

Accomplishing the cycle demands several talents: hitting ability, speed, power, and, often, sheer luck. The single and the double? The easy parts. The homer is far more common than the rarity of a triple. In his cycle, Hall saved the toughest component for last, tripling off Astros' closer Dave Smith in his ninth-inning at-bat. He'd already touched Houston starter Jim Deshaies for the first three legs.

That triple was one of just eight career triples for Hall, but four came that season. So did three of his five career home runs, in 772 big-league at-bats. Only three other major leaguers hit for the cycle that season, all big names: Andre Dawson, Candy Maldonado, and Tim Raines. Yet to that list, add little-known Albert Hall, who recalled when he slid head-first into third, "Russ Nixon [Atlanta's third-base coach] told me what I'd done. And it flashed up on the board: 'Albert Hall Hit for the Cycle.'

"But I still didn't know I was going for the cycle," Hall said. "I was just running hard." Running right into history.

It would be 21 years—a relative blip in time, given the Collins-Hall gap—before another Brave hit for another cycle. On August 14, 2008, Mark Kotsay took no chances. He tripled in the second inning, hit a leadoff homer in the fourth, and singled in the sixth. The veteran outfielder completed the sixth cycle in franchise history by doubling—for his 1,500th career hit—in the seventh inning.

"It takes some luck to do that," Kotsay said that night after adding a fifth hit for good measure. "But I did have some good at-bats."

He also had a unique witness to history. "I saw both of them," said Braves pitcher Tom Glavine, who was a rookie call-up in 1987 for Hall's cycle and a rehabbing veteran in '08.

"It's obviously a very rare thing," Glavine told MLB.com's Mark Bowman. "And when you see it, it's very exciting. It's pretty much as exciting as seeing a no-hitter."

66 Unlikely Heroes

Most fans know the no-name biggies, lesser lights who saved their moments for the bright lights of the World Series. Even during day games of old.

Howdy, Hank Gowdy, the .243 banjo-hitting catcher for the Boston Braves who went all Albert Pujols in the 1914 World Series and hit .545 for those Miracle Braves. Of more recent vintage, there's Oly and Lemmer: Greg Olson and Mark Lemke, the unlikely catalysts for the worst-to-first Braves run to the 1991 National League pennant and Game 7 of the World Series.

And, of course, there's the ultimate one-hit wonder: Francisco Cabrera, whose two-out, "Braves win!" two-run pinch-single won the '92 pennant.

There's been more heroism during the postseason, especially since 1991. Unlikely heroes like Eddie Perez and Mike Devereaux, Walt Weiss and John Burkett.

For most of his career, Perez was the every-fifth-day personal catcher for Greg Maddux, who didn't want Javy Lopez catching him. Come the 1999 postseason, Perez caught on a daily basis; Lopez was injured.

Perez made the most of his opportunity. He homered twice: a solo in Game 1 of the NLCS, a two-run blast in Game 2, both Braves victories. In the decisive Game 6 Perez had a key eighth-inning single that helped tie the game. It went into extra innings, and in the 11th the Braves scored the winning run on a bases-loaded walk by—of all people—Andruw Jones, courtesy of the Mets' Kenny Rogers. The winning run was scored by another unheralded player—Gerald Williams, who doubled to start the 11th.

Perez was named the MVP of that NLCS. A .249 hitter in the regular season, he batted .500 against the Mets (10-for-20). In addition to those two homers, he hit two doubles and drove in five runs. His on-base percentage: .524. Slugging percentage: .900. Not bad for a career .253 hitter.

In the World Series Perez turned back into a pumpkin, hitting just .125 (1-for-8), with three strikeouts. But he had his NLCS Most Valuable Player trophy. It's even sweeter than his 2005 appearance in Milwaukee, as the bratwurst in Miller Park's sausage race. He finished out of the money in that one.

Four years earlier, Mike Devereaux was a similarly surprising NLCS MVP. The outfielder was acquired in August from the Chicago White Sox as a little late-season insurance. The Braves made good on their policy in the playoffs. In Game 1 of the NLCS in Cincinnati, Atlanta rallied to tie the game 1–1 in the top of the ninth. In the 11th Devereaux singled in the winning run.

In Game 4 Devereaux, pressed into the starting lineup after an injured knee sidelined right fielder David Justice, broke open a tight game with a three-run homer in the seventh. The Braves shut out the Reds 6–0 and completed a four-game sweep, thanks in large part to Devereaux.

In 1988 Walt Weiss was the AL Rookie of the Year with Oakland. The shortstop would later sign with Atlanta in 1998, start at short, and make his only appearance in the All-Star Game. As his average plunged to .226 in '99, Weiss lost his starting job but proved invaluable during one postseason game.

In Game 3 of the NLDS in Houston, with the score tied 3–3 in the 10th, the Astros had the bases loaded with one out. Tony Eusebio hit a smash up the middle, but Weiss made a sensational play, diving to his left and throwing home to Perez for the out. After getting out of the inning, the Braves won it 5–3 in the 12th.

Once a 22-game winner with San Francisco, John Burkett came to Atlanta in 2000 and resurrected his pitching career. Although his win in the 1996 ALDS was the first postseason victory in Texas Rangers franchise history, Burkett was probably better known as a part-time professional bowler.

He has at least 12 sanctioned 300 games to his credit, and willingly gave out such bowling tips as, "Never eat french fries with your bowling hand." After going 10–6 in 2000, Burkett made the NL All-Star team in '01 when he went 12–12. In the NLDS that season, with the help of light-hitting backup catcher Paul Bako's homer and relief help from four relievers, Burkett got the 6–2 win over Houston to complete a three-game sweep. It's the last postseason series the Braves have won.

67 Check out OLPH

No, that's not another newfangled statistical formula by which baseball's stat mavens can measure a player's performance. No OPS or WHIP here. OLPH stands for Our Lady of Perpetual Help Home. It's a cancer home run by Catholic nuns that sits in the shadow of Turner Field, answering to a far higher calling than ball or strike, fair or foul, safe or out.

Our Lady is one of the very few places in Atlanta where people live and die with baseball in the most literal sense.

It was particularly so on Sunday, October 1, 2006. The day of the regular season finale and, for the first time since 1990, the end of the line for the Braves. After 14 consecutive division titles, there would be no playoffs. No more baseball. That absence was acutely felt at Our Lady, where most of the eight nuns in residence are rabid baseball fans. Most patients are, too. If not, they quickly become so.

"The patients just love baseball," said Sister Mary Edwin, a Cleveland fan as a kid but now on the Braves bandwagon big-time. "They like going to games but also just watching on TV."

The home was established in 1939 by the Hawthorne Dominicans, an order of nuns devoted to caring for patients with terminal cancer. "Servants of Relief for Incurable Cancer" is their official title. Patients must apply for admission to OLPH with a diagnosis of incurable or terminal cancer and also with proof that they're unable to afford adequate nursing care elsewhere.

Once admitted, they find a loving atmosphere, a highly capable nursing and care-giving staff, and no shortage of folks who can explain the infield fly rule, like manager Bobby Cox, an occasional drop-in, and especially Dewsy—Bobby Dews, the Braves' former third-base coach who's been in the organization for decades in a variety of roles and is a frequent visitor to OLPH. "The most amazing operation in the world," Dews said. "And really, almost in another world from time to time."

Several times each season, when the Braves play mid-week matinee games at Turner Field, Dews (now a team consultant) drops off tickets at OLPH. A handful of patients attends, accompanied by staff, relatives, and volunteers, sometimes even a nun or two.

"The patients love to go to games," said Sister Miriam, the superior at the home who's known to occasionally wear a pink Phillies cap. "Baseball gives them something to look forward to. Even if they're sick, they can go over in a wheelchair. Even if it's only for an hour, it's being out and going to a game. You have your treats over there.

"Maybe your beer and your hot dog," she added, smiling.

More often, most residents watch the Braves on TV while lying in their beds. For Friday night home games, some nuns will sit on the second-floor porch to enjoy the postgame fireworks. Earlier in the evening they can hear the crack of the bat on the stadium public-address system, the roar of the crowd, and may even sing along to "Take Me Out to the Ballgame" during the seventh-inning stretch.

But primarily the Sisters for the Relief of Incurable Cancer are there to provide palliative care, to lessen the pain for the terminally ill. "To help them find some comfort here," Sister Miriam said. "Just some TLC. Sounds simple, doesn't it?"

OLPH, like its other six sister homes around the country, is supported solely by private donations. From its brochure: "No remuneration is accepted from the patients or their families, even though they may be able to contribute something. The Sisters place their trust in the loving providence of God, and that trust has never failed. Donations large and small from groups and individuals have provided the necessary funds from the very beginning."

So drop by Our Lady. If possible, make a donation. Even better, donate your time and help a patient cross Bill Lucas Drive and catch a Braves game.

Our Lady of Perpetual Help Home
760 Pollard Blvd., SW
Atlanta, GA 30315
Phone: 404-688-9515
Email: olphhome.org

68 The Turner Field Turnaround

In its own way, the Turner Field Turnaround of 1996–1997 was almost as remarkable as the Atlanta Braves' worst-to-first about-face of 1991. In terms of architecture and construction—and later destruction and reconstruction, too—the transformation of an 85,000-seat Olympic stadium into a 50,000-seat baseball park was much like those legendary 1914 Boston Braves of yore.

A miracle.

In baseball terminology, the Braves turned two of sorts: turning old Atlanta-Fulton County Stadium into a gigantic pile of rubble, then downsizing and turning Centennial Olympic Stadium into beautiful Turner Field.

When Fulton County Stadium opened in the spring of 1965, it symbolized Atlanta's big-league sports aspirations and the city's can-do spirit. The circular multipurpose stadium was completed in just 50 weeks at a bargain cost of $18 million. Originally, it was intended as the future home of the Kansas City Athletics, whose owner, Charlie Finley, agreed in terms to a 10-year lease with city officials to move the club to Atlanta. Not surprisingly, Charlie O. reneged and moved the A's to Oakland. Atlanta instead wooed and won over the Milwaukee Braves' ownership group. The minor league Atlanta Crackers opened the sparkling new ballpark in 1965 before the Braves overcame legal obstacles to move south in '66. They shared the stadium with the NFL expansion Atlanta Falcons.

At Atlanta's elevation of 1,057 feet above sea level, the ballpark soon became known as the Launching Pad. Home runs took flight—and not just those off the bat of Hank Aaron—as regularly as Delta departures from Hartsfield Airport. From 1970 through 1977, more National League homers were hit in the Launching Pad than anywhere else.

In 1991 the stadium got a new nickname, the Chop Shop, for all those Braves fans doing the Tomahawk Chop and Chant that wondrous summer and fall. By then, the city had been named the unlikely host of the 1996 Centennial Summer Olympics. The big question: where to build the Olympic Stadium? The solution:

across the street from Atlanta-Fulton County Stadium. The biggest quandary: how to convert Centennial Stadium into a ballpark in time for the 1997 season? And then what to do with the old joint?

On July 19, 1996, Centennial Olympic Stadium officially opened in grand style. Muhammad Ali, hands trembling from Parkinson's disease, took the Olympic torch and lit a cauldron that looked like a giant McDonald's french fries box. Later that summer, after Michael Johnson raced to Olympic gold, after Carl Lewis leaped to a fourth gold medal in the long jump, and once the Summer Paralympic Games ended, the real work began—converting and downsizing.

The decision was made to "retrofit" the stadium for baseball by removing thousands of temporary seats in what would become the outfield stands. Those plastic seats took up nearly half the stadium. They were removed and sold, and permanent outfield seating was built, along with other facilities and the Braves' new office building beyond left field.

Janet Marie Smith, the vice president of planning and development for the Braves, was very involved in not only the design of the Olympic stadium but also the retro look and redesign of Turner Field. She'd played a great role in the building of Camden Yards, the mother of all retro ballparks. She would later work wonders in the refurbishing of Fenway Park.

Turner Field, now with an official capacity of 49,743, opened on time to rave reviews on April 4, 1997. A newspaper poll determined that most fans wanted the new park to be named Hank Aaron Stadium. Instead, it was named for Braves owner Ted Turner and quickly got the nickname "The Ted."

On a sunny Saturday morning, August 2, 1997, the Launching Pad was imploded in a "3-2-1" matter of seconds. The park where Sid slid, Glavine won the Series, and Ted chopped while occasionally nodding off was gone in seconds.

An over-the-top TV reporter, giving his eyewitness account from a helicopter overhead, said, "The dust rising, from home runs to home rubble."

Then they paved paradise and put up a parking lot where Atlanta-Fulton County once stood.

69 Charlie Leibrandt...Reliever?

Yes. Not once, but twice.

Two years in a row. Both times in the World Series. Each time in Game 6. Each time in extra innings. Each time a similar result—ouch.

"A couple of my good friends, golfing buddies, still give me a hard time about it," Leibrandt said over the phone. "You've got to be remembered for something, I guess."

Try two things. Two painful outings and decisive innings, especially the first: an 11th-inning, game-winning homer Leibrandt gave up to Minnesota's Kirby Puckett in the penultimate game of the 1991 World Series, the home run that forced an epic Game 7.

The second: another rare relief appearance for the veteran Leibrandt, this time in Game 6 of the 1992 World Series in Atlanta. The two-out culprit this time? Toronto's Dave Winfield, whose two-run double broke a 2–2 tie in the 11th and gave Canada its first World Series championship, 4–3 over the Braves.

In neither instance was Leibrandt the ideal man for the job. He was, after all, a starting pitcher. In each instance, Braves manager Bobby Cox felt he had no choice but to turn to Leibrandt. In both instances, the moves misfired.

When Atlanta acquired Leibrandt, the club knew what it was getting—a crafty lefty whose best days were largely behind him. In

1985 Leibrandt went 17–9 for Kansas City with a 2.69 ERA, and he helped the Royals beat St. Louis in the World Series.

After coming to Atlanta in 1990, Leibrandt was the No. 4 man in those Young Guns' '91 and '92 rotations. He was expected to provide leadership, stability, and double-digit wins. Pitching in relief wasn't really in the job description.

In 1991 Leibrandt and the two kid lefties, Tom Glavine and Steve Avery, each won 15 games. The last time a team had three left-handed 15-game winners? The 1917 New York Giants. In the opening game of the World Series, Leibrandt started and got knocked out in the fifth inning of the Twins' 5–2 win.

In Game 6 Leibrandt, who'd made 36 starts in the regular season, made his only relief appearance all year. The score was tied 3–3 when Cox turned to his veteran starter.

"I wasn't surprised," Leibrandt recalled. "Whether I should have been out there, I don't know. But we didn't have a lot of experience in our bullpen. We were pretty green." Alongside him in that bullpen was another left-hander, Kent Mercker, and righties Jim Clancy and young Mark Wohlers. "As the game went on," Leibrandt said, "I looked down the bench and thought, *I'm the one who's probably going in next.*"

On Leibrandt's fourth pitch, a change-up that he left up, Puckett ripped it over the wall for a walk-off homer. In the aftermath of that crushing 4–3 defeat, Cox said, "Why not Leibrandt? We'd be pretty stupid if we were resistant to bringing in a 15-game winner."

The Twins won the Series the next night with a dramatic 10-inning, 1–0 win behind starter and World Series MVP Jack Morris.

The next year Leibrandt found himself again in similar circumstances. Of his 32 appearances, only one came in relief. His only appearance during the '92 World Series was his outing in Game 6. He came on in the top of the 10th inning and retired the Blue Jays. "I got in trouble in the 11th," said Leibrandt, who'd put two Blue Jays on. "I didn't make a good pitch to Winfield."

Winfield's two-run double won it for Toronto, the Braves managing to score once in the bottom half. "I was happy to get in and hoping to do a better job," Leibrandt said years later. "If we'd scored in the bottom of the 10th, I could've been a hero. But I am who I am. That's okay. To pitch as long as I did, that's great."

70 The Eric Gregg Game

For St. Louis Cardinals fans, it's Don Denkinger. A quarter-century later, Cardinals fans still live with the umpire's blown call at first base that cost St. Louis the 1985 World Series championship. They'll forever feel royally…Denkingered.

On Chicago's North Side, it's Steve Bartman and his foul ball, fan-interference horror of 2003. It may be a century—if ever—before long-suffering Cubbies fans get over it, or the Cubs finally—if ever—win a World Series again.

For Braves fans, it's Eric Gregg. To this day, many still gag at the mention of his name. Yes, Atlanta blew some scoring chances in Game 7 of the 1991 World Series. Yes, Mark Wohlers threw that ill-considered slider in Game 4 of the '96 Series. Yet it was just one pitch and one swing of Jim Leyritz's bat that tied the game, though it turned the tide of that World Series.

But Eric Gregg? His was a game-long gaffe, lasting literally from first pitch to last.

October 11, 1997. Game 5 of the NLCS. The Braves and the Florida Marlins, tied at two games apiece. The starting pitchers: Atlanta's Greg Maddux, the greatest pitcher of his era, who won four consecutive NL Cy Young Awards from 1992 to 1995. For Florida? A 22-year-old rookie right-hander named Livan Hernandez, starting in place of flu-ridden ace Kevin Brown.

The home-plate umpire? Eric Gregg, a gregarious, fun-loving guy who weighed well over 300 pounds. On this day, his strike zone was as generous as his girth.

How big? His was the Louisiana Purchase of strike zones. It was, like Gregg's waistline, larger than life intended.

"It was bad today," Fred McGriff, the Braves' first baseman and cleanup hitter, said of the strike zone. "It was bad."

The Crime Dog said this after taking a called third strike for the final out in Florida's tense 2–1 victory. For Hernandez, it was his 15th strikeout of the game, setting a new NLCS record. For McGriff, it was much like his first at-bat of the game—indeed, much like many of those 15 Ks: nowhere near the strike zone. At least not baseball's universally recognized strike zone.

In the very first inning McGriff took a called strike on a pitch that was at least six inches, and perhaps a foot, outside. McGriff growled. But the tenor of the game was quickly established. Gregg's strike zone was the size of the Eastern Time Zone. Hernandez adjusted accordingly. Maddux? Not so much.

"Above all, pitchers and hitters demand consistency from an umpire, and Gregg's strike zone was consistent, if bizarre," Buster Olney wrote in the *New York Times*. "For right-handed batters, he generally called strikes on pitches an inch or two off the outside edge of the plate. But for left-handed batters, his strike zone was a little bit higher than usual, and anywhere up to a foot outside, based on television replays. Gregg was consistent, but the circumstances created a distinct disadvantage for the Braves—the first six batters in the Atlanta lineup batted left-handed, while only three hitters in the Florida lineup hit that way. The strike zone altered the game completely, like raising a basket to 11 feet."

After Kenny Lofton's leadoff triple in the first inning, not one Atlanta left-handed batter pulled a ball to the right side the rest of the game. The Braves managed just two more hits and flew home furious.

"I'm not trained to hit pitches there," Ryan Klesko, who struck out twice, said of Livan's outside offerings to left-handers.

"I swung at pitches that were a foot outside," said the switch-hitting Chipper Jones, who batted left-handed that day. "I turned around and asked if they were strikes, and he said yes. I couldn't help but give a little chuckle. I'm so mad, I can't see straight."

In a rare postgame interview—rare for an umpire, at least—Gregg vigorously defended his performance. "If you know me, you know my strike zone," he said. "I'm consistent on both sides of that strike zone. I've been that way for 25 years. Next question."

Okay, had there been a change in the strike zone? "The strike zone has been the same for 100 years," Gregg replied. "Next question."

The Braves, including Bobby Cox, disagreed. "I haven't seen the replays," said the manager, "but most of our hitters were coming back saying the pitcher's six to 10 inches, a foot and a half to the other batter's box."

Yet Cox and some of his players also credited Hernandez and his catcher, Charles Johnson, for quickly recognizing the enlarged strike zone and using it to their advantage—outside pitch after outside pitch. Although Keith Lockhart walked after Lofton tripled to start the game, Hernandez fanned Chipper Jones, McGriff, and Klesko to end the threat. At least one Brave struck out in every inning.

So did 10 Marlins batters during the game, but that was no consolation to Atlanta. In the ninth inning, Marlins manager Jim Leyland never considered pulling Hernandez, even if he'd already thrown 129 pitches. "There were 50,000 people here, and I did not want to get snipered," said Leyland.

Don Sutton, the 300-game winner and Hall of Famer–turned–Braves broadcaster, called the first 4½ innings of the game on radio with Pete Van Wieren. With two out and none on, with the crowd roaring and an 0–2 count on McGriff, Sutton told

Van Wieren, "All he has to do now is throw that curveball. It can be a foot outside, but as long as he doesn't bounce it, it'll be a strike."

It didn't bounce. It was outside by a good eight inches. Strike three called.

Back in Atlanta for Game 6, the Marlins jumped on Tom Glavine immediately and won 7–4. Hernandez was named the MVP of the NLCS. Florida went on to win a thrilling World Series with Cleveland in seven games.

Baseball America later chose Eric Gregg's Game 5 work as the third-worst umpiring performance in the era from 1975 to 2000. Gregg was one of 22 umpires who resigned in 1999 in a labor action by their union. In 2001 he unsuccessfully sought reinstatement. Gregg died June 5, 2006, after a massive stroke.

71 Buy a Brick

The Atlanta Braves Foundation Legacy Brick Paver Program at Turner Field enables fans to buy individually engraved commemorative bricks to be installed in Monument Grove. They're inlaid among the statues of such Braves legends as Henry Aaron, Phil Niekro, Warren Spahn, and a party-crasher named Cobb.

Ty Cobb, the Georgia Peach, a native of Royston, Georgia, never played for the Braves. Perhaps that's why there are no engraved bricks by his statue. Still, Cobb's forever cast in iron in a rare pose: sliding in spikes low, not high, as a nameless infielder applies the tag too late. "Leading Batsman of All Major League History," proclaims his plaque, heralding Cobb's 4,191 hits. Too bad Felix de Weldon, de sculptor, finished his Cobb in 1977, nine years before Pete Rose retired with 4,256 hits.

But below the other sculptures, literally at the feet of three of the greatest Braves, are more than 1,000 bricks—baseball bric-a-brac, if you will, many of the most personal and heartfelt kind.

We Miss You!
Skip Caray 2008
The Mierzwas

I Saw Otis
Make The Catch!
Jack Munnell

Amy Battimore Watson Is
Beating Breast Cancer in 2008!
Praying 4 You,
Rick J. Nehls

The bricks range in price from $150 to $325. There are four basic types, two three-liners and two four-liners. The stylized Braves *A* costs extra. (For information, call 1-877-ABF-BRIX.). Each purchase includes one complimentary replica brick, complete with its message. Most engravings are fairly obvious. Some require a little thought. Like this one:

31-47-29-33
Fawn Drucker

Remember? The uniform numbers of the Braves' nonpareil pitching rotation in the mid-'90s: Maddux. Glavine. Smoltz. Avery.

Familia Ramirez
1979–2010

Patty Rasmussen
Chop Talk Ace

There's a reason baseball remains our national pastime. It grabs us when we're young and, if we're among the lucky ones, never lets go. People from everywhere, young and old, read these bricks and see their stories. Better yet, buy one yourself and tell your own tale.

Mary Schnirring
My Mom, My Hero
Love, Your Girls

#1 Braves Fan
North Pole, AK
Jesse Edmisten

Toby and Christina From Las Vegas
He Proposed On 9-9-09
She Said Yes!

"Weichelsbaum"
Wax & Tee 2008
Kiss Our Brick
For Good Luck!

There are beginnings…

Cathy & Cass
1st Date 4–4–01

1st Birthday
Riley Hughes
12-01-06

1st Braves Game
April 17, 1996
Neil Sheinin

And endings…

In Loving Memory
Of Elmer R. Gould
Braves Usher

John Beckham Jr.
6/20/84–2/15/07
Our Big Leaguer

#1 Braves Fan
Cecil L. Caylor
In Heaven

A Loyal Braves Fan For Eternity
Bettie Ann Lordahl
1926 To 2007

In Memory of Tracy Rupp
(Cousin of Chipper Jones)

Some are virtual brick business cards…

Walter Banks VIP Usher
Working and Supporting the Braves
For Over 40 Years

Gary Caruso
Spahn's #1 Fan

Shepard Porter
Atlanta Black Braves
Played 1949–1951

…and some are sheer fun…

Put Me N Coach!
Corey Yates

Yes, We McCann!
The Dements '09

Hotlanta Baseball
A Long Strange Trip It's Been
Gratefully, Dr. Azmi Tawardos

They came from everywhere to see America's Team…

Duke Boiz
Father and Son World Tour

Iowa Braves Fan. #1 Braves Fan in Oklahoma! AZ fans!

From near…

Joe Hutcherson
3rd Base Hanes High

Alex Hunt
Braves Bat Boy
2005–2008

From far…

Kyle Dinkel
Mile-High City!

Irish Brave Fan
Padraig McKeown
Dundalk Ireland

Fishy & Jamila Habbaniyah Iraq

Go Braves
USA To Africa
Laura & Kyle

…and from Far East.

Chiba Japan
Maki Suzue

Braves Rules!!!
Do-Hyeon Kim
S. Korea 2007

They know what they like…

'74 & '95 Best Years Ever!
Keely Chow

Dale Murphy Fan Forever!
Jeff Donovan

I Love The Boys of Summer
Bridget—'08

...and dislike.

Beat the Mets
Dana DeMarco

Beat the Mutts!
Kevin Nelson

One has been around for a century...

Edith B. Fox
100th Birthday
January 28, 2010

And another speaks for, well, all of them...

Yvonne Lilze Loves Baseball
& Bobby Cox THNX

72 Help Revive Sid & Frankie Day

Back in the day, Sid & Frankie Day was a veritable Holy Day of Obligation. At least it was for a small group of folks, mostly charter members of the Braves 400 Club who'd suffered through so much brutally bad baseball before the calendar finally flipped from 1990 to 1991.

And then to 1992. Especially October 14, 1992.

That starry night in Atlanta-Fulton County Stadium, the Braves trailed Pittsburgh 2–0 in the bottom of the ninth of Game 7 of the NLCS. Then Chico Lind made the rarest of errors. Jim Leyland lifted his ace, Doug Drabek, for submariner Stan Belinda. Atlanta drew within a run, and then…

Close your eyes and recall how Francisco Cabrera—Skip Caray called him "Frank" on the radio—lined a two-out single to left, easily scoring David Justice. And then came the Impossible Bream: Sid Bream, the lumbering first baseman rounding third, headed for home, encumbered by a knee brace. But Sid slid, and home plate umpire Randy Marsh signaled that he'd beaten—barely—Barry Bonds' throw. (See? There is a God). Then all heaven broke loose.

Somehow, the Braves had won 3–2. Somehow, they were going back to another World Series. Somehow, Bream beat the unbeatable throw. To run where that Brave dared to go? Like he's gonna stop at third.

"The most magical moment in franchise history," Gary Caruso calls it. He should know. He wrote the book on the Braves, *The Braves Encyclopedia.* A lifelong Braves fan, Caruso was editor and publisher of *Chop Talk*, the best fan magazine in baseball. He also started Sid & Frankie Day in 2000.

"It was the most exciting moment in Atlanta sports history, I'd say," Caruso said on October 14, 2002, when a couple of dozen devotees gathered in a parking lot, on the site of what was once the baseball diamond in Atlanta-Fulton County Stadium. That was the 10th anniversary of Game 7 and the third annual Sid & Frankie Day.

"This is the one [game] everybody remembers," Johnny Tallant, a retired judge from Cumming, Georgia, and then the president of the Braves 400 Club.

People like John Padgett, a Braves fan from Canton, Georgia, who wore his 1992 National League Champions T-shirt he bought outside the old park when Frankie swung and Sid slid, remember that day.

"I was sitting right over there that night, four rows behind the Braves dugout," Padgett, pointing across the parking lot, told Tim Tucker of the *Atlanta Journal-Constitution* in 2002. "I remember that my voice was gone for two or three days from all the hollering."

Exactly a year later, standing where home plate once was at the old ballpark, Mary Lou Brooks told Carroll Rogers of the *Journal-Constitution*, "You've got to have something to cheer for because our guys sure didn't do it 'til the end." That was not just another Sid & Frankie Day gathering, but yet another disappointing end to a Braves season. Having finally won the World Series in 1995, 2003 marked the eighth straight year in which Atlanta won the NL East but was eliminated in the playoffs.

"I'm beginning to feel like Cubs fans: wait 'til next year," Brooks told Rogers.

That day, as at every Sid & Frankie Day, Brooks and her fellow celebrants enjoyed eating a baseball-themed cake. One year, it was circular and designed like the old stadium. Another year, the icing on that Publix cake was a copy of the famous photo of Bream sliding home safely. Every year, fans like Jean Berken listened to the last few innings of Game 7, speaking the words in sync with Skip's voice blasting out of a boom box. Some even "slid" into home plate: the infield and foul lines are still marked in the paved parking lot.

Caruso was inspired to stage Sid & Frankie Day by a group of Pirates diehards who still gather every October on the site of old Forbes Field. October 13 is the anniversary of Bill Mazeroski's ninth-inning, walk-off homer that beat the New York Yankees and won the 1960 World Series. In October 2010 about 2,000 people—including some of Mazeroski's old teammates—celebrated the 50th anniversary of his historic home run.

Popular for a time, Sid & Frankie Day petered out once Caruso moved to San Diego. Last October 14 was a gorgeous autumn in Atlanta. At noon, I drove over to the site of Sid's slide. One person was there: a security guard riding in a cart. I was crestfallen, having eaten some Sid & Frankie cake and slid myself a few times. But no one was there to mark the anniversary.

What a shame. Sid & Frankie Day should live forever. Help revive it.

73 Take a Tour of the Ted

A guided tour, that is, of Turner Field, the Braves' home since 1997. At $12, it's one of the best buys in the ballpark, certainly better than a $7 beer. It's an hour-long, behind-the-scenes, 360-degree look at one of the baseball's finest stadiums. More important, it's not Atlanta-Fulton County Stadium, so you won't have to dodge rats while walking in the tunnel in the bowels of the park. Unless, of course, Barry Bonds unexpectedly shows up one night.

The guided tours, which are offered year-round, begin at the top of the hour. The first stop is the Braves Museum and Hall of Fame, a rich treasure trove of Braves baseball history run by its estimable director, Carolyn Serra. Linger there and ask Carolyn a question or three; she knows everything about the Braves.

No reservations are necessary for individuals or groups of fewer than 20 people. Walk-ups can buy tickets on the day of the tour at the Turner Field ticket windows. Free—repeat, free—parking is available in the Green Lot, where Atlanta-Fulton County Stadium once stood before it was imploded following the 1996 season. Groups of 20 or more, and school groups, must make reservations two weeks in advance. Call (404) 614-2311 or email: turnerfieldtours@braves.com.

Once you've enjoyed the museum and hall—make sure to savor a replica of the train cars in which the Boston and Milwaukee Braves once traveled—a nine-inning stop ensues.

The Atlanta Braves, right, and the New York Mets stand on the baselines at Turner Field during Opening Day ceremonies in 2005.

There's the Coca-Cola Sky Field, high atop left field, where kids run amok during the season, play games, run the bases, and get sprayed with water on hot summer days, and where twice a year dogs can bark in the park on—what else?—Bark in the Park days. Check out the enormous Coke bottle and, of course, the Tomahawk Choppin' Chick-fil-A cow.

Down in Scouts Alley, you can take BP, throw your fastest fastball, and read how a bird-dogging scout evaluated a high school kid named Chipper Jones. (He liked him. Go figure.) Next stop, the broadcast booths, named for two Braves broadcast icons. The Skip Caray TV Booth, where Skip famously repeated one summer, "And there's another double for Andruw Jones." And the Pete Van Wieren Radio Booth, where the Professor shared his 24-carat "Diamond Notes" before each game.

Turner Field Tour Info

During the baseball season (April–September), tours are given Monday through Saturday, 9:00 AM to 3:00 PM, and Sunday, 1:00 PM to 3:00 PM. No tours on days when the Braves play home matinee games.

Off-season (October—hopefully late October—through March), Monday through Saturday, 10:00 AM to 2:00 PM.

Closed: MLK Day, Thanksgiving, December 23 through January 2.

The Museum opens 2½ hours before each game and closes in the middle of the seventh inning. Sing along to "Take Me Out to the Ballgame," and you might be able to linger a little longer.

Admission:
Adults $12
Children (3–13) $7
Military $7
Museum only (no tour) $5
Admission to museum during game: one token ($2)
The whole shebang, the Full Teddy: priceless

Drop by a luxury suite and enjoy it while you can, then move on to the press box. Which, as of this writing, was still unnamed. It should, of course, be the Furman Bisher Press Box, in honor of the legendary *Atlanta Journal-Constitution* sports columnist. Along with the late Ivan Allen Jr., one of the city's great mayors, Bisher was instrumental in helping to get a stadium built that brought Major League Baseball and the NFL to Atlanta.

In the Braves' clubhouse, which is likely bigger than your house, picture the champagne sprayed after the 1995 World Series, and again when the 2010 Braves gave retiring, soon-to-be Hall of Fame manager Bobby Cox one last postseason. Alas, the artificial-turf putting green put in for Tom Glavine, John Smoltz, and Greg Maddux when Turner Field opened in 1997 is kaput.

Out in the plaza, gaze up in wonder at the size of the photo of Hank Aaron's 715th home run. From a distance, enjoy the five statues in Monument Grove (two of Aaron, one each of Warren

Spahn, Phil Niekro and…Ty Cobb? Yes. Go figure). Back in the Braves dugout, imagine Leo Mazzone rocking on the bench while one of his pitchers rocked the house once more. Or picture Coxie standing on the top step of the dugout, urging you on in your first at-bat: "C'mon, Humm-dog! C'mon, kid!")

Lastly, hit the Museum Store. There are lots of goodies in there.

74 Make a Pilgrimage to Poncey

Poncey. That's what old-time Atlantans called Ponce de Leon Park, once the venerable and beloved old ballpark on Ponce de Leon Avenue, forever the ancestral home of professional baseball in the city of Atlanta.

To Paul Hemphill, the late, great Atlanta author and lifelong baseball fan, it was, "My generation's field of dreams."

To Jimmy Carter, it was big-league hardball long before those Milwaukee Braves ever moved South. "Before we had the Braves, the Crackers were our team," said the 39th president of the United States.

"As a wide-eyed boy, I watched Lindsay Deal rattle the signboards in right field, Eddie Mathews field ground balls off his chest, and Country Brown fly to first after a perfect drag bunt," former U.S. Senator Zell Miller wrote in praise of Tim Darnell's fine history, *The Crackers—Early Days of Atlanta Baseball.*

Back in the day, the Atlanta Crackers were the biggest show in town. The ballpark's address was 650 Ponce de Leon Avenue in midtown, right across the street from the enormous Sears Building. The original park opened in 1907 but was destroyed by fire in 1923. Rebuilt in 1924 and renamed Spiller Park for team owner Tell J. Spiller, the stadium had a seating capacity of more than

15,000 and served as the playground of one of the most celebrated minor league franchises.

The Crackers played there in the Southern Association from 1908 to 1961, and later in the Triple A International League (1962 to 1964). After reverting to its original name in 1933, Poncey later became baseball nirvana, a bettor's paradise in the left-field bleachers, and home to an eternal landmark still standing, the magnolia tree in deep, deep center field.

The original Yankee Stadium's "Death Valley" in center had nothing on Poncey and its famous magnolia. The distance from home plate to the center-field scoreboard: 462 feet. In front of the scoreboard stood the magnolia, like a leafy sentinel. In 1949 Crackers president Earl Mann built a hedge from left to center field, significantly cutting down the distance to the wall. In exhibition games Babe Ruth and future Braves star Eddie Mathews reportedly hit home runs that disappeared into the magnolia.

"It seemed not just the park's symbol, but the baseball South's," the late Baseball Hall of Fame broadcaster Ernie Harwell once recalled in *Storied Stadiums: Baseball's History through Its Ballparks* by Curt Smith. Ernie would've known. As a boy, he went to Poncey to watch his heroes play and later became the Crackers' play-by-play man from 1943 to 1947 before being "traded" to the Brooklyn Dodgers for a catcher.

By then, the segregated ballpark had also been the home of the Atlanta Black Crackers of the Negro Leagues. Whenever the Crackers went on the road, the Black Crackers had Poncey to themselves. When Jackie Robinson and the Brooklyn Dodgers stopped in Atlanta one weekend, barnstorming their way up north after spring training, thousands and thousands of black Atlantans packed Poncey to see the Georgia native who'd broken baseball's color line. They had to sit down in the far right-field bleachers, or on the four-deck tiers of wooden ad signs in right, or stand up on the Southern Railway tracks on the plateau high above right field. Many even

An Atlanta Moment in Time

A commemorative marker, mounted atop a three-dimensional concrete home plate near the base of the old magnolia, reads:

Ponce De Leon Ball Park 1908–1966

Here on the grounds at Ponce De Leon Ball Park, the Atlanta Crackers and the Atlanta Black Crackers began a tradition of baseball championship and athletic excellence which set the high standard we enjoy in Atlanta now. The Atlanta Crackers, known as the "Yankees of the Minors," were led by Luke Appling, Eddie Mathews, Bob Montag, Ralph "Country" Brown, and many others.

For many years, they were owned and operated by "Mr. Atlanta Baseball," Earl Mann, who rose from peanut vendor to owner. Mann led Atlanta in becoming a Major League city, and was instrumental in bringing the Braves to Atlanta. The Atlanta Black Crackers fielded many of black baseball's superstars, including Norman "Geronimo" Lumpkin, James "Red" Moore, James "Gabby" Kemp, and Vinicus "Nish" Williams. The Rev. John and Billie Harden owned the Atlanta Black Crackers for many years, and the team played on these grounds when the White Crackers were away. The marker continues:

An Atlanta Moment in Time
Preserved by The Native Atlantans Club, Inc.
May 2004
With the Cooperation of Whole Foods Market

stood deep in the outfield, behind ropes, ownership trying to squeeze in as many paying customers as possible.

In 1965, with sparkling-new Atlanta Stadium built but the Milwaukee Braves prevented by a court order from moving south until '66, the Atlanta Crackers were the first tenants of the new ballpark. By 1966, they were history, and so was Poncey. The cherished old ballpark was torn down to make room for a shopping center.

Lee Walburn, then an Atlanta sportswriter, covered the last game in Ponce de Leon Park for the *Atlanta Journal*. Years later, he wrote, "It was sad, like a death, to see this beautiful old stadium neglected, ravaged by peeling paint and broken bleachers, and finally, a broken heart."

But the magnolia lives on. And you should make a pilgrimage to pay homage to a time, a team, and a tree. Its trunk is hidden now behind a Borders bookstore and a Whole Foods market, but you can see the leaves above the roof line. And if you walk behind that row of stores, you can still touch the magnolia that the Babe and Mathews reached, that the city and its baseball fans loved so much. As much as they loved Poncey itself.

75 Ernie

Or rather, Uncle Ernie. That's how Pete Van Wieren and Skip Caray often referred to their on-air partner, and how millions of Braves fans came to regard and revere Ernie Johnson. As Uncle Ernie: the gentlemanly, homespun ballplayer-turned-broadcaster who helped make the Atlanta Braves "America's Team" on TBS. Not bad for a tall, lanky kid from Vermont, the son of Swedish immigrants.

"That's what it felt like when you worked with him," Van Wieren says. "Just like sitting alongside a kindly uncle."

"With his soothing voice and over-the-back-fence delivery," *Atlanta Journal-Constitution* columnist Ron Hudspeth once wrote, "Ernie Johnson is as comfortable as an old shoe."

Or, while watching all those night games on TBS, as a well-worn slipper.

The 6′4″ right-hander signed with the Boston Braves right out of Brattleboro High in 1942. After serving with the U.S. Marines from 1943 to 1946, Johnson rejoined the Braves and began working his way up the farm system, landing with the parent club in 1950. At season's end, the top batting average in the National League belonged to...Ernie Johnson. The rookie reliever hit .500, going one-for-two.

"I was just a middle reliever," he liked to say in his self-deprecating way. "Couldn't start, couldn't finish."

Johnson moved with the franchise from Boston to Milwaukee in 1953. He easily made the transition from New England to the Midwest. Whether on the diamond or in the broadcast booth, his transitions were always seamless.

As an important member of the Braves' 1957 World Series champions, Johnson went 7–3 in 30 relief appearances with four saves and an ERA of 3.88. In three games against the New York Yankees, he allowed just one earned run in seven innings. In Johnson's nine-year big-league career (he spent the last season with Baltimore), he was 40–23 (a .635 winning percentage) in 273 games, all but 19 in relief. His career ERA: 3.77.

He tried selling insurance for a while before returning to the Braves in the early '60s, working in the front office and as a Braves color commentator for a local TV station. Although he'd retired from pitching, Johnson was a key player in the club's move from Milwaukee in 1966. He moved to Atlanta in 1965 to set up the Braves' radio network throughout the Southeast.

But Johnson wasn't a goodwill ambassador. He was a greatwill ambassador, making inroads and friends wherever he went. In Atlanta's inaugural season of '66, Ernie was in the broadcast booth.

For a quarter-century, he was one of the most popular and beloved broadcasters in the Southeast and, thanks to TBS, across the country. Initially, Johnson worked with the egocentric Milo Hamilton, who always did six innings of play-by-play to Ernie's three. By chance, Johnson got to call Hank Aaron's 500th homer...and his 600th...and finally his 700th. After that, Hamilton insisted he call Aaron's at-bats.

So it was Hamilton behind the mike the night Aaron hit No. 715 to break Babe Ruth's record. And it was Hamilton who made a perfectly pedestrian call of baseball's milestone moment.

In December 1975, after Hamilton was fired, Johnson helped hire two young broadcasters: Skip Caray and Pete Van Wieren. In January Ted Turner bought the ballclub. The new broadcast crew and outrageous owner would get along great, with Ernie, Skip, and Pete once donning racing silks as jockeys in a pregame ostrich race. They hung out together on the road and socialized with their families in the off-season.

That chemistry and convivial tone, which drew rave reviews from TV sports critics across the country, was set by Johnson in their first spring training. During a broadcast, tossing back the play-by-play, Caray said, "And here again is the voice of the Atlanta Braves, Ernie Johnson." Afterward, Johnson told his young cohorts, "We're *all* the voices of the Atlanta Braves." And so they were.

It was Johnson who nicknamed Van Wieren "the Professor," not so much for Pete's professorial approach to the game as for his resemblance to Jim Brosnan, a pitcher in the '50s who had a scholarly appearance. If the Braves played an afternoon home game that went into extra innings, Johnson advised his wife on the air, "Take the roast out of the oven, Lois. I'm going to be a little late."

Once, when Phillies third baseman Mike Schmidt reached out and somehow golfed a one-handed home run, Caray gushed, "Man, that shit sure is strong!" Aghast, Caray kept talking nonstop, hoping viewers hadn't noticed. Johnson called a few pitches on the next batter, then casually asked, "What was that batter's name again?"

On a September night in 1989, in another dreadful season in which the Braves lost 97 games and averaged just over 10,000 fans a game, more than 40,000 turned out on Ernie Johnson Night to show their affection for everyone's Uncle Ernie. A beloved broadcaster who, on those rare times when the Braves didn't lose, would sign off with his trademark, "And on this winning night, so long everyone."

76 Genuflect at the Left-Field Fence

Or at least what's left of it. Actually, it's a replica of the old chain-link, outfield fence at Atlanta-Fulton County Stadium. Like the classic baseball-green facsimile of the bullpen wall standing behind it, the fence marks the spot. It's hallowed ground. It's the site where Henry Aaron's 715th home run cleared the fence before landing in the Braves bullpen and passing on into immortality.

There in the Turner Field green lot, once the home of the old ballpark and now parking area 10 for the Ted, history took flight with one swing of Aaron's bat. On the evening of April 8, 1974, Aaron lined No. 715 and surpassed Babe Ruth's seemingly insurmountable 714 homers. In the old city of Jerusalem, millions have prayed at the Wailing Wall for centuries. In Atlanta, baseball fans are drawn to this spot and some even take a knee. You should, too. Particularly if you're a Braves fan, and especially if you revere baseball's true home run king, Henry Louis Aaron.

Mounted on the green bullpen wall is a sign, a large white baseball, painted with red stitching and these words:

HANK AARON
HOME RUN
715
APRIL 8, 1974

That's all. No embellishment. Succinct and to the point like the Hammer himself.

In front of the blue, 10-foot-high chain-link fence are inlaid light-brown bricks to simulate the warning track. Between the fence and the concrete wall is a patch of green grass, just as it was in the bullpen that night.

Stand there, close your eyes, open your imagination, and you can recall it all. Perhaps you can hear Al Downing's voice. "He knows what I can throw. He hit two home runs off me last year," the Dodgers starting pitcher said before the game. "But I'm not going to change my pattern. I can't go against what I've been successful with." Picture Aaron, who never took the bat off his shoulder before walking in his first at-bat, now using his remarkably strong, quick-wristed swing to turn on a fastball. Envision L.A.'s Bill Buckner and teammate Jimmy Wynn converging in futile pursuit of the drive. (Afterward, Buckner admitted, "We kind of wanted Aaron to get it over with so he could go back to being a human being.")

See the ball clearing the fence and...what, no mad scramble? No. None at all. The fan who'd caught Aaron's 700th homer the previous season was given $700 for returning it. Entertainer Sammy Davis Jr., had offered $25,000 for the record-breaking 715th, but Aaron declined. Nearly everyone assumed it would land in the Braves bullpen.

That's why Chief Noc-a-Homa, the team's oh-so-politically incorrect mascot, a Chippewa Indian whose name was Levi Walker and whose teepee stood in the left-field stands, brought a lacrosse stick to the stadium. He hoped to lean over the railing and into the bullpen to catch 715. Not a chance.

When the ball touched down, it did so in the glove of Braves reliever Tom House. "Blew my mind," House, who was standing approximately 350 feet from home plate, said of the ball's path as it came right toward his glove.

"That ball was rising on a line," he recalled. "If I'd frozen like a dummy, the ball would've hit me in the forehead. The only problem, though, was a guy above me who had a fishnet on a pole. He couldn't get it operating in time." Teammate Jamie Easterly was out of luck, too. He ran into a cannon parked behind the fence.

House ran in from the bullpen and gave the ball to Aaron right after the Hammer crossed the plate. The relievers had all agreed to do this, although House took good-natured grief from friends who, knowing he was pursuing a master's degree in marketing, had missed out on an opportunity to market the 715 ball.

Many people can still picture all of this. You can, too. All you need do is go to the left-field fence, genuflect, and use your imagination.

77 .438

No, that's not Atlanta's aggregate winning percentage in the 1970s and '80s. It's a batting average, and it belongs to a relatively little-known, little man named Hugh Duffy. He was one of baseball's greatest hitters in the late 1890s and a star for the Boston Beaneaters, the franchise now known as the Atlanta Braves.

In 1894 Hugh Duffy batted .438. Well more than a century later, that remains the highest single-season batting average in baseball history.

That's not bad for a 5′7″, 168-pound kid from Cranston, Rhode Island, a textile mill worker who first played semipro baseball on weekends. Not bad for the professional who later joined the National League in 1888 for Cap Anson's Chicago White Stockings, despite the manager's initial brush-off. "We already have a batboy," Anson scoffed at Duffy. But Cap signed him, using him mainly as an outfielder for two seasons. After plying his services as a free agent, Duffy joined the Beaneaters in 1892 and became one of baseball's earliest stars.

A fine hitter and base stealer, Duffy excelled in center field. Right fielder Tommy McCarthy was also a good defensive player, and the two were nicknamed the "Heavenly Twins." For Duffy, the 1894 season was precisely that: heavenly.

The ball was purportedly juiced that year. The National League's composite batting average of .309 reflected that suspicion. "However," Gary Caruso wrote in *The Braves Encyclopedia*, "everyone hit the same ball, and no one hit it like Duffy did."

He led the league in home runs (18), RBIs (145), hits (237), doubles (51), and slugging percentage (.694). Although it wasn't recognized as such back then, Duffy won the Triple Crown—the only player in franchise history ever to do so.

And, of course, there was his historic batting average that season. But was it .438 or .440? Depending on which reference you use—Elias Sports Bureau, the Baseball Encyclopedia, Total Baseball—Duffy hit either .438 or two percentage points higher. But .438 is generally the accepted figure.

"All I know is that I led the league [in batting]," Duffy once said, "and that was the important thing."

As that memorable season was ending, not even Duffy was keeping track of his statistics. The pennant race, the team, that's what mattered most back then. Indeed, entering the season finale, "Sir Hugh," as he later came to be called, didn't know what his exact average was, or how much of a cushion he had in the race for the batting title. After base hits in his first two at-bats, teammates encouraged Duffy to take the rest of the day off. He didn't, and got three more hits.

Duffy won the NL batting title by an astounding 33 percentage points. He was the third batting champion in club history, and in the off-season was treated like royalty.

The Bleacher Club held a banquet for him and gave him a gold watch engraved to the "Great Run-Getter." The Beaneaters gave Duffy a watch charm inlaid with five diamonds and engraved thusly: "Presented to Hugh Duffy, champion batsman of the world, by his fellow players and manager."

Although he won the home run crown again in 1897 with 11, Duffy never again won the batting and RBI titles. In nine seasons as a Beaneater, he had 100 or more RBIs eight times. He continued to play a fine center field, and is also credited with being the first player to take two bases on a sacrifice fly. He scored from second on such a play in 1894, and the home crowd at the South End Grounds erupted.

Hugh Duffy, who batted .324 for his career, scouted for the Boston Braves from 1917 through 1919. He later coached for the Boston Red Sox and became a longtime Red Sox scout—but not before becoming one of the first hitting coaches for a young Boston outfielder later hailed as "the Kid" and "the Splendid Splinter." In just his third big-league season, Ted Williams batted .406. He remains the last man to hit .400. His .406 was merely 32 percentage points behind Hugh Duffy, who was inducted into the Baseball Hall of Fame in 1945.

78 Get Some Culture, Catch a Sculpture

As galleries go, this ain't the Louvre. It's more homer than MOMA. It's Monument Grove on the plaza outside Turner Field. If it's not a Henry Moore sculpture garden at the Atlanta Botanical Gardens, well, the Brit Bad Henry never went yard, unlike our Bad Henry, as the Dodgers admiringly called Henry Louis Aaron, cast in bronze not once but twice in Monument Grove.

Let's take a quick tour of the five baseball works of art on display. Starting with…

1. A Bust of Hank. At least the head and shoulders of Aaron, who stood head and shoulders above virtually every player he ever faced. The plaque reads: "Presented to the City of Atlanta in commemoration of the outstanding contribution of Henry Louis Aaron to the game of baseball and to this city. Presented by C&S Bank. Sculptor: N.M. Matoda, '74." (Note: 1974 was a good year for N.M. and Hank, who hit his record 715th homer that April.)

2. Knucksie. A full-length, larger-than-life sculpture of Phil Niekro, the beloved Braves knuckleballer, 318-game-winner, and enshrinee in the Baseball Hall of Fame. It's not really abstract art, just a tad modernized, especially Knucksie's face. But not the knuckleball grip, as old as the game itself. The baseball in his right hand, the nails of his forefinger and index fingers digging into the ball before he released it and made it dance. Just ask his 3,342 strikeout victims.

From the plaque is a quote from Niekro himself: "There's no better Braves fan anywhere than I."

3. The Spahn Statue. A nine-foot-high tribute to Warren Spahn, the greatest left-hander in baseball's history, but also a labor of love for Gary Caruso. As a kid growing up, Caruso was captivated by Spahn—not just his 363 victories (including two no-hitters) and 2,583 strikeouts, but his majestic windup and delivery. It was captured perfectly by sculptor Shan Gray: Spahn's right-foot, sky-high kick that even a Radio City Rockette would envy. The baseball below in his hand, nearly scraping the dirt on the mound. Then the release...and an invisible swing and a miss.

In the summer of 2003 Spahn was a frail, 82-year-old World War II hero (wounded by shrapnel in the Battle of the Bulge) when I visited him in his Broken Arrow, Oklahoma, home outside Tulsa. The next week, he flew to Atlanta for the annual Braves Hall of Fame induction and the unveiling of his statue. That was Caruso's cause: he raised nearly $100,000 for the sculpture from patrons of the art of pitching, including everyone from Stan Musial, a foe and fan of Spahn who faced him many times, to...Elton John? Yes. Caruso persuaded the entertainer, a big Braves fan, to kick in big money.

Other donors, as listed, included Greg Maddux, Tom Glavine, John Smoltz, disabled American Veterans, Bobby Cox, Joe Torre, Carmen and Yogi Berra, and Lois and Ernie Johnson (a Braves reliever and teammate of Spahn's before becoming a broadcaster).

The Spahn statue was unveiled on August 12, 2003. The marker said it all: "Winningest Left-Hander in Major League History W-363 L-245."

Yes. Spahnie was a genuine work of art, both pitcher and sculpture.

4. The Full Henry. This was finally finished and dedicated on September 7, 1982, eight years after Aaron's milestone, six years after he'd retired as a Milwaukee Brewer.

> Henry Louis "Hank" Aaron
> 715th Home Run
> April 8, 1974
> Atlanta-Fulton County Stadium

That's where the statue stood before Turner Field opened in 1997. A full-sized, larger-than-life sculpture captures Aaron, eyes on the prized ball, following through on the swing that launched 715. Well done, Ed Dwight Jr., sculptor.

5. Lastly, a statue of...a sliding Ty Cobb? A native of Royston, Georgia, one of the game's greats, Cobb never played for the Braves but died in Atlanta. Thus:

> Tyrus Raymond Cobb 1886–1961
> Known as the Georgia Peach
> Charter Member of Baseball Hall of Fame
> Leading Batsman of All Major League History
> .367 Average, 4,191 Hits
> Felix de Weldon Sculptor 1977

79 Gold and Silver

As pitching-potent as Atlanta was from 1991 and beyond, those Braves could not only fling it but field, too. Swing the bat, as well. They were not alone.

Since 1957, when Rawlings, the St. Louis sporting goods manufacturer, began awarding Gold Gloves, only two teams—St. Louis and Baltimore—have won more Gold Gloves than the Braves. Since the Louisville Slugger bat company began presenting Silver Sluggers for hitting excellence in 1982, 14 different Braves have polished the silver.

In 1992 Terry Pendleton won his Gold Glove as the best fielding third baseman in the National League. That began Atlanta's 16-year streak in which at least one Brave won a Gold Glove every year from 1992 through 2007. In nine of those seasons two Braves won Gold Gloves.

Of course, Braves began winning Gold Gloves in 1958. Milwaukee Braves, that is. In '58 catcher Del Crandall won the first of his three straight Gold Gloves, and four overall. A young outfielder won his first of three consecutive Golds, too. The kid also hit a few home runs in his time: Hank Aaron.

Joe Torre won the last of Milwaukee's seven Gold Gloves in 1965, the team's final season in Wisconsin before moving to Atlanta. Torre, who also played third base during his 18-year career, became the second Braves catcher to go for the Gold.

Felix Millan is the only Braves second baseman so honored. He won it twice, in 1969 and again in '72, to become one of the franchise's eight multiple winners.

Knuckleballer Phil Niekro won five Gold Gloves in six seasons from 1978 to 1983, missing out only in 1981. Outfielder Dale

Murphy, the most complete player in the National League for the first half of the 1980s, was golden five straight seasons from 1982 to 1986, including his back-to-back NL Most Valuable Player campaigns of 1982 and '83.

Another multiple-year honoree is Marquis Grissom, the great center fielder, in the world championship season of 1995 and an encore in '96. The other one-timers range from the slick-fielding third baseman Clete Boyer in '69 to pitcher Mike Hampton (2003) and right fielder Jeff Francoeur (2007).

And then there's Greg Maddux and Andruw Jones. Undoubtedly the finest-fielding pitcher in baseball history, and one of the greatest defensive center fielders of all time.

In his 11 seasons in Atlanta (1993–2003), Maddux won the Gold Glove for pitchers 10 time. In all, including his time with the Chicago Cubs and later Los Angeles and San Diego, Maddux won an unprecedented 18 Gold Gloves—a record that will never be equaled. Who knows how many Gold Gloves Tom Glavine, a great fielder in his own right, might have won had the 300-game winner not played at the same time as Maddux all those years?

Andruw Jones was a phenom with the glove even as a teenager from Curacao. The center fielder won 10 consecutive Gold Gloves from 1998 to 2007. A golden decade of climbing the outfield wall at Turner Field, charging and diving to turn bloopers into outs, throwing out runners at the plate.

Jones also won a Silver Slugger in 2005, in which he hit a career-high 51 homers and won Major League Baseball's Hank Aaron Award as the top hitter in the National League. Thirteen other Braves have won Silver Sluggers, including four multiyear winners.

Three were four-timers: Murphy (1982 to 1985), the versatile Glavine (1991, 1995, 1996, 1998), and catcher Brian McCann (2006, 2008, 2009, 2010). Third baseman Chipper Jones won in his NL MVP season of 1999 and repeated in 2000.

Braves Gold and Silver Winners

The 13 players who won Gold Gloves for the Braves:

Del Crandall, C, 4 (1958–1960, '62)
Hank Aaron, OF, 3 (1958–1960)
Joe Torre, C, (1965)
Felix Millan, 2B, 2 (1969, '72)
Clete Boyer, 3B, (1969)
Phil Niekro, P, 5 (1978–1980, 1982–1983)
Dale Murphy, OF, 5 (1982–1986)
Terry Pendleton, 3B (1992)
Greg Maddux, P, 10 (1993–2002)
Marquis Grissom, OF, 2 (1995–1996)
Andruw Jones, OF, 10 (1998–2007)
Mike Hampton, P (2003)
Jeff Francoeur, OF (2007)

Braves Who Won a Rawlings Gold Glove Award (Listed by Position)

P
Phil Niekro (1978–1980, 1982–1983)
Greg Maddux (1993–2002)
Mike Hampton (2003)
C
Del Crandall (1958–1960, 1962)
Joe Torre (1965)
2B
Felix Millan (1969, 1972)
3B
Clete Boyer (1969)
Terry Pendleton (1992)
OF
Hank Aaron (1958–1960)
Dale Murphy (1982–1986)
Marquis Grissom (1995–1996)
Andruw Jones (1998–2007)
Jeff Francoeur (2007)

Braves Who Won a Louisville Slugger Silver Slugger Award (Listed by Position)

P
Tom Glavine (1991, 1995–1996, 1998)
John Smoltz (1997)
Mike Hampton (2003)
C
Javy Lopez (2003)
Brian McCann (2006, 2008–2010)
1B
Fred McGriff (1993)
SS
Jeff Blauser (1997)
3B
Chipper Jones (1999–2000)
OF
Dale Murphy (1982–1985)
Ron Gant (1991)
David Justice (1993)
Gary Sheffield (2003)
Andruw Jones (2005)

80 The Longest Night

We hold this truth to be self-evident, that the Braves-Mets game on July 4, 1985, was the longest and looniest in the annals of Atlanta-Fulton County Stadium. A long night's journey nearly into day.

Actually, the sun hadn't quite risen yet when that marathon mercifully ended. How long had this been going on? For 19 innings, two rain delays, and the most improbable pinch-hit since, well, ever.

The Braves stunk, as they did throughout most of the '80s, and the Mets were starting their young right-handed phenom, Dwight Gooden, who'd go 24–4 that year. An Independence Day crowd of some 45,000 came out for a little baseball and a lot of traditional postgame fireworks. Yet not before rain delayed the first pitch for one hour, 24 minutes. After another rain delay of 41 minutes in the third inning, play resumed.

After midnight, things got sideways. Braves closer Bruce Sutter couldn't protect an 8–7 lead in the ninth inning and was charged with another blown save, his sixth in 21 opportunities. In the 13th Howard Johnson hit a two-run homer off Terry Forster, whom David Letterman would later famously call, "That fat tub of goo." But Atlanta's Terry Harper smacked an 0–2 pitch from Mets reliever Tom Gorman for a tying, two-run home run.

The patrons of pyrotechnics would have to remain patient. In the 18th the Mets finally scored to regain the lead, 11–10. In the bottom half, with two out, none on, and a reliever due up in the pitcher's spot in the order, manager Eddie Haas had only one pinch-hitter left: Rick Camp, a starting pitcher with an .060 (10-for-67) career batting average at the time. Just as Haas had no choice, Camp had no chance.

Earlier that year, during a futile Camp at-bat, John Sterling (then a Braves broadcaster) quoted legendary broadcaster Russ Hodges of "The Giants win the pennant!" lore thusly: "Any man is dangerous up there swinging a shillelagh." To which Sterling's on-air partner Skip Caray replied, "Obviously, he never saw Rick Camp."

Yet on an 0–2 pitch from Gorman, Camp swung and somehow lined the ball over the left-field wall. "This can't be happening!" Sterling screamed. "I don't believe it!" He'd later call this, "The wildest, wackiest, most improbable game in history."

Camp's one and only career homer tied the game. It sent Mets left fielder Danny Heep slumping to the ground, stunned. The scoreboard clock read 3:12 AM.

Mercifully, the Mets scored five times in the top of the 19th, then held on for a 16–13 victory. Camp not only took the loss, he struck out to end the game as the stadium clock clicked to 3:55. No game in major league history had ever ended so late.

With some 7,000 fans still in the stands, the Braves decided to go on with the postgame fireworks show. It began at 4:01 AM. The surrounding Summerhill neighborhood was not amused. Many residents were frantic and panicked, suddenly awakened in the middle of the night and terrified that their neighborhood was under siege. Some called the police.

"I thought," one neighbor later recalled, "we were being attacked."

The next day a Pennsylvania transplant named George Krall, a Mets fan who lives in Atlanta's Morningside–Lenox Park neighborhood far from any postgame fireworks, showed up for another Mets-Braves affair. Krall wore a homemade sandwich board sign. It read: "I Survived Last Night's Game."

Pete Van Wieren showed up for it, too. To work. "As I recall, we had a game that afternoon," said the Braves broadcaster. "So we had to sleep fast."

And Lenny Dykstra, dude, spoke for everyone. "Man," said the Mets outfielder, "it's not easy playing baseball at 3:30 in the morning."

81 The Homeric Odysseys... and Oddities

For all the pitching heroics of the 1990s and on into the early 2000s, the Braves have a heralded homer-rich history—one that literally runs from AA to Z (Guy Zinn hit one home run in 1913, the only season he played for the Boston Braves). So let's go yard, from...

The aging Babe's 714th and last homer as a Boston Brave to the Hammer and Eddie Mathews mashing moon shots in Milwaukee in the '50s. From Tony Cloninger's two grand slams in one game (not bad for a pitcher) to Hank's historic 715th. From 40-40-40 in the Launching Pad to Atlanta's "And Justice for All Time" World Series title in '95, when David Justice put his wallop where his mouth was. From the fiery Crime Dog, the switch-hitter Chipper, and the precocious Andruw to Jason Heyward and…Brooks Conrad?

Yes. Absolutely yes. Despite the three-error horror of 10/10/10, the longest night in the 30-year-old rookie's life, the Braves would not have reached the playoffs in Bobby Cox's final season if not for Conrad.

His parents named him, ironically, for Brooks Robinson, the best-fielding third baseman in baseball history. By the last weekend of the 2010 regular season, and through the first three games of the Braves-Giants NLDS, Conrad couldn't field at all. Not at third base, not even when Cox switched him to second.

He made three errors in Game 3, leading to two unearned runs. The last error, on a sharp grounder that skidded between his legs, allowed the eventual winning run to score. Turner Field fans screamed in disbelief, venting their anger. One writer lampooned the choice of Conrad's namesake: "Perhaps Buckner Conrad was already taken."

Yes, Conrad's best glove was his batting glove. Yet without him, Cox would never have sniffed one last October.

In 2009, finally called up from Triple A Gwinnett, the switch-hitting Conrad hit his first big-league homer: a three-run, pinch-hit shot in a 9–8 win over Washington.

In 2010 he homered in an 11–3 victory over Milwaukee on May 11. He started again the next day, smacked another homer, and had four RBIs. On May 20 came Conrad's memorable walk-off, pinch-hit grand slam—the one that initially left Conrad holding his hands to his head, thinking it had been caught above the left-field wall. No. It bounced atop the wall and then over, completing a seven-run, ninth-inning rally to beat Cincinnati 10–9.

It was Atlanta's third straight walk-off win, and the Braves' first walk-off grand slam when trailing by three runs since Del Crandall did it in 1955. On July 24 Conrad smacked another pinch-slam, this one against Florida. He's just the fifth player in 60 years to hit two pinch-hit grand slams in a season, joining Davey Johnson of Philadelphia, the Giants' Mike Ivie, Darryl Strawberry of the Yankees, and Cleveland's Ben Broussard. Conrad is the only rookie in major league baseball history to accomplish that feat.

Wait, there's more.

On August 10 his two-run pinch-home run off Houston's Matt Lindstrom keyed the Braves' three-run rally in the ninth to win 4–2. Conrad is the first player to hit three go-ahead homers in the eighth inning or later since Rusty Greer of Texas in 1995. He's also a stand-up guy. After his 3-E nightmare, Conrad faced the media at his locker, answering questions. Many players would've hid. Not him.

"I wish I could just dig a hole and sleep in it," the shell-shocked Conrad said in a deathly silent clubhouse. He'd committed eight errors in his last seven games, going back to the last week of the regular season. And still, without him? There's no postseason.

And then there's Jason Heyward, who formally introduced himself on Opening Day in the most spectacular way. The date: April 5, 2010. The count to the next face of the franchise for, say, 15 years: 2–0. Caray's perfect call of Heyward's first major league at-bat: "Swing and a drive!...Belt to right!...Welcome to the show!"

On the just the third pitch of the rest of his big-league life, Heyward crushed a 470-foot, three-run homer off the Cubs' Carlos Zambrano. It was the perfect start for a certain All-Star of the future, and one of J-Hey's 18 home runs. Welcome to the show, indeed.

The Braves Greatest Hits

Despite his late-season fielding gaffes, Brooks Conrad hit himself into the Braves record book. In a few categories:

No. Grand Slams	Player	Season
4	Sid Gordon	1950
3	Wally Berger	1935
3	Del Crandall	1955
3	Hank Aaron	1962
3	Chipper Jones	1997
2	30 players, including: Brian McCann (2007) and most recently Brooks Conrad (2010)	

No. Pinch-Homers	Player	Season
5	Butch Nieman	1945
4	Tommy Gregg	1990
3	Eight Players, including most recently Brooks Conrad (2010)	

A switch-hitter, Conrad's power comes mostly from the left side. One of his eight homers in 2010 was hit right-handed, however. Maybe he'll join a select list of four Braves who've homered from both sides of the plate in the same game.

Jim Russell: July 7, 1948, at Chicago.

Chipper Jones: Six times, the first on May 1, 1999, against Cincinnati (one of three times Jones did so that season, when he was the NL MVP).

Rafael Furcal: Twice, both in 2005, the first on April 15 at Philadelphia.

Mark Teixeira: Twice in 2008, the first on June 22 vs. Seattle (he homered three times that game).

Jason Heyward made some history of his own. When he debuted with a three-run home run on Opening Day, Heyward became just the sixth player in franchise history to homer in his first at-bat. He joins:

Joe Harrington: Boston Beaneaters, September 10, 1895 (One of his three career homers).

Johnny Bates: Boston Beaneaters, April 12, 1906 (One of his six that season).

Chuck Tanner: Milwaukee Braves, April 12, 1955 (The future manager of the Atlanta Braves hit the first big-league pitch he saw for a pinch-hit homer).

Jermaine Dye: Atlanta Braves, May 17, 1996 (vs. Cincinnati).
Jordan Schafer: Atlanta Braves, April 5, 2009 (at Philadelphia).

Although Heyward was still 20 on Opening Day when he bid Atlanta hello with a homer, he wasn't close to being the youngest Brave to homer as a rookie:

Lew Brown: Boston, 1876. 18 years, 169 days.
Bill Southworth: Milwaukee, 1964. 18 years, 328 days.
Andruw Jones: Atlanta, 1996. 19 years, 115 days.

It's unlikely Heyward will be the oldest to homer, either. But just in case:

Babe Ruth: Boston, 1935 (a three-homer game). 40 years, 108 days.
Warren Spahn: Milwaukee, 1964. 43 years, 90 days.
Julio Franco: Atlanta, 2005. 46 years, 355 days.

82 Attend a Braves Hall of Fame Luncheon

Since 1999, high above the diamond in the 755 Club at Turner Field, it's been a mid-summer day's dream every year but one. There was no inductee into the Braves Hall of Fame in 2008. But then, this isn't like some sports halls that seem to welcome one and nearly all.

It's a distinct honor, and it's a highly selective group of 22 men who've already been inducted, from baseball immortals to broadcast royalty, fine front-office management to eagle-eyed scouts, great players to good company men. This short list of greats includes old-time heroes now long gone and recent inductees who look like they could still own the outside corner.

Of the 22 members of the Braves Hall of Fame, 16 are former Braves players. Seven have had their numbers retired. In numerical order, left to right, as displayed high above left field at Turner Field, they are: Dale Murphy (3), Warren Spahn (21), Greg Maddux (31), Phil Niekro (35), Eddie Mathews (41), Henry Aaron (44), and Tom Glavine (47).

Three more numbers are surely soon to be retired: manager Bobby Cox (6), who took the ballclub back to the postseason in his 2010 farewell; pitcher-turned-broadcaster John Smoltz (29); and third baseman Chipper Jones (10).

Go to this season's luncheon and you may well see Cox inducted into the Braves Hall of Fame. Or you might end up sitting at Smoltz's table, or next to Jones. The entire ballclub, including the front office, always attends the luncheon where broadcaster Joe Simpson has been the entertaining emcee in recent years.

From 2001 through 2003, Braves broadcast icon Pete Van Wieren handled those duties. In spring of 2004 Van Wieren was approached by Braves president Terry McGuirk. When he mentioned the date for that season's HoF luncheon, Van Wieren assumed McGuirk wanted him to work it again. Instead, the Professor learned that he and on-air partner Skip Caray were two of that year's inductees. Stunned, Van Wieren was still in disbelief as the August 13 date neared.

"What a tremendous feeling that was," Van Wieren recalled in *Of Mikes and Men*, his 2010 autobiography. "Talk about going from the outhouse to the penthouse! A year earlier, Skip and I were being booted off the telecasts, and now we were to receive the highest honor that the Braves could bestow."

Skip Caray was there that Friday, too, to be inducted with his longtime on-air partner, Van Wieren. The previous Sunday, Caray had left the Braves in Arizona and flown to St. Louis, where his younger brother, Chris, was terminally ill with an inoperable brain tumor.

"One of the last things he said was, 'Isn't Skip's Hall of Fame thing about to happen?'" Caray said after that 2004 luncheon. "That assured me my place was here." He flew home to Atlanta on his 65th birthday and was inducted into the Braves Hall of Fame that day.

The following day, Chris died at age 57. Skip flew back to St. Louis for the funeral, helped bury his baby brother, then got back to the business of broadcasting baseball.

Yet not before doing himself, and his brother, proud. You'll hear sincere thanks at these luncheons, lots of humor—highbrow and otherwise—and, at times, real eloquence and pure heart. Caray, like Van Wieren, was thrilled about being inducted into the Braves Hall and joining former broadcast partner Ernie Johnson, who helped hire Skip and Pete for the 1976 season. He thanked Uncle Ernie, and then:

"If you are people who pray," Caray told the hushed audience, "a prayer for Chris Caray would be very much appreciated right now. Because the odds are stacked against him."

Afterward, Caray said, "One of Chris' goals was to be here. It's a strange day in that your heart is so full on one hand, and then so empty on the other. I've never been afraid of making a speech in my life, but today I was."

All this was a side of Skip Caray the public rarely, if ever, heard or saw. Then again, that's part of the atmosphere and appeal, the class and charm of the Braves Hall of Fame Luncheon.

In his acceptance speech that Friday, Van Wieren recalled Chipper Jones' words one time following his walk-off homer to beat the New York Mets: "Words can't describe it. I just wish everyone could experience such a moment just so they could know how it feels."

Turning toward Jones in the luncheon crowd that day, Van Wieren said, "Well, Chipper, now I know. Now I know."

Braves Hall of Famers

Class of 1999

Henry Aaron—Career average of .305, 755 HR, 2,297 RBIs. 1957 NL MVP and still the peoples' choice as the all-time home run king.

Eddie Mathews—Career average of .271, 512 HR, 1,453 RBIs. Braves manager (1972–74). The only Brave to play for the franchise in all three cities.

Phil Niekro—Won 318 games, lost 274 (268–230 as a Brave). Threw a no-hitter in 1973. Holds or shares 13 Atlanta career pitching records.

Warren Spahn—Won 363 games (most by a left-hander in baseball history), lost 245 (356–229 with Braves). 1957 Cy Young Award winner. Threw two no-hitters (1960 and '61).

Class of 2000

Dale Murphy—Career average of .265, 398 HR, 1,266 RBIs. Two-time NL MVP (1982 and '83). The most revered Brave throughout the dismal 1980s and the one Brave who isn't but should be in the Baseball Hall of Fame.

Ted Turner—Owner from 1976 to 2000. Founded TBS, the SuperStation that made the Braves "America's Team." Managed one game in 1977 (Career record: 0–1). Atlanta won its only World Series title (1995) under his ownership.

Class of 2001

Lew Burdette. Won 203 games, lost 144 (179–120 as a Brave). 1957 World Series MVP, when he beat the New York Yankees three times, including Games 5 and 7.

Ernie Johnson—Beloved broadcaster from 1962 to 1999. Reliever for the Boston and Milwaukee Braves (1950–1958). Was 7–3 for '57 World Series champs, 40–23 career.

Class of 2002

Bill Bartholomay—Chairman of the Braves board since 1962. Instrumental in moving the franchise to Atlanta in 1966.

Johnny Sain—Won 139 games, lost 116 (104–91 with the Boston Braves). Later became one of the most acclaimed pitching gurus and coaches in baseball history.

Class of 2003

Del Crandall—Career average of .254, 179 HR, 657 RBIs. Catcher and cornerstone for 1957 World Series champions.

Class of 2004

Tommy Holmes—Career average of .302, 88 HR, 581 RBIs. Outfielder spent all but the last of his 11 seasons with Boston. Hit over .300 annually from 1944 to 1948, .352 in 1945. Second in that NL MVP voting and struck out nine times all year. Set modern NL mark in '45 by hitting safely in 37 straight games; it stood until 1978.

Kid Nichols—Won 360 games, lost 205 (328–180 with Boston). Baseball's most accomplished 19th-century pitcher and key to the Beaneaters' five pennants from 1891 to 1898. Won 27 games as a rookie in 1890, then had seven 30-win seasons in the next eight years. Threw 533 complete games (fourth all-time), 502 for Boston.

Skip Caray—Broadcaster from 1976 to 2008. Son of the legendary Harry Caray, father of current Braves broadcaster Chip Caray. Not too keen about pregame show callers seeking an explanation of the infield fly rule.

Pete Van Wieren—Broadcaster from 1976 to 2008 and the professorial half of the immensely popular duo of "Skip & Pete" on TBS. His Diamond Notes on pregame broadcasts were true baseball gems.

Class of 2005

Herman Long—Boston Beaneaters shortstop from 1890 to 1902. Career average of .277, 2,127 hits, 91 HR in the dead-ball era, 1,055 RBIs, 1,455 runs scored.

Paul Snyder—Player, coach, and scout from 1958 to the present. One of the most respected player personnel men and talent evaluators ever in baseball.

Class of 2006

Ralph Garr—Outfielder known as "the Roadrunner," played from 1968 to 1975, starting in left field from 1971 to 1975. A hitting machine who had three 200-hit seasons. Led the NL with 214 hits in '74. Former coach and a Braves scout since '85.

Bill Lucas—Highly respected and popular front-office executive from 1976 to 1979. Director of player personnel, he was the first African American general manager in baseball history.

Class of 2007

David Justice—Career average of .279, 305 HR, 1,017 RBI. 1990 NL Rookie of the Year. Outspoken outfielder who criticized Braves fans before Game 6 of the 1995 World Series. Homered in that 1–0 win to give Atlanta its only world championship.

Class of 2008

No inductees

Class of 2009

Greg Maddux—Won 355 games, lost 227 (194–88 with Braves from 1993 to 2003). First of only two pitchers to win four consecutive Cy Young Awards (1992 to 1995). Eighth on the all-time victory list, 10th in strikeouts (3,371). Won 18 Gold Gloves, 10 with Atlanta. A true craftsman and baseball's most dominant pitcher as a Brave.

Class of 2010

Tom Glavine—Won 305 games, lost 203 (244–147 as a Brave from 1987 to 2002 and 2008). NL Cy Young winner in 1991 and '98. As a New York Met (2003 to 2007), became baseball's 23rd 300-game winner in 2007, beating the Cubs 8–3. A 10-time NL All-Star. MVP of the 1995 World Series, beating Cleveland twice, including an eight-inning, one-hit, no-run masterpiece in Game 6 for Atlanta's only World Series title. Now a special assistant to Braves president John Schuerholz.

83 The Brave Who Belongs in Cooperstown

Murph. Dale Murphy. I'll admit I'm biased. Not a homer, but biased. When I moved from Manhattan to Atlanta in early May 1983, I quickly thought, *Good grief, what the hell have I done?* Then I realized, *I can watch Dale Murphy play every day, either at Atlanta-Fulton County Stadium, or on TBS, the SuperStation.*

Familiarity bred not contempt, not boosterism. Rather, familiarity bred, well, familiarity with—and appreciation for—a player who was arguably baseball's best for most of the '80s. Says who? Says Joe Posnanski, the superb and knowledgeable baseball writer and columnist for *Sports Illustrated.*

Before the 2010 Hall of Fame voting was announced that January, Posnanski wrote, "From 1980 through '87, Murphy was smack in the discussion as the best player in baseball. I'm not sure he ever was quite the best—Mike Schmidt was awfully good—but you could make a viable argument for him. He was, in his prime, a Gold Glove center fielder who got on base, hit with power, stole bases, and willingly was the face of baseball as the (only) star attraction for Ted Turner's Atlanta Braves."

Nolan Ryan put it another way: "I can't imagine Joe DiMaggio was a better all-around player than Dale Murphy."

In 1982 Murphy was chosen the National League's Most Valuable Player after helping Atlanta win its first National League West Division title since 1969. He hit 36 homers, drove in 109 runs, batted .281, and won both a Gold Glove and Silver Slugger award. In '83 he repeated as the NL MVP. Again, he hit 36 homers with 121 RBIs and a .302 average. Again, he won a Gold Glove (the second of his five consecutive) and Silver Slugger. With 30 stolen bases, he was also a 30-30 guy when that truly meant something. He was, simply, the best.

Murphy's finest season was likely 1987. On a dreadful team that lost 92 games, he belted a career-high 44 homers with 105 RBIs and hit .295. This was one season after he'd finally taken a night off and ended a 740 consecutive games streak.

My favorite Murph season, and moment, came early in 1984. He got off to a very slow start after his back-to-back MVPs. The paper I then worked for had already done a couple of stories on that topic, but in mid-May it was my turn to write it. I waited in the clubhouse until Murphy flew in, uncharacteristically a little late and carrying his golf bag over his shoulder.

I walked over, said hello, and explained what my assignment was for the next day's paper. Murphy began talking as he hurriedly got dressed in his uniform, then said, "I've gotta hit," but agreed to talk again after BP. I didn't panic, but I began looking for anyone

Dale Murphy leaps high against the wall to rob the Los Angeles Dodgers' Pedro Guerrero of a home run in September 1983 in L.A. That year Murphy hit 36 homers with 121 RBIs and a .302 average and was named the NL MVP for the second consecutive year.

to discuss Murph's slow start—even Luke Appling, the ancient Hall of Famer then serving as a Braves hitting consultant.

We were still talking when I heard a voice across the clubhouse: "Jack, do you still want to talk some more?"

Murphy knew exactly what I wanted to discuss: why he was stinking it up so badly. Yet he still offered to talk about it. Let's just say not many baseball players would do that. He did. Vintage Murph.

Another thing to admire: Murphy was then and remains a devout Mormon. He was very upset when female reporters were first allowed in the clubhouse, yet wore a towel or robe to comply. Unlike many athletes, Murphy never wore his religion on his uniform sleeve like so many clubhouse zealots. Never proselytized. He lived his faith, and that's all you had to see to know it and admire it. That was his unspoken testimony.

In 1987 Murphy was chosen as the *Sports Illustrated* Co-Sportsman of the Year. Two years earlier he'd won the Lou Gehrig Memorial Award. In 1988 he won the Roberto Clemente Award, named for the late Hall of Famer and humanitarian.

Murphy's performance declined sharply in 1988 (.226, 24 homers, 77 RBIs) and continued as such. In 1990 he approved a trade to Philadelphia, where he spent one full season before knee problems limited him to 18 games in '91. In 1993 he played just 26 games in Colorado. Although needing just two homers to reach 400—a true milestone in those pre-steroid days—Murphy retired. If he couldn't go deep in 42 at-bats in Denver's rarified air, he knew was done.

In his second year of eligibility for the Hall of Fame Murphy maxed out at 23 percent in the voting, declining every subsequent year. If he ever makes it to Cooperstown, it will be via the Veterans Committee. The veterans take into consideration a player's character. No player's was ever better than Murph's. And in these times, shouldn't that count for even more?

84 The Pearl of the Braves

She lived in Canton, Georgia, due north of Atlanta, but her real address was Seat 1, Row 9, Section 105.That's where you could always find Pearl Sandow. That's where she was happiest: in her usual seat on the aisle, right behind the home dugout in Atlanta-Fulton County Stadium, watching the Atlanta Braves play another game of baseball.

Oh, Pearl loved her baseball. She had to. How else to explain such extraordinary devotion? From 1934 on, for 55 years, she attended every professional baseball game in Atlanta except one.

And you thought Lou Gehrig was the Iron Horse and called Cal Ripken even more enduring.

Pearl came by her baseball passion naturally. Her mother took her to her first Atlanta Crackers game when Pearl was an infant. The Crackers were Atlanta's original hometown team, the celebrated minor league club that played in Ponce de Leon Park in Atlanta. Pearl missed one Crackers game in 1961, the first she'd missed in nearly a quarter-century. Her excuse? Her mother had suffered a stroke. It was another quarter-century before Sandow missed another game.

During her remarkable streak, Pearl saw more than 1,850 Crackers games. Once the Milwaukee Braves moved south in 1966, Sandow attended 1,889 Atlanta Braves games in a row, starting with Opening Night in 1966 and on to 1989.

For years, Pearl was the best fan of the worst team in Major League Baseball. All that Braves ineptitude during all those summers? Even the awful 1980s? No matter. If they played, she was there.

For 33 years, Sandow worked as a department head of a federal government housing program in Atlanta. She structured her schedule and her life around her Braves. During the season, Pearl left her office at the end of each workday and went straight to the ballpark. Usually, she arrived in plenty of time to see batting practice. Yet she always felt having to work for a living interfered with being a Braves fan.

In 1975 the Braves honored Sandow with a lifetime pass to the ballpark, a watch, and a night held in her honor at Atlanta-Fulton County. The omnipresent Pearl was easily identifiable by her hair: A white beehive of sorts, stacked high in what she preferred to call "snow-cone style." During one 24-year period, she attended spring training annually.

In 1989 Pearl's loyalty was rewarded in baseball nirvana: Cooperstown, New York, at the National Baseball Hall of Fame. On the third floor of the Hall, in a section devoted to an exhibit of the grand old game's greatest, most extraordinary fans, Sandow was among them. She was one of several legendary fans honored with their own papier-mâché figures. There was Brooklyn's Hilda Chester from Ebbets Field; Yoyo, the superfan from Philadelphia; and Pearl, in an orange-and-white-striped dress, wearing headphones (gotta follow the game on radio, right?), white sunglasses to match her hair, and a Braves pennant over her shoulder.

In early 1990, however, Sandow suffered a severe shoulder injury. No, not a torn rotator cuff, but two broken shoulders, suffered in a fall. The Braves' last bad season was a bummer for Pearl, too. She didn't see a single game in person. She did continue to follow the club religiously, however, via TV and radio.

On May 12, 2002, the Braves invited Pearl to Turner Field to celebrate her 100th birthday. She was given a gigantic birthday card signed by the team and a cake. Pearl served as the honorary team captain for that game during the pregame meeting at home plate and the exchange of lineup cards.

The Pearl of the Braves died in her hometown of Canton on April 17, 2006—the season that ended the Braves' record run of 14 straight division titles. Coincidence? You make the call.

85 I-285 Perez

On the evening of August 19, 1982, the Braves were in a freefall, if not outright panic. Buoyed by their 13–0 start, they'd now blown a

10½-game lead over Los Angeles. Having lost 19 of their previous 21 games, the Braves were four games behind the Dodgers in the National League West. Their once-high hopes were fading. Even worse, their scheduled starting pitcher was AWOL.

Donde está Pascual Perez? The kid right-hander from the Dominican Republic who'd been called up in late July from Triple A Richmond, where he was 5–0, was a no-show. What in the name of San Cristobal—his hometown—was going on?

That morning Perez had moved into a new suburban apartment after recently getting his Georgia driver's license. Emboldened by his new digs and driving privileges, Perez decided to drive himself to the ballyard that afternoon. At about 4:30 PM, some three hours before he'd throw the first pitch against Montreal, Perez set out on I-285, the perimeter highway that encircles the city. It wasn't long before the kid from Triple A needed help from AAA, the American Automobile Association.

The perimeter is a 60-mile interstate loop around Atlanta. Perez was positive that Atlanta-Fulton County Stadium was right off I-285. One full loop and an hour later, he found himself back where he'd started. Would he go round in circles? Yup. Confident that he'd merely missed the ballpark, Perez kept driving. Lap 2 was as confounding as the first. On his third go-round, and now running out of gas, Perez exited the perimeter and drove to a service station. He had to borrow $10 for gas from the attendant, who'd been following the Braves' pregame show.

"Hey, man, they're looking for you," said the attendant. Indeed, the Braves had already notified the police in the event that Perez had been in an accident. Not to worry. The attendant pointed Perez in the right direction. The pitcher finally got off at the correct exit and arrived at the ballpark at 7:50—10 minutes after the first pitch.

Again, not to worry. Phil Niekro, the Braves' tireless knuckleballer, was the emergency starter in Perez's absence. Atlanta rallied for a 5–4 win, and the escapade lightened up a tense clubhouse.

The next day Perez had some new nicknames—"Perimeter Perez" and "Wrong Way Pascual"—and a new number on the back of his blue Braves jacket. It was traveling secretary Bill Acree's idea to put "I-285" on the wayward pitcher's jacket.

A commemorative cartoon poster soon appeared, too—a road map of his route, with Perez driving aimlessly on the perimeter and a caricature of manager Joe Torre standing outside the stadium, frowning at his watch.

The Braves won 13 of their next 15 games, beginning with Perez's on-time arrival and 2–1 victory over the Mets the following night. They regained first place and held off L.A. to win their first NL West title since 1969 by one game.

Perez went 4–4 that season, then 15–8 in 1983, when he was named to the National League All-Star team. After a 14–8 record in '84, Perez pitched for Montreal and the Yankees. After violating baseball's drug policy, he was out of baseball by 1991. At least his driving record was clean.

86 Road Trip!

Actually, make that plural. There are numerous road trips just waiting to be taken throughout Braves Country and beyond. That was the marketing campaign for the 2010 season: "This is Braves Country." And it said so right there on the outfield wall in Turner Field. Bobby Cox said so, too, up on the big video screen before each game.

But there are other stops along the way in Braves Country, other road trips to be taken in 2011.

Take a trip to Lynchburg, the new Virginia home of the Braves' Advanced-A franchise that was formerly based in Myrtle Beach,

South Carolina. Good-bye, Myrtle Beach Pelicans. Hello, Lynchburg Hillcats of the Carolina League.

The surfing's not as good in central Virginia as it is in Myrtle Beach, but Atlanta Braves general manager Frank Wren loves everything else about Lynchburg and the new four-year player development agreement. "We wanted to stay in the Southeast and the Mid-Atlantic," Wren said. "All of that works really well for us, and the logistics [work] for our players and staff."

Lynchburg's also much closer to Danville, Virginia, the Braves' Rookie Advanced team in the Appalachian League. You can easily catch both teams in action on successive days. Lynchburg's home opener is April 15. For tickets, call (434) 528-1144 or go to the website, www.lynchburg-hillcats.com. For Danville, call (434) 797-3792 or go to the website: www.dbraves.com.

Atlanta's other minor-league affiliates remain the same:

The Triple A International League Gwinnett Braves are about a 30-minute drive north of Turner Field, right up I-85. Gwinnett Stadium is a beautiful 10,000-seat facility with a very cool grassy berm beyond the right-field fence. Bring a blanket, sit down, and enjoy the action. For tickets, call (678) 277-0338 or go to their website, www.gwinnettbraves.com.

Trustman Park, the home of the Double A Mississippi Braves in Pearl, Mississippi, is a terrific park in a great setting and a fine organization. It's a five-hour drive from Atlanta, but well worth the trip. Contact (601) 932-8788 or www.mississippibraves.com.

The Rome Braves of the Class A South Atlantic League play in gorgeous State Mutual Stadium, about a 40-minute drive northwest of Atlanta. General manager Mike Dunn does a fine job running the affiliate. Contact (706) 368-9388 or www.romebraves.com.

The Gulf Coast League Braves, the club's Rookie affiliate, plays its home games in Champion Stadium—the spring training home of the Atlanta Braves in Kissimmee, Florida, right next door to

Disney World. It's ideal for a vacation with the kids or even a long weekend. For tickets and information, call (407) 939-2301.

The Braves 400 Club, the team's longtime official fan club, makes an annual road trip to a different major league city each year. The 2010 weekend trip to breathtaking Target Field in Minneapolis was a huge success. For information, call the 400 Club's 24-hour hotline: (770) 416-4539. By mail: Braves 400 Club, P.O. Box 7689, Atlanta, GA 30309.

And start researching, planning, and reserving your upcoming road trips to Cooperstown, New York. At least three or four Atlanta Braves will be inducted into the Baseball Hall of Fame in the next few years: Bobby Cox, who retired after last season as the fourth-winningest manager in major league history; Greg Maddux, the four-time Cy Young Award winner who won 355 games, is eligible for the Hall in 2013; Tom Glavine, the two-time Cy Young winner and 305-game winner, is eligible in 2014; and John Smoltz is the only pitcher in baseball history with more than 200 wins and 150 saves.

And then there's Chipper Jones, a shoo-in once he retires, too.

87 No-Hit Wonders

As great as they were throughout the 1990s and early in the next decade, none of the Braves' Big Three ever pitched a no-hitter. Not Tom Glavine. Not Greg Maddux. Not John Smoltz. Not even while they were winning six consecutive National League Cy Young Awards from 1991 through 1996 and a seventh in '98.

Glavine won his first in '91, becoming the first Brave in 34 years to do so since Warren Spahn won it with Milwaukee in 1957. Glavine captured his second Cy in '98. In 1992 Maddux won the first of his four straight NL Cy Youngs as a Chicago Cub before coming to Atlanta and repeating in 1993 through 1995. Smoltz was simply overwhelming in his Cy Young year of 1996, winning 24 games and four more in the postseason.

Yet none of the Braves' Big Three ever threw a no-no. But Jack Stivetts did, as did "Big Jeff" Pfeffer. Tom Hughes did, too, and even Jim Wilson, who'd nearly been waived. And, of course, Knucksie, Phil Niekro.

Here's a look at the 14 no-hitters pitched in Braves history:

Jack Stivetts, August 6, 1892—The best of Stivetts' 35 wins that season was this 11–0 shutout of Brooklyn. The 24-year-old right-hander walked five but held Brooklyn hitless and led Boston to the pennant.

Vic Willis, August 7, 1899—Known as the "Delaware Peach," the second-year pitcher beat Washington 7–1. He's the only Brave whose no-hitter wasn't a shutout. Willis, then 23, was no fluke. He led the league with five shutouts and a 2.50 ERA that season.

Frank Pfeffer, May 8, 1907—The pitcher nicknamed "Big Jeff" won just 31 games in a six-year career and had only six wins in the 1907 season. But one of those was a 6–0 no-hitter against Cincinnati. Go Pfigure.

George Davis, September 9, 1914—He was smart (a Harvard Law School student at the time) and talented. Strong, too, hence the nickname, "Iron." In between classes Davis no-hit Philadelphia 7–0 in the second game of a doubleheader for a key victory in the Miracle Braves' run to a World Series title. It was Davis' only shutout in a seven-win career. Released by the club at age 25, he graduated from law school and lawyered up in Buffalo.

Tom Hughes, June 16, 1916—Primarily a reliever in his nine-year career, Hughes hurled a 2–0 no-no against Pittsburgh. The 32-year-old led the league in winning percentage that season (16–3, .842), which was cut short by a broken hand.

Jim Tobin, April 27, 1944—Tobin was the first Braves knuckleballer to pitch a no-hitter. He was not only the first Braves pitcher to homer in a no-no, going deep to beat Brooklyn 2–0, but was also the first pitcher in major league history to do so.

Vern Bickford, August 11, 1950—The night time was the right time for Bickford. His 7–0 shutout of Brooklyn was the first night no-hitter by a Brave, and the only no-hitter in either league that season.

Jim Wilson, June 12, 1954—A month earlier, in their first season in Milwaukee, the Braves tried to waive Wilson. No one wanted him, so manager Charlie Grimm gave Wilson a start in the opener of a June 6 doubleheader. Nice move, Charlie: Wilson threw a shutout. Six days later Grimm gave him another start. Even better move, Charlie: Wilson no-hit Philadelphia 2–0. The first no-hitter at Milwaukee County Stadium jump-started Wilson to an eight-game winning streak and earned him a spot on the National League All-Star team.

Lew Burdette, August 18, 1960—This was not merely a no-hitter, but near-perfection. The only Phillie to reach base in Burdette's 1–0 masterpiece was Tony Gonzalez, hit by a pitch in the fifth inning. After the ensuing double-play, Burdette faced the minimum 27 batters, had two hits himself, and scored the game's only run.

Warren Spahn, September 16, 1960—Less than a month later, and not to be trumped by his good buddy Burdette, Spahn also no-hit Philadelphia 4–0. Near the end of his 16th season, the great lefty finally threw a no-hitter, overpowering the hapless Phils with 15 strikeouts. It was the first Braves no-hitter thrown by a left-hander. A meager Milwaukee crowd of 6,117 was most appreciative.

Warren Spahn, April 28, 1961—The wait for Spahn's second no-hitter was much shorter. He held the San Francisco Giants' potent lineup hitless, winning 1–0 for his second no-hitter in seven starts. Spahn turned 40 five days earlier; at the time, that made him the second-oldest pitcher to throw a no-hitter. Another meager Milwaukee crowd (8,518) was again appreciative.

Phil Niekro, August 5, 1973—Welcome to the fraternity, Knucksie. Niekro's no-hitter was a 9–0 breeze over San Diego. It was the first no-hitter in Atlanta Stadium, the first by a Brave since the franchise headed south and included a one-of-a-kind, inside-the-park homer by lumbering Braves catcher Paul Casanova.

Kent Mercker, Mark Wohlers, and Alejandro Pena, September 11, 1991—The first combined no-hitter in National League history was also a critical win in an unlikely pennant race. Mercker pitched six innings, Wohlers two, and Pena, the veteran obtained two weeks earlier, completed the 1–0 win. Terry Pendleton homered for the only run. He was also involved in a highly controversial official scorer's ruling. With two out in the ninth, Pendleton backed off a chopper to the left side that then glanced off shortstop Rafael Belliard's glove. Pendleton later admitted he'd lost the ball in the stadium lights, but the play was ruled an error. When Tony Gwynn flied out, the historic no-hitter was official.

Kent Mercker, April 8, 1994—Mercker needed no help this time. After winning the fifth spot in the starting rotation, he threw a no-hitter in Dodger Stadium, winning 6–0. Mercker struck out 10 and walked four for his first career complete-game win. It was also the Braves' first—and still only—road no-hitter in modern history.

88 The Managing Judge

Long before Ted, there was Emil. Almost a half-century before Ted Turner put on a Braves uniform and managed a game in Pittsburgh, another owner beat Ted to it: Judge Emil Fuchs.

In 1929 Fuchs, a German immigrant who owned the ballclub from 1923 to 1935, decided to double as the Braves' manager, too. This, after the club's 50–103 fiasco in '28, its seventh straight losing year and fourth 100-loss season during that span. Fuchs, a New York lawyer—hence the "Judge" handle—had no professional baseball experience as a player, coach, or manager. He became a New York City magistrate in 1915, later a deputy attorney general for the state of New York. In 1922 Fuchs went to work for Ralph Day, the federal prohibition director for the New York district.

He was also the attorney for the New York Giants, further fueling his passion for baseball. That also enabled Fuchs to buy the Braves in 1923 from George Washington Grant, a friend of legendary Giants manager John McGraw. His partners were legendary pitcher Christy Mathewson, now the club president, and James McDonough. Fuchs was the vice president, although he owned most of the team's stock. Six years later, despite no actual baseball experience, he decided to come down to the dugout and manage. At least Fuchs had enough sense not to wear a uniform.

"The time has gone when a manager has to chew tobacco and talk from the side of his mouth," Fuchs proclaimed in a press conference. "I don't think our club can do any worse with me as manager than it has done the last few years." In a courtroom, such language would have been stricken from the record, or regarded as magisterial misconduct. In baseball, it was sheer hubris. From magistrate to manager? Good luck, your honor.

At least Fuchs had enough sense to name Johnny Evers his assistant manager. For his baseball farewell, the once-great, future Hall of Fame second baseman made a brief appearance in one game in '29. Throughout that season Evers was the technician who ran the ballclub. Miraculously, the awful team with the attorney/owner-turned-manager somehow managed to win eight of its first 10 games. Quickly, however, the Braves began playing down to form. And after the first few miserable weeks, Fuchs let Evers run a wretched club.

As usual, Fuchs was in dire financial straits in 1929. The Red Sox were Boston's ballclub of choice, by far. Unlike the Sox, the Braves were badly hurt by the city's ban on Sunday baseball. The attorney in

Fuchs fought that ban vigorously. Sunday baseball was eventually legalized in '29, but not before more problems for the owner. Fuchs was charged with improperly influencing the vote on Sunday ball. Translation: he paid people to help change the law. Fuchs pleaded no contest. The ballclub was fined $1,000 in municipal court.

Like Ted Turner in his early years after buying the Braves in 1976, Fuchs was a rabid promoter, trying anything to lure fans to Braves Field. He held the first Ladies Day in Boston. He staged Knot Hole Days for children. He approved the city's first radio broadcast of a baseball game. He lavishly courted local sportswriters with food and drink. His "board of directors," Fuchs called them.

Nothing worked, at least not for long. Fuchs was widely ridiculed for his ridiculous decision to "manage." As a result, he was often out of town, hardly ever down in the dugout even while in Boston. His players rarely paid the owner any mind when he deigned to sit in the dugout. Somehow, those '29 Braves won 56 games, six more than the previous season's 103-game losers. Saddled with 98 defeats, personal financial problems due to the stock market crash of 1929, and a foolish image, Fuchs returned to the front office where he presumably belonged.

His 1935 decision to bring Babe Ruth back to Boston as a box-office attraction proved disastrous. Two months after Ruth retired on June 2, Fuchs forfeited his majority share of the franchise. Fourteen months later, he filed for bankruptcy, $300,000 in the red.

Those abysmal Braves lost 115 games in 1935. They won just 38—two less than Casey Stengel's 1962 expansion New York Mets. Those Amazin's were 40–120, a winning percentage of .250. The '35 Braves were 38–115, a .248 winning percentage. Thus, they were the worst National League team of the 20th century. Imagine how much worse it would've been had Fuchs stayed in the dugout.

The judge returned to practicing law and eventually paid off his debts. He died at age 83 in 1961, thus never getting to root for those original Mets to break his Braves' record for futility.

89 The Natural

Says who? Said *SI.* Right there on the cover of the August 26, 2005, issue of *Sports Illustrated.* Right beneath "The Natural" headline, just like the title of the Robert Redford baseball film, based on the novel by Bernard Malamud. There was also a photo of the real-life "Natural" himself. And this sub-headline, which begged the question: "Atlanta Rookie Jeff Francoeur Is off to an Impossibly Hot Start: Can Anyone Be This Good?"

Uh, no, as it turned out. At least not this preternaturally talented 21-year-old Georgian.

Just how hot was Frenchy's start? After being called up by the Braves on July 6, Francoeur was in the starting lineup the next day in the second game of a doubleheader against the Chicago Cubs. In the eighth inning the right fielder with the Uzi of an arm got his first major league hit: a three-run homer to center field. On TV, his parents, David and Karen, rejoiced with family and friends. At the plate, their son kept on swinging.

In his first 12 games Francoeur hit five homers. Not even the most prolific home run men in Braves history could compare with his impossibly hot start. It took the precociously talented teenager Andruw Jones 15 games to hit five homers.

Bob Horner? 26 games.

Chipper Jones? 28 games.

The immortal Hank Aaron? 32 games.

Two-time NL MVP Dale Murphy? 83 games.

Only one Brave hit five homers more quickly than did Francoeur. In 1994 a relatively obscure third baseman named Jose Oliva hit five home runs in his first 11 games, before fizzling.

Jeff Francoeur hit five home runs in his first 12 games during his debut 2005 season and held strong numbers through 2007, but his numbers fizzled, and he was traded in 2009 to the Mets.

Not Francoeur, though. At least not initially. He was a 6′4″, 220-pounder who turned down a football scholarship at Clemson as a strong safety to play baseball. You would, too, if the Braves had made you their first-round pick in the 2002 baseball draft and signed you for $2.2 million. When he was called up in 2005, the gushing began.

"Winner written all over it," Atlanta manager Bobby Cox said of Francoeur's fresh young face.

"He's like Roy Hobbs," Braves pitcher Tim Hudson told Mike Farber, the outstanding *SI* writer working on that cover-story profile. "I'm waiting for him to come out of the bullpen and start striking guys out, throwing 98 [mph]. Or to start hitting bombs left-handed."

Francoeur was born in 1984, the year *The Natural* hit the big screen. At least he knew Hudson was referencing the Redford character in the film who hits the stadium light tower in the movie's finale. When Farber explained to Francoeur that in Malamud's novel the tragic hero strikes out, the kid laughed and shouted, "That's why books suck!"

It didn't take long for opponents to learn the book on Frenchy. He was an aggressive, impatient hitter who looked for fastballs and flailed at breaking balls down and away. In 2006, his first full season, Francoeur batted .260 with 29 homers and 103 RBIs while playing in all 162 games. He didn't miss a game in '07 either, hitting .293 with 19 homers and 105 RBIs while winning a Gold Glove.

But in 2008, in the midst of an awful slump, Francoeur was sent down to the Double A Mississippi Braves to work with his old hitting coach, Phillip Wellman. That helped some but didn't last. Neither, eventually, did Francoeur. On July 10, 2009, he was traded to the New York Mets. In 2010 he was dealt at the trade deadline to the World Series–bound Texas Rangers.

While his attitude was excellent, the part-timer Francoeur's numbers were down in all categories. His combined slugging percentage for both the Mets and Rangers was just .383. His OPS was .683. Over his last 61 regular season games for the Mets, Francoeur batted .198 with four homers and 19 RBIs in 187 at-bats. All this, after that unnaturally hot start to begin his career. He's now a Kansas City Royal.

90 Mound Rushmore

It came to Marty Noble in the Turner Field press box one afternoon, during yet another virtuoso pitching performance by yet another Hall of Famer–in-waiting. Might've been Maddux. Could've been Glavine, or maybe Smoltz? Didn't matter. Looking down at the infield, Noble—Jersey guy by birth but an esteemed veteran New York baseball writer—spied the pitcher's mound and had a great notion.

"Mound Rushmore." Yes.

This was the site of incomparable pitching excellence in the late '90s and early to mid-2000s, the red Georgia clay canvas for the art of pitching. It's where Tom Glavine won his second National League Cy Young Award in 1998. It's where Greg Maddux, he of the record four straight Cy Youngs, out-foxed everyone, proving, as he put it, that movement and location are more important than velocity. It's where John Smoltz, a year after his overwhelming 1996 Cy Young performance across the street, continued to dominate, especially in the postseason.

"Mound Rushmore." Yes, indeed.

Those three men, the Big Three of the Atlanta Braves, were permanent pitching fixtures looming as large and imposing to opposing batters as the famous faces on Mount Rushmore. That lineup of George Washington, Thomas Jefferson, Teddy Roosevelt, and Abraham Lincoln, carved into the granite face of a South Dakota mountain—back in the four-president rotation days—was rigid. Literally cast in stone. Not so Mound Rushmore.

It actually had its genesis across Ralph David Abernathy Boulevard, in old Atlanta-Fulton County Stadium. That's where the Big Three, the permanent trio on the original Mound Rushmore, had their greatest moments together.

Glavine was just a kid when he won his first Cy Young in '91, the first Brave to do so since Warren Spahn in 1957. Then Maddux, the big-money free agent who'd won the Cy Young with the Cubs in '92, captured the next three straight in Atlanta. Then Smoltz, overpowering in '96, won an Atlanta-record 24 games and four more in the postseason. He was the winning pitcher in the All-Star Game that year, giving him 29 victories in all.

Those three were fixtures, pitching perennials. The fourth face on Mound Rushmore varied. Initially, it appeared Steve Avery would round out the mound quartet for keeps. Ave was "Poison Avery" in the early '90s (thank you, Andy Van Slyke), especially in his 18-win campaigns of '91 and '93, and while winning the '91 NLCS MVP.

Later, the No. 4 man rotated to Denny Neagle. Kevin Millwood. Mark Wohlers in relief, if briefly. A reborn John Burkett. Russ Ortiz. Tim Hudson. Smoltz again, only in relief. Now, Jair Jurrjens and Tommy Hanson. Good-bye, Billy Wagner. Thanks and godspeed.

Under pitching coach Leo Mazzone's rockin' tutelage and now Roger McDowell's fine guidance, Mound Rushmore pitches on. It was Ground Zero for so much of the greatest collective, prolonged pitching the game has ever witnessed. And likely ever will.

Maddux and Glavine, both 300-game winners, are Cooperstown locks as first-ballot Hall of Famers. The Braves have already retired their numbers, 31 and 47, respectively. Smoltz's 29 will be next. As the only pitcher in baseball history with more than 200 victories and 150 saves, Smoltz will join Mad Dog and Glav in the Hall, too, very likely in his first year of eligibility.

Yet even before then, and for years afterward, that threesome should be immortalized—in bronze, out there in Monument Grove at Turner Field. There already are individual statues of Aaron, Spahn, Niekro. There should be a bronzed Big Three, too, a three-man sculpture of Maddux, Glavine, and Smoltz. Not pitching, just standing beside each other. Maybe one guy's hand on his hip, another's elbow up on the third guy's shoulder. Whatever the makeup, the title will be easy: "Mound Rushmore." Yes, indeed.

91 Oly

"I had steak tonight."

The ear on the other end of the phone call wasn't sure it had heard properly. So…

"Excuse me?"

"I had steak tonight," the woman's voice repeated. And then Lisa Olson and her husband's Boswell both roared with laughter.

Oly. Ahhh, Oly. If it's October of 1991, the best month in Atlanta Braves history, this must be Oly. Greg Olson, opining about, well, almost everything from the World Series to waterbeds.

It was titled "Greg Olson's Playoff Diary," and it quickly became required daily reading in the *Atlanta Journal-Constitution*, as did its sequel, "Greg Olson's World Series Diary." I know. I was Olson's diarist. Each morning he regaled readers with his daily doings, his game exploits, his seemingly endless supply of freebies. Oly's philosophy: if it's free, it's for me. Rental cars for the in-laws. Krispy Kremes. A complimentary hotel room for a relative. The catcher pitched unabashedly, and why not?

In essence, each was the Diary of a Glad Backstop, of a minor league lifer who came to the Braves as a 29-year-old rookie, won the starting catcher's job and the hearts of a city, then packed more into four years than some White House administrations do. And did so with a real sense of joy.

Oly was an opportunist in every sense, but in the very best sense of the word. Given an opportunity, he seized it, whether it be a starting position or a free pizza.

For a while, he tattooed the baseball with his bat as deftly as he autographed it.

"I thought, *If I don't take advantage of these opportunities now, I'll say, why didn't I do that?*" said Olson, who quickly became a congenial fan favorite at signings and card shows. "It wasn't that I was money-hungry. I liked it. I'm a people person. I actually like doing that stuff....

"That was my mentality: do what you can at the time."

In a four-year career with the Braves, Olson played in one All-Star Game, one World Series, and two National League Championship Series. "You look back at some Hall of Fame players," he said, "they'd kill to play in one World Series."

In 1990 Olson somehow made the club as the last man on the roster. He worked one game with Tom Glavine, who liked how Olson caught him. So did some other pitchers. Olson got hot with the bat—hitting a career-high .262—and became the first Braves rookie since 1968 named to the National League All-Star team. In '91, when newly acquired catcher Mike Heath developed bone chips, the job was all Oly's.

He got several clutch hits during the out-of-nowhere pennant drive that captivated Atlanta. "Absolutely bazonkers," was Olson's take on the city's frenzy over its worst-to-first Braves. When they clinched the NL West on the penultimate day of the season, Olson provided the perfect photo op—leaping into the arms of winning pitcher John Smoltz. Or "Schmoltzie," as Oly still calls his old battery mate.

In the NLCS Olson led the team in hitting (.333) and free testimonials. In Game 3 he belted a two-run homer and even stole a base in a 10–3 rout of Pittsburgh. Afterward, when Olson held court at his locker, a local sportscaster sarcastically asked, "Who does he think he is, Johnny Bench?"

"He was today," said Braves coach Pat Corrales, who should know. A career backup catcher, he'd spent four seasons as Bench's caddie.

In the World Series in his native Minnesota, Olson had another frozen-in-time photographic moment. The Twins' Dan Gladden barreled home and flipped Olson on his head. To this day, Oly still signs several dozen prints of the photo at the annual off-season Twins Fest. To this day, he still watches the magnificent Game 7 pitching duel between Jack Morris and Schmoltzie on ESPN Classic, still hoping against hope that "somebody edits that thing and we score a run." But Minnesota still wins 1–0 every time on a base hit by Oly's good friend and hunting buddy Gene Larkin.

In 1992 Olson shared the catching duties with Damon Berryhill. He missed the postseason after fracturing his right leg on September 18. Carted off the field wearing an air cast and neck brace, Olson reassured his wife—who he knew was watching on TV—by doing the Tomahawk Chop. In Game 7 of that epic NLCS Olson threw down his crutches and, thigh-to-ankle cast and all, hopped from the dugout to the plate after Sid Bream slid home safely to win the pennant.

Following one more season with the Braves, Olson went home to Minnesota in '94 after being released by the Mets in spring training. And he went home gladly to be with his family and to sell real estate. It was time. And as Oly knows, "Timing is everything, isn't it?"

92 The Catcher's Box Brouhaha

On the last June weekend in the 2000 season, the Milwaukee Brewers came to Turner Field. Once Friday night's game ended, Brewers manager Davey Lopes walked out to home plate to talk to John Shulock, the chief of the umpiring crew working that series. The two men were looking down and gesturing at the area behind the plate. The white-lined area where a catcher plies his tools of the trade.

Upstairs in a broadcast booth, Pete Van Wieren and other broadcasters took notice. The official rules of baseball dictate that the chalk-lined catcher's box be precisely 43 inches wide. Davey Lopes thought the Turner Field catcher's box was a little too wide. That, of course, would enable catchers—specifically Braves catchers—to set up just a bit further off the plate, the better to get more called strikes on the corners. As baseball knew all too well, pitchers Greg Maddux and Tom Glavine made a living on the corners, benefiting from borderline called strikes.

Van Wieren and others in the broadcast booth had a hunch, but called down to the TBS truck and asked them to record all this. Just in case.

The following night, Atlanta catcher Fernando Lunar was called for a catcher's balk—a real rarity in baseball. Lunar had lined up with one foot out of the catcher's box. Manager Bobby Cox came out and was promptly ejected for arguing the rare call. Banished to the clubhouse, Cox was watching on TV and listening as the broadcasters related what they'd seen the night before between Lopes and Shulock. TV then superimposed the Friday night catcher's box over Saturday's version. The Saturday box was smaller.

As Van Wieren later recalled, no one was certain which box was the right size, but the broadcasters had their suspicions. To wit, he suggested the "possibility that the Braves had gotten caught bending the rules a bit." Though he also considered the possibility that "a simple mistake had been made by the ground crew on one of those nights."

Cox heard all this and was, well, not amused. Neither were general manager John Schuerholz and team president Stan Kasten. The broadcasters—Van Wieren and Skip Caray, Don Sutton and Joe Simpson—were merely doing their jobs, reporting a developing story. Simpson's timing was particularly bad. He was talking on the air when the banished Cox turned on the TV in the clubhouse.

That Sunday the front office took out its anger—or maybe embarrassment?—on the messengers, not the message. The four broadcasters were banned from flying on the team charter. Said Van Wieren, "This seemed a strange way to punish us, if that's what they were trying to do."

With the Braves flying to Montreal the next day, the club had to buy four commercial airline tickets for the broadcasters—all four in first class, as stipulated in their contracts. They'd have to be reimbursed for cab fare to the team hotel and for airport parking back home. The broadcast crew was told not to tell any of this to the media.

Beat writers Carroll Rogers of the *Atlanta Journal-Constitution* and Bill Zack of the *Gwinnett Daily News* knew something was up, however, when they boarded their Monday flight to Montreal. Pete, Skip, Don, and Joe were sitting in first class.

The front page headline in Tuesday's *Journal-Constitution* read, "Truth Won't Fly On Braves' Plane?"

The following day the situation was resolved by team and TV officials, but not before the broadcasters, who'd booked tickets for the entire road trip, had a three-game stop in New York for that series before flying home. Besides the extra travel expenses, the Braves also paid a significant fine for illegally lining the catcher's box. Or was it simply an accident?

"We were never really able to find out exactly what happened here," Van Wieren recalled years later. "In fact, if you want to have a conversation end quickly, just ask Bobby Cox or any other Braves official about the catcher's box incident in 2000."

93 The Babe a Brave?

Yes. So was Casey. Big Poison, too. Also Hornsby and Rabbit, Ducky and Cy. Yes, that Cy. As in Denton "Cy" Young.

Those are seven of baseball's immortals who, in their career twilights, wore the uniform of the Boston franchise that eventually became the Atlanta Braves. The greatest, of course, literally being the biggest. "The Bambino." "The Sultan of Swat." Once and forever the game's greatest star, personality, performer. The Babe.

"You have been a great asset to baseball…your greatest value to a ballclub would be your personal appearance on the ball field," wrote Judge Emil Fuchs, owner of the Boston Braves, in a letter dated February 23, 1935, welcoming George Herman "Babe" Ruth to the ballclub.

In the grip of the Great Depression, Fuchs, who bought the Braves in 1923, was nearly broke after the stock market crash of 1929. By 1935, his franchise was near bankruptcy. Financially desperate, Fuchs planned to put a dog-racing track in the outfield and run races there when the Braves were playing on the road. The National League was not amused and nixed the plan. Desperate for money, for fans, Fuchs needed a cash cow.

His target: Babe Ruth, the game's greatest attraction. Having hit his 700th homer late in the '34 season, Ruth had announced that his days as an everyday player were over. He was 40, overweight, not adroit enough to play the field. He still had his classic swing, but even that would soon desert him. Fuchs wanted the Babe as a draw in Boston, where Ruth began his career with the Red Sox in 1914 before being traded to the Yankees in 1920.

The Babe, however, hoped to manage the Braves. That would never happen. Nor would his home run swing return, although he delighted some 25,000 fans on Opening Day with a two-run homer off the great New York Giant Carl Hubbell in a 4–2 win. So much for that. Even in spring training, Ruth admitted, "Kids were striking me out or getting me to pop up on pitches I would have hit out of the park a few years earlier. And it was more and more of an effort to move at first base or run the bases. It was just torture."

Torturous, too, for fans to see the great Babe bottom out. As part of the $25,000 contract he'd signed with Fuchs, Ruth also was an assistant manager to Bill McKechnie, but Babe never managed a game and had a limited partnership in the franchise. Also, McKechnie was neither retiring nor looking to become the team's general manager. On May 12 Ruth told Fuchs and McKechnie he was done.

Yet Fuchs had all sorts of promotions planned around Ruth. Opposing teams had scheduled their own Babe Ruth Days, too, with big advance ticket sales.

"You can't quit now," said Fuchs, so Ruth didn't. While his average plunged to .181, he still had his moments, especially a three-homer game one day in Pittsburgh. The last one, an estimated 600-footer, was the 714th and last of Ruth's career.

Ruth, as he'd promised Fuchs, remained on the active roster for the last two stops—Philadelphia and Cincinnati—on the road. He went hitless in three games in Cincinnati, striking out three times in the first, and left the second with a bum knee. In Philly, two more games, two more strikeouts, and, after hurting his knee chasing a fly ball in the first inning, Ruth took himself out of the game. The 2,503rd and last of his 22-year career.

There was one final indignity. With the Giants and Dodgers coming to Brooklyn and, perhaps, drawing big crowds with Ruth facing his old New York rivals, Fuchs wanted Ruth to play one more week. But the Babe, with his bad knee, was going to New York, to a reception in honor of the arrival of the ocean liner *Normandie*. Fuchs was livid. Ruth said his knee was too sore to play and called the owner "a dirty double-crosser." Fuchs promptly released him, then got in the last jab—blaming the Babe for Boston's 9–27 record and ongoing 1–10 slump.

Charles Dillon "Casey" Stengel played his last two seasons (1924–1925) as a Boston Brave. His '25 farewell was a cameo: 12 games, 13 at-bats, one hit, and an .077 average, slightly below his lifetime .284 mark.

In 1938 "the Old Professor" succeeded McKechnie as the manager. He'd been living in Texas, where he'd made a killing investing in the oil business after being fired as Brooklyn's manager following three lousy seasons (1934–1936). Bob Quinn, the new GM of the newly named Bees, wanted Stengel's showmanship, his "Stengelese" way of speaking, and also some of his oil money.

Quinn convinced Casey to invest in the club, as well as manage it. Stengel also gave Boston fans a show, as he had in the mid-1920s, when he took off his cap for the National Anthem one game and a sparrow flew out. While chasing a fly ball in the outfield during an exhibition game, Stengel disappeared down a manhole. His ballclubs, however, were far less entertaining. The Bees weren't talented to begin with—the World War II talent drought only exacerbated that.

In 1942 Stengel had the pleasure of managing Paul "Big Poison" Waner, Pittsburgh's Hall of Fame outfielder. Waner, 39, got his 3,000th hit as a Bee in '42 (he finished with 3,152). He'd hoped to bow out in style in '43, primarily as a pinch-hitter. But Stengel kept Waner in that weak lineup, even playing him in both ends of a series of doubleheaders that August. Finally, when a hit rolled by him, Big Poison fell down and stayed there, the ball lying just a few feet from him.

Stengel was fired following the 1943 season; he missed the first two months after being hit by a car, his leg badly broken. In five-plus seasons Stengel was 373–491. His postmortem, courtesy of Dave Egan of the *Boston Record*: "The man who did the most for Boston in 1943 was the motorist who ran Stengel down two days before the opening game and kept him away from the Braves for two months."

In 1942 a rookie named Warren Spahn pitched in four games for the Bees before entering the military during World War II. In the 1957 and '58 World Series Spahn faced Stengel, who managed the mighty Yankees during their dominance. Spahn's final season in 1965 began as a New York Met, managed by…Casey Stengel, in his last season in baseball with, as he called them, the "Amazin' Mets."

Spahn, never enamored of Casey, said, "I'm probably the only guy who worked for Stengel before and after he was a genius." Stengel died at age 85 in 1975.

"Rajah" was a Brave, too. Rogers Hornsby, one of the game's greatest right-handed hitters—and to some still its greatest second baseman—played in 1928 for the Braves. He also managed them for most of that season. He batted .387, winning the last of his seven NL batting titles, but that was no anomaly. His career average of .358 is second only to Ty Cobb. His .424 average in 1924 is a 20th-century record.

Hornsby was haughty, too. Early in the '28 season he said he'd seek a trade rather than continue playing for first-year manager Jack Slattery. Owner Emil Fuchs fired Slattery and made Hornsby a player/manager. His inaugural address to his teammates: "I don't smoke, drink, or chew. I can hit to left, center, and right. They call me a great player. If you do like I do, you can be a great player, too."

Hornsby's alienated club went 39–83 under his tutelage, the club finishing with 103 total losses. Just four other Braves teams fared worse: 1935 (115 losses), 1909 (108), 1911 (107), and 1988 (106). After the season, Hornsby talked his way out of town, telling Fuchs, "Judge, you need a young club, and I have about one year left in me. Why don't you let me make a deal for myself with Chicago?"

So at age 33, Hornsby went to the Cubs, for whom he hit .380 in 1929, the first of his four seasons in Wrigley Field. In 1933 Hornsby returned to St. Louis, where he'd begun his career in 1915 and spent 12 years as a Cardinal. He split the '33 season with the Cards and St. Louis Browns before retiring as a Brown in '37.

Rabbit, run? You bet. Rabbit Maranville stole 194 bases for the Braves, for whom the little Hall of Fame shortstop played 15 seasons in a 23-year career. But it was his glovework that made Maranville memorable. The 5′5″, 155-pound sparkplug of the 1914 Boston Braves helped make those wunderkinds the world champion "Miracle Braves."

Rabbit and second baseman Johnny Evers combined to lead the league in double plays that year. Maranville hit .308 in the four-game sweep of the powerful A's in that World Series.

On his Cooperstown Hall of Fame plaque, his nickname's listed as "Ducky Wucky." But his fellow "Gas House Gang" members of the 1930s St. Louis Cardinals merely called him "Ducky," which Medwick wasn't when he joined the Boston Braves midway through the 1945 season. It had been eight years since the left fielder won the 1937 Triple Crown and was voted the NL MVP. A notorious bad-ball hitter, Medwick led the league with a .374 average, 31 homers, and 154 RBIs. Things weren't ducky in Boston—in 66 games, he hit .284 with 26 RBIs and no homers. But Ducky, too, was a Boston Brave.

And old Cy Young was, too. It's almost criminal that the winningest pitcher in baseball history finished his incomparable career with the Boston Rustlers. Moving from Cleveland to the Rustlers in 1911, the 44-year-old Young got the last four of his record 511 victories with Boston. He'd had 15 20-win seasons, including nine consecutive from 1891 to 1899. Five of those were 30-win seasons, and his career ERA was 2.63. Although Young was just 4–5 as a Rustler, there's a reason—511 reasons actually—his name is on the trophy presented annually to the top pitcher in each league.

Lloyd "Little Poison" Waner, younger brother of Paul "Big Poison" Waner, spent one year with the Boston Braves in his waning years. In 1941, playing just 19 games, Little Poison batted .412, the once-speedy slap hitter going 21-for-51.

Christy Mathewson, the turn-of-the-20th-century pitcher whom some still call the greatest ever, was the Boston Braves team president from 1923 to 1925. Mathewson, nicknamed "Big Six," won 373 games (still third all-time) with the New York Giants, losing 188. He completed 434 of 551 career starts. In failing health when he took the Braves' presidency, Mathewson died in 1925 at age 45.

94 Go on a Braves Field Field Trip

Or at least what's left of it. While you're in Boston, you can also visit other sites where the Boston Braves once played. The South End Grounds. The Congress Street Grounds. Even Fenway Park, the home of the Red Sox that the Braves used on occasion. But you must begin at Braves Field. Now part of multisport Nickerson Field at Boston University, it was once baseball's biggest, brightest ballpark jewel.

"It is the last word in baseball parks," John K. Tener proclaimed on August 18, 1915. The National League president helped hoist the 1914 Miracle Braves NL pennant that day, in conjunction with the grand opening of the new stadium. With a seating capacity of 43,400, Braves Field was the largest ballpark in America. To James

Gaffney, it was the "perfect ballpark." At least to the Braves owner who built Braves Field to his specifications. "Obviously," Braves historian Gary Caruso wrote in *The Braves Encyclopedia*, "he was a pitchers' owner."

The original dimensions: 402 feet down the left- and right-field lines. Straightaway center: 520 feet. Deep right-center: 550 feet. With a stiff wind often blowing in from center off the Charles River.

When Ty Cobb took a look from home plate, he predicted, "No home run will ever go over that fence. This is the only field in the country on which you can play an absolutely fair game of ball without the interference of fences."

It's not that Gaffney didn't dig the long ball, he just preferred inside-the-parkers. It took nearly a decade before Frank "Pancho" Snyder cleared the left-field wall. Until the distances were dramatically shortened in 1928, only seven home runs were hit over the wall, as opposed to 209 inside-the-park homers. In 1922 the Giants hit four in one gusty game.

Gaffney spent $1 million to build his spacious palace. Some features included a trolley line that dropped off and picked up fans inside the stadium, and the celebrated "Jury Box," as the 2,000 vocal fans in the right-field bleachers came to be known and to cheer on right fielder Tommy Holmes.

Although the Braves never played a World Series, a young Red Sox left-hander did during the 1916 World Series when Gaffney let the Sox use his larger park. Babe Ruth threw 13 scoreless innings after allowing a run in the first to beat Brooklyn 2–1 in Game 2 of the Series. The Babe later homered in his first game as a Brave in 1935, when his career was ending.

By 1936, the team was under new ownership and called the Bees, with the ballpark known as the Beehive. It had its moments: the first National League victory in an All-Star Game in '36. One game ended when a hurricane struck. Outfielder Sam Jethroe broke the color barrier in Boston baseball there. After owner Lou Perini and his two co-owners, "The Three Little Steam Shovels," made $500,000 worth of stadium improvements in 1946, nearly 1 million fans turned out. Some sat in new skyboxes on the grandstand roof.

Nearly 1.5 million savored Boston's "Spahn and Sain" 1948 pennant winners, but saw only one World Series win in person—Johnny Sain's 1–0 duel with Bob Feller in the opener before Cleveland prevailed in six games. By 1952, though, season attendance bottomed out at 281,278. Just 8,822 watched the season finale, but that was the Braves' second-largest crowd all season. Milwaukee beckoned.

Perini sold Braves Field to Boston University in 1953 for $500,000. It became the home of BU football, and its name later changed to Nickerson Field. Just the original right-field pavilion portion, since refurbished, remains now and has been incorporated into the stadium. The university dropped football in 1997, but the field is home to BU's men's and women's soccer teams, and women's lacrosse.

In Boston, you can also visit the site of the South End Grounds, once a grassy field with a small wooden grandstand built just before the Boston Red Stockings, as the club was known in 1871, began play. It later became the double-decked "Grand Pavilion" to accommodate crowds itching to see Boston's "$20,000 Battery" of King Kelly and John Clarkson. It also became the Atlanta-Fulton County Stadium of its time.

Unlike the situation with the fire that destroyed only part of the stadium press box in Atlanta in 1993, the old wooden ballpark was burned to the ground on May 15, 1894, after a fire accidentally began under the stands. Everything was destroyed, including some 170 buildings in 12 acres around the park. Even the 1893 pennant went up in flames. Damages were estimated at $1 million, with 1,000 people left homeless. Amazingly, the park was rebuilt in just over a month, and play resumed on July 20. But the new park was smaller and not well maintained.

In the interim, Boston played at the Congress Street Grounds next to Boston Harbor. The Beaneaters, as the club was then called, loved the 250-foot left-field fence. That was especially true of Bobby Lowe. Between games of a Memorial Day doubleheader, the little second baseman went to a local restaurant for lunch. Then, after striking out in his first at-bat in the second game, Lowe hit four consecutive homers over the 250-foot wall in left, two coming in a nine-run third inning. He was the first player in baseball history to hit four homers—whatever the distances—in a game.

95 Do the Fredi

As managerial successions go, this one seems as seamless as it appears addressed for success. Bobby Cox retires. What's a front office to do? Do the Fredi. And so they did.

Less than 48 hours after Cox retired following his 25th season as manager of the Braves, the club hired a familiar face—Fredi Gonzalez, Cox's third-base coach from 2003 to 2006 before becoming the Florida Marlins manager. It was a foregone conclusion that Gonzalez would eventually succeed Cox once he was fired last June by Florida.

He was the skipper-in-waiting, if not fully in residence, although Gonzalez and his family still maintained their Marietta home once he took the Marlins job. Fredi was familiar with the team, the terrain, and the tradition.

"Our goal is simple," he said at his reintroductory press conference. "We want to keep putting flags on that façade up there"—the one high above left in Turner Field, where flags commemorate the record 14 consecutive division titles the Braves won from 1991 to 2005. That's 13 yellow pennants for divisional titles, and one red flag for the 1995 World Series champions.

"I don't think there's a person alive who can replace Bobby Cox," Gonzalez said. "We just want to continue the winning tradition and go from there."

"Let me just say this," Cox offered at that October press conference, sitting deferentially by his protégé's side and drawing a Dodgers comparison. "Walter Alston was replaced by Tommy Lasorda. Tommy did a great job and they forgot all about Walter Alston. That is what's going to happen here."

"This is perfect for us on so many levels," said Braves general manager Frank Wren, who's known the Cuban-born Gonzalez for two decades. Wren was the Marlins' assistant GM when the club hired Gonzalez in 1992 to manage their Class A Erie team.

"He's got a great personality." Wren said. "Players gravitate toward him. They like playing for him. It's important that guys like playing for you, because they'll usually play even better. We've seen him over the course of time. Managing at the major league level is different, but we saw what he did at Florida. He ran a good game."

Gonzalez was 276–279 in three and a half seasons as the Marlins manager. He's the winningest manager in the history of a dysfunctional franchise that has won two World Series but now labors under the frugal ownership of Jeffrey Loria. It was Loria who fired Gonzalez the previous June after the manager benched shortstop Hanley Ramirez for not hustling. After confronting his best player in the dugout, Gonzalez yanked him. Loria was angry. Most of baseball was impressed. Fredi was nonplussed.

"That's the way I was brought up," said Gonzalez. "I know the way the game should be played. If you don't do something, you're going to lose those 24 other guys. For me, it was a simple thing to do."

It enhanced his reputation and résumé and got props from lots of baseball people. Fredi's cred. That's what they said.

Then-third-base coach Fredi Gonzalez congratulates Chipper Jones on a solo home run against the Phillies in a 2004 game in Philadelphia. Gonzalez was the natural choice to succeed Bobby Cox as manager, and he did so after Cox's retirement following the 2010 season.

When Cox announced after the 2009 season that 2010 would be his last, the Braves began compiling a list of 15 or 16 potential managerial candidates. Gonzalez, at 46, was atop that wish list even then.

"He was on our radar before he was available," Wren said. "We thought there may come a time when we were going to have to ask the Florida Marlins for permission to talk to their manager. We really thought Fredi was the best candidate for us."

Barely a week after Gonzalez was fired in Florida, he and Wren drove to the GM's lake cabin in Alabama. They talked baseball and managing for nearly six hours. After that, Wren never talked to another candidate. A few days later, team president John Schuerholz interviewed Gonzalez. He, too, came away highly impressed. In September, the two executives conducted a final interview that was a mere formality. Fredi was their guy.

"It was kind of a perfect storm," Wren told Braves beat writer David O'Brien. "An upheaval in his life when it happened, but I think at the same time, it worked out very well for us.

"It's perfect for us because of the job he's done in Florida, but also the familiarity, the players' familiarity [with Gonzalez]."

When Gonzalez took the Marlins job in 2007, Cox advised, "You are who you are. You've got to be yourself." That's true now, too.

"Fredi's got the right makeup to be a great manager. He has all the respect around baseball that you can get. I just want to be in the background," said Cox, who has a five-year consultant's contract with the Braves. "There's always going to be new starts, and Fredi is getting a new start here."

"For me, it was a really easy decision," said Gonzalez, the *Sporting News* Manager of the Year in 2008, when the Marlins went 84–77 while saddled with the lowest payroll in the majors. Returning to the Braves was so appealing that Gonzalez, after overtures from at least four teams—including the cash-rich Chicago Cubs—declined to even be interviewed.

"It's a hell of an organization," he said of the Braves. "It's a good fit.... I don't feel any outside pressure because I'm the next guy after Bobby. It never crossed my mind to shy away from being that guy. Somebody's got to do it. I'm honored they asked me to do it."

Gonzalez said he wouldn't make "a lot of crazy changes.... Whoever comes in has their own little way of doing things." Like many teams, the Braves will now stretch on the field before taking batting practice. Cox, old-school, never did that.

There were immediate changes in the coaching staff. Longtime first base coach Glenn Hubbard and bench coach Chino Cadahia were fired. Terry Pendleton, no longer the hitting coach, took Hubbard's role. Carlos Tosca, who coached under Gonzalez in Florida, replaced Cadahia. Three coaches were retained in their respective jobs: pitching coach Roger McDowell, third-base coach Brian Snitker, and bullpen coach Eddie Perez.

Don't expect to see Gonzalez riding his Harley to Turner Field, like he and good buddy Pendleton often did while on Cox's staff. Do expect Fredi to be his own man.

"He can't be Bobby," Wren, who stressed that to Gonzalez, told Dave O'Brien. "There's not going to be another Bobby Cox. Fredi needs to do things just as he did them in Florida, even if it's different than the way we have done things here for the last 20-some years.

"Fredi needs to do things his way. That's how he's going to be most natural and most genuine, by being himself."

"He knows the game of baseball inside-out," Cox said. "He's got a great personality with players. His communication skills are excellent. Anything you'd want in a young manager, Fredi possesses. It'll be an easy transition."

96 Why Love a Parade?

Why not? How could you not? Certainly not if you were in downtown Atlanta on Tuesday, October 29, 1991. It was an absolutely gorgeous autumn afternoon, the kind that reminds Atlantans, "This is why we live here and love it here. This is one of the golden days." Golden, yes, yet unlike any other in the history of the city.

The official estimate: 750,000 people. That's three-quarters of a million people. That's how many people city officials estimated had come downtown to say thank you and to embrace their worst-to-first Braves.

Two nights earlier, in a domed stadium in chilly Minneapolis, the Atlanta Braves very nearly completed the greatest, most unlikely turnaround in baseball history. Now back home in Georgia, on a beautiful Indian summer day, the Braves got to cruise down Peachtree Street in style, in a two-mile-long lovefest down Atlanta's main artery, in a caravan of top-down convertibles and a few open-air trucks that would've seemed ludicrous seven months earlier.

"If you would have told me I'd be riding through downtown Atlanta in a parade," catcher Greg Olson said, "I would have told you you're nuts."

The Braves had captured the city, and now Atlanta was trying to return the favor. By far the largest congregation of people in the city's history, the crowds were as thick as they were jubilant. The Lemmer, Mark Lemke, a rock star? You betcha. David Justice won thousands of hearts that day. Oly the catcher, the unlikely hitting hero of the National League Championship Series, doffed his white Braves cap again and again and again.

The noise was deafening, the shrieks of teenage girls a sound once reserved for the Beatles. Tickertape and confetti and plain pieces of paper fell from the sky from office buildings along the parade route. The crowds slipped past police lines and barricades, anything to get closer to their heroes.

Terry Pendleton, who would be voted the National League's Most Valuable Player later that year, wore a brown suit and a permanent smile and waved from a convertible. A memorable photograph by Joey Ivansco, a photographer for the *Atlanta Journal-Constitution*, showed four pairs of shoes and eight lower legs standing on the hood of a white pickup truck. The caption read: "Boys on the Hood."

"Imagine if we'd won the Series," hitting coach Clarence Jones said in wonder.

No matter. Atlanta had fallen under the spell of its never-quit ballclub months earlier. Fans were now still chopping and chanting for their Boys of Autumn. So they'd lost, agonizingly so. So what of it? Of the hundreds and hundreds of handmade signs along that Peachtree corridor, one spoke for many: "It's Better to Have Chopped and Lost than Never to Have Chopped at All!"

At long last, the parade was nearing its end at City Hall. No one wanted it to end. Brian Hunter, the rookie first baseman, turned and looked back up Peachtree Street. "I wish," he said, "I could turn around and go through it again."

"There is no feeling in the world like this. Nothing, no way," said John Schuerholz, the general manager and architect of it all. "It has to be one of baseball's all-time great stories."

And one of Atlanta's most golden days ever. Why love a parade? You had to.

97 Meet Matthew, the Music Man

He's the ballpark organist who plays "Feliz Navidad" for Pedro Feliz, the Looney Tunes theme for James Loney, "Stairway to Heaven" for Floyd Bannister, and the theme from *Blazing Saddles* for Chase Headley—as in Hedley LaMarr.

He serenaded Adam LaRoche with "La Cucaracha," Wladimir Balentien with "My Funny Valentine," Miguel Cairo with "Walk Like an Egyptian," and did "The Hokey Pokey" for Hiroki Kuroda. For Placido Polanco? "La Donna e Mobile," which renowned tenor Placido Domingo always knocks out of the park.

He's also an organ grinder, a needler who once improvised "Satin Doll" when Cameron Maybin fouled a ball off his ankle and left the game. It's "Mighty Mouse" when 5′7″ David Eckstein comes to bat, "This Old Man" for 41-year-old Brad Ausmus.

After pitcher Tim Lincecum was cited for misdemeanor marijuana possession following the 2009 season, the two-time NL Cy Young Award winner was welcomed back to Turner Field last August with "Puff the Magic Dragon." When the Giants complained, Matthew Kaminski quickly switched to "The Joker" by the Steve Miller Band. Or was it "Purple Haze" by Hendrix? Maybe both.

For the past two seasons, Kaminski, 34, has been the wildly popular organist at Turner Field. A professional musician and music teacher, he came by his musicianship naturally. The Chicago native is the son of Polish immigrants. His father, grandfather, and great-grandfather all learned to play the accordion and other instruments by ear back in Poland. Matthew is trained and versatile, and his is a thoroughly modern milieu.

Not only does he play with a jazz combo, he regularly moonlights on Saturday nights with Orquesta MaCuba, a Cuban salsa band that packs the dance floor at Loca Luna, a club in midtown. It's at Turner Field, however, that Kaminski has his most devoted following.

A 21st-century musician, he's on Twitter. Sitting in his press box aerie, he regularly gets tweets from fans during Braves games, suggesting songs for opposing players who come to bat. Or tweeters will respond to ditties that Kaminski comes up with himself. "That is brilliant!" one replied last season to "Mighty Mouse" for Eckstein.

A perfectionist who was once very shy, Kaminski graduated from Georgia State in 2000, then expanded his musical horizons. As he told Atlanta writer Michelle Hiskey, he played the accordion for an Edith Piaf impersonator in Birmingham. He played for a burlesque group called The Dames Aflame. He played with a polka band, Lawrentz Un Die Katzen.

In 2009, when one of his piano students mentioned the Braves were looking for an organist, Kaminski applied and got the job. In baseball parlance, he's already become at least a four-tool player, and the latest in a fine line of Braves organists.

In 1988, fresh out of high school, Carolyn King, 18, was hired by Ted Turner. The piano player on Sunday mornings at Ebenezer Baptist Church, King was the one who led the crowd in the Tomahawk Chop in the heady early '90s. In the late '80s, after San Diego pitcher Bob Knepper complained in a national publication about women being allowed in the clubhouse, King played Helen Reddy's "I Am Woman" when he walked to the plate.

She stopped playing in Turner Field in 2004 to spend more time with her family.

Her predecessor, Lowery Ballew, played for the Braves before becoming the Florida Marlins' organist.

A footnote, or grace note, if you will: in 1954, the Braves' second season in Milwaukee, a woman was hosting a local TV show called *Jivin' with Jarvis* while doubling as the staff pianist and organist at WTMJ. The team wanted her to play the organ at Milwaukee County Stadium; she did so for eight years before moving to Manhattan in 1962, the year the Mets were born. In New York, Jane Jarvis became the celebrated organist for the Mets, famous for playing "Meet the Mets" and "The Mexican Hat Dance" during the seventh-inning stretch at Shea Stadium.

She'd come a long way from her job interview with the Milwaukee Braves. As she told a *New York Times* writer in 1984, Jarvis wondered when she'd get to perform during games, and the Braves official answered, "When the umpire says, 'Three outs.'" To which Jarvis replied, "And when would that be?"

An accomplished musician and performer, Jane Jarvis died in 2010 at age 94.

98 The Mann on the PA

In this age of bombast and buffoonery on public-address systems throughout the world of sports, Marshall Mann would not have fit in. Proudly so. For 30 years, he'd been the voice from on high, the PA man at Atlanta-Fulton County Stadium, the only one Atlanta Braves fans had ever known since Opening Night on April 12, 1966.

Three decades later, October 24, 1996 was a bummer of a Thursday evening for Braves fans everywhere, but especially those in the old bowl of a ballpark. The Braves, reigning world champions and seemingly in control after dismantling the New York Yankees in the first two games of the '96 World Series, had just lost Game 5 1–0. The Yanks' third consecutive win not only sent them back to the Bronx in command, it also ruined the finale at Atlanta-Fulton County Stadium. The 30-year-old stadium was scheduled for demolition at season's end.

As usual, Mann gave the final totals for the game. As in, "For the Braves, no runs, five hits, one erra." Marshall always said "erra," never "error." Then he said, in his familiar baritone, "And for the last time, this is Marshall Mann saying good night, thank you for coming, and drive home carefully."

Little did we know that he was not just saying good night, but good-bye.

Eight days into the new year was a big day in Griffin, Mann's hometown about 25 miles southeast of Atlanta. Wednesday, January 9, 1997, was Marshall Mann Day in town. WKEU, the local AM radio station where Mann had broadcast for many years, was broadcasting the Mann Day festivities live from the Elks Lodge.

More than 300 came for the luncheon and program, including Mann's two sons, many of his friends, and Kiwanis Club brethren. Braves broadcasters Ernie Johnson, Pete Van Wieren, and Skip Caray were there, along with a busload of 40 Braves employees, even new Hall of Famer Phil Niekro. Everyone, it seemed, but Mann himself. A longtime smoker, he had cancer. He was home, in pajamas, in his recliner in the living room.

"Marshall Mann is very, very sick," emcee Jim Hall told the luncheon audience. "We need your prayers for Marshall. He wanted to be here so bad."

So did Dale Murphy, by then retired but forever a Marshall Mann fan. After the crowd sang "Take Me Out to the Ballgame," a familiar voice crackled on the speakerphone: "Hello, Marshall? This is No. 3, Murph." Calling from Utah. Mann listened on the radio at home. "We all feel you are a Hall of Famer. When I left the Braves, I never felt the same when I came up to hit and heard my name."

"To hear him say, 'Ladies and gentlemen, your Atlanta Braves', when the team takes the field got to me every night," said Jim Schultz, then the team's PR director and ever a gentleman himself. Van Wieren did the math and learned that since moving to Atlanta, the Braves had gone through one ownership change, seven GMs, 16 managers, and 15 broadcasters. "There was never a change needed in the public-address booth," he said. "We had the best."

"There's two voices in my life I'll never forget," said Niekro, the knuckleballer who won 318 games. "Jack O'Connell of the Baseball Writers Association calling me the other night to tell me I was elected to the Hall of Fame. And Marshall Mann's: 'Pitching for the Atlanta Braves tonight, No. 35, Phil Niekro.' When you heard Marshall's voice, it was done as professionally as it could be. Whether there were 40,000 in the stands or 4,000. He made me feel like a big-league ballplayer."

Later, Niekro and several others drove to Mann's home. Niekro said softly, "Hello, my friend," as he knelt and shook Mann's hand.

They talked a bit, and then the Hall of Famer pulled out a baseball and asked the PA man for his autograph.

Mann was too weak to sign. His wife, Patsy, put the ball in her husband's left hand. She gently placed his right hand on hers, and the two of them signed Marshall's name.

"I don't know if that was the right thing to do," Niekro said afterward. "But I had to do it."

Schultz brought along the microphone Mann used for 30 years. When he also presented him with his very own Braves jersey, No. 98 for Marshall's seat in the press box, Mann replied, "Bless your heart."

"I hope you know," Schultz said, "how many people care for you."

"I do," said Marshall Mann, who died a month later.

99 Off His Rocker

Every franchise has its cross to bear. Atlanta's was John Rocker. He was the left-handed loon of a closer and a serial disparager who wore out his welcome nearly as fast as he'd bull-rush in from the bullpen.

During the 1999 postseason, Rocker alienated both Mets and Yankees fans in the NLCS and World Series, respectively. They booed and cursed him, threw objects at him, too. Rocker responded by spitting at them, cursing, and giving them the finger as he strode from the mound to the dugout. A hate-hate relationship was born.

That winter, an article appeared in *Sports Illustrated.* It was written by Jeff Pearlman and was an accidental manifesto of sorts for Rocker, demonstrating man's inhumanity to man and denigrating, well, the entire city of New York. East Side, West Side, all around the town, Rocker torched New Yorkers of all stripes, races, ethnicities, and persuasions with equal impunity. Idiocy, too.

That December in Atlanta, asked by Pearlman if he'd ever play for the Mets or Yanks, Rocker replied, "I'd retire first. It's the most hectic, nerve-racking city. Imagine having to take the 7 train to the ballpark looking like you're riding through Beirut next to some kid with purple hair, next to some queer with AIDS, right next to some dude who just got out of jail for the fourth time, right next to some 20-year-old mom with four kids. It's depressing.... The biggest thing I don't like about New York are the foreigners. You can walk an entire block in Times Square and not hear anybody speaking English. Asians and Koreans and Vietnamese and Indians and Russians and Spanish people and everything up there. How the hell did they get in this country?"

Commissioner Bud Selig suspended Rocker for the first 30 days of the 2000 season for his remarks "that offended practically every element of society." He also levied a $20,000 fine and ordered Rocker to undergo sensitivity training. When the Player's Association appealed the penalties, an independent arbitrator reduced them to 15 days and a $500 fine. Neither that nor a meeting Henry Aaron arranged between Rocker and Andrew Young, the ex-mayor or Atlanta, former U.S. ambassador to the United Nations, and a prominent longtime figure in the Civil Rights movement, had any lasting effects.

After serving his suspension, Rocker rejoined the Braves in mid-April. He earned three saves during a 10-game homestand. On the first day of a West Coast road trip, however, Rocker reverted to form. He heckled San Diego Padres fans in Jack Murphy Stadium. When a photographer from the *San Diego Union-Tribune* took photos of this, Rocker was furious. He railed at the photographer, belittling him.

The next day's *Union-Tribune* reported it all. Braves broadcaster Pete Van Wieren read it and was livid. For his April 29 "Diamond

Notes," the popular three-minute segment on the pregame radio show, Van Wieren uncharacteristically wrote an editorial ripping Rocker but also the Braves for allowing "this situation to fester." He even wondered if another Braves trip to the World Series would be "tainted" should Rocker's act continue all season.

The Professor was lauded nationally but expected a reprimand from his employer. Instead…nothing. No one criticized Van Wieren. They all knew he spoke the truth.

Later that year, Tom Glavine told the *Atlanta Journal-Constitution*, "That, coming from Pete, meant something. It was like, hey, E.F. Hutton's talking. Let's listen."

A few weeks later, Pearlman was in Atlanta on an assignment for *SI*. Rocker confronted him, cursing and threatening him. The Braves sent Rocker down to the minor leagues. When he got the word, the livid reliever left the clubhouse and was talking on a cellphone at the end of a hallway leading to the field. Marlene Karas, then a *Journal-Constitution* photographer, approached Rocker with trepidation.

"What the [hell] are you doing, bitch?" Rocker asked.

"I'm taking your picture," replied Karas, who clicked and kept on walking and got a memorable photo of an angry man.

Rocker returned shortly from the minors, resumed his closer's role, and led the Braves with 24 saves that season. Yet the demotion changed nothing; if anything, Rocker got worse, even criticizing some teammates. On June 29 Rocker returned to Shea Stadium for the first time since his *SI* tirade. More than 700 police officers were assigned to Shea that night. The fans were vile and vicious, but there was no violence. Not even when Rocker came on in the eighth inning of a 6–4 Atlanta win. He left Shea about a half-hour after the team bus did, riding in a black van escorted by three security vehicles for the trip back to the Grand Hyatt. Whenever the Braves played in New York, a plainclothes cop occupied the hotel room next to Rocker's, and Rocker rode to and from the ballpark in an unmarked car with two other cops.

John Rocker celebrates at the end of the Braves' 1–0 win over the Mets in Game 3 of the 1999 NLCS in New York. Though his pitching efforts may have led to some success, his attitude was too much for the team to bear, and he was traded in 2001.

By mid-June of 2001, although Rocker had 19 saves, the Braves had had enough. They traded him to Cleveland. There, a Jesuit priest, Father Edward Glynn, then the president of John Carroll University, was openly critical of Rocker's arrival. In a newspaper article Father Glynn wished Rocker nothing but ill. The reliever finished the season with the Indians, but his pitching continued to decline.

Rocker was traded to Texas, where he later refused a minor league assignment and was released. In 2003 he pitched two games with Tampa Bay before being released again. Rocker attempted a comeback with the Long Island Ducks, an independent minor league team. When he signed with them, longtime baseball writer Marty Noble, who'd previously worked for years for *Newsday* on Long Island, concocted a headline that was so right, on so many levels:

> Rocker signs,
> Long Island ducks

That comeback bid bombed out, too. Rocker was gone for good, and baseball was the better for it.

In March 2007 Rocker was implicated in a steroid ring that involved Applied Pharmacy of Mobile, Alabama. He was listed on the client list. His publicist said that while Rocker admitted taking Human Growth Hormone, he only used HGH for medical reasons.

100 Bravo!

"The Misfits." That's what the Giants called themselves last season when they won the World Series, the first for the franchise since 1954. The Atlanta Braves knew those Misfits by another name: the team the battered, injury-depleted wild-card Braves nearly beat in a dramatic four-game NL Division Series.

Each game was decided by one run. In Game 4 at Turner Field Atlanta led 2–1 in the seventh. But the Giants scored twice off relievers Peter Moylan and Jonny Venters after a tough throwing error was charged to shortstop Alex Gonzalez. It was one of seven Braves errors in the NLDS, four by infielder Brooks Conrad.

In the ninth Atlanta had two men on, the crowd roaring. Both runners were stranded to end the series and Bobby Cox's career. The manager began to break down in a postgame press conference, composed himself, and returned to the field to acknowledge the fans and salute rival manager Bruce Bochy. When the Giants saw Cox, they stopped celebrating and applauded the Hall of Famer-to-be.

Although the loss was painful, the Braves returned to the playoffs for the first time since 2005. In that '05 NLDS, in his first career postseason at-bat, rookie catcher Brian McCann crushed a three-run homer off Roger Clemens. That was the first of five consecutive seasons in which McCann made the NL All-Star team—the only Brave ever to start his career in such fashion. In last year's All-Star Game McCann's three-run double gave the National League a 3–1 win at long last.

That 2005 NLDS ended in agonizing fashion. Reliever Kyle Farnsworth imploded, blowing a 6–1 lead, allowing an eighth-inning grand slam and a solo homer in the ninth. After another 8½ scoreless innings, rookie Joey Devine gave up a home run in the 18th, and Houston won 7–6.

The Braves didn't sniff the playoffs again until last fall. Somehow, they won 91 games despite an injury-ravaged roster to give Cox one last October.

What if Chipper Jones hadn't torn his left ACL again last year? What if infielder Martin Prado, a revelation with a .307 average, 184 hits, and his first All-Star Game selection, hadn't suffered a hip pointer and torn left oblique muscle in late September? What if closer Billy Wagner hadn't injured his oblique in Game 2 of the NLDS? Then he would've been on the mound in the ninth inning of Game 4. Instead, after compiling 37 saves and a career-best 1.43 ERA, Wagner retired fifth on the career saves list with 422—just two behind leader John Franco among left-handers. A man of his word, Wagner returned to his family and farm in his native Virginia.

Bobby Cox waves to fans after his final game in Major League Baseball, a 3–2 loss to the San Francisco Giants in Game 4 of the 2010 NLDS.

What if the Braves hadn't been sold, and Ted Turner had remained the owner? For all his early daffiness, Ted became a great owner with deep pockets, hired good people, and let them do their jobs. What if Mark Wohlers hadn't thrown that slider in '96? The Braves would've almost surely won their second World Series, and Wohlers wouldn't have lost his control—so painful to watch. What if Andruw Jones, the center fielder who won 10 consecutive Gold Gloves from 1998 to 2007 and hit 368 of his 407 homers as a Brave, was more disciplined at the plate? What if Jair Jurrjens, the splendid young pitcher, wasn't injured part of the previous season?

Yet the Braves were resilient and hit remarkably in the clutch. Jason Heyward, second in the NL Rookie of the Year voting, will be a star for years. The J-Hey Kid hit .277 with 18 homers and 72 RBIs.

Then there's Huddy: Tim Hudson, the veteran right-hander who had Tommy John surgery in August of 2008 and returned to make seven starts late in '09, was sensational in 2010. Hudson went 17–9 with a 2.83 ERA and was fourth in the NL Cy Young Award voting. He won the MLB Comeback Player of the Year Award and was named the Braves Player of the Year. The Hudson Family Foundation, run by Kim Hudson and her husband, is one of the finest and most philanthropic in Atlanta.

In the off-season Atlanta acquired Dan Uggla from Florida, then signed the slugging second baseman to a five-year, $62 million contract extension. Uggla hit 33 home runs last year with 105 RBIs. He has 154 homers in five seasons.

The morning after the 2010 World Series ended, David O'Brien, the Braves beat writer for the *Atlanta Journal-Constitution*, wrote:

"I've always said injuries are part of the game. Every team has them. So I usually hate it when people point to a couple of injuries during the course of a season as the main reason a team didn't reach its goals.

"That said, what happened to the Braves in the second half of this season was a bit beyond the usual litany of pain.

"As well as the Giants played, as deserving as they are of their World Series title, I would not blame Braves fans for wondering aloud what might have been if the Braves hadn't played without injured Martin Prado, Chipper Jones, Eric O'Flaherty, Jair Jurrjens, Kris Medlen, and Takashi Saito for all or part of the stretch drive, then lost closer Billy Wagner in the playoff series versus San Fran.

"The Giants beat the Braves three games to one.... What might have been? Who knows? Doesn't matter, though. And to the Giants' credit, they played better with each step of the playoffs. Would the Braves have done the same with a healthier team? Don't know. Maybe..."

Bibliography

I worked for four major newspapers in a nearly four-decade sportswriting career: the *Miami News*, *Chicago Daily News*, *New York Daily News*, and the *Atlanta Journal-Constitution*. As such, I'm an inveterate newspaper reader—primarily because my late father, Jack, drove a newspaper truck for a living and brought home at least a half-dozen New York/Long Island papers each morning. That instilled in me a love and respect for newspapers and baseball. My affection for both continues to this day. Thanks, Dad.

Among the many papers and publications I researched for this book are the *Atlanta Journal-Constitution*, the *New York Times*, *New York Daily News*, *Newsday*, the *St. Louis Post-Dispatch*, the *Pittsburgh Post-Gazette*, the *Chicago Tribune*, the *Chicago Sun-Times*, the *Houston Chronicle*, the *Philadelphia Inquirer*, the *Philadelphia Daily News*, the *Boston Globe*, the *Miami Herald*, the late *Gwinnett Daily News* and other papers in the Morris Communications chain, the *Washington Post*, the *Los Angeles Times*, and the *San Francisco Chronicle*. Also, *Sports Illustrated*, *ESPN The Magazine*, *Time Magazine*, *Newsweek*, and *ChopTalk*, the Atlanta Braves' excellent fan magazine.

Baseball-Reference.com and Retrosheet.org were vital, authoritative sources of instant baseball information. So, of course, was the ever-helpful Atlanta Braves media relations and public relations staff. MLB.com, particularly Braves beat writer Mark Bowman's work, was a ready, accurate source. Video clips of great calls of memorable Braves moments by broadcasters Pete Van Wieren, Ernie Johnson Sr., the late Skip Caray, Skip's son Chip, and Joe Simpson were also invaluable. So were media guides from the Braves and several other Major League Baseball teams.

The baseball books, leading off with Derrick Goold's superb *100 Things Cardinals Fans Should Know & Do Before They Die* (Chicago: Triumph Books, 2010), which served as an excellent model to follow.

Others include:

Aaron, Hank with Lonnie Wheeler. *I Had a Hammer: The Hank Aaron Story*. New York: Harper Collins, 1991.

Allen, Ivan Jr. with Paul Hemphill. *Mayor: Notes on the Sixties*. New York: Simon and Schuster, 1971.

Appel, Marty. *Slide, Kelly, Slide*. Lanham, Maryland.: Scarecrow Press, 1996.

Bryant, Howard. *The Last Hero: A Life of Henry Aaron*. New York: Pantheon, 2010.

Caruso, Gary. *The Braves Encyclopedia*. Philadelphia: Temple University Press, 1995.

Darnell, Tim. *The Atlanta Crackers: Early Days of Atlanta Baseball.* Athens, Georgia: Hill Street Press, 2003.

Harwell, Ernie with Tom Keegan. *Ernie Harwell: My 60 Years in Baseball.* Chicago: Triumph Books, 2002.

Hope, Bob. *We Could've Finished Last Without You*. Marietta, Georgia: Longstreet Press, 1991.

Kahn, Roger. *The Head Game: Baseball Seen from the Pitcher's Mound.* New York: Harcourt, 2000.

Klapisch, Bob and Pete Van Wieren. *The World Champion Atlanta Braves: 125 Years of America's Team*. Atlanta: Turner Publishing, 1995, 1996.

Kurkjian, Tim. *Is This a Great Game, or What?* New York: St. Martin's Press, 2007.

Olney, Buster. *The Last Night of the Yankee Dynasty*. New York: HarperCollins, 2004.

Reichler, Joseph L. *The Baseball Encyclopedia (7th edition)*. New York: MacMillan Publishing Company, 1988.

Rosenberg, I.J. with Al Tays. *Miracle Season!* Atlanta: Turner Publishing, 1991.

Smith, Red. *Red Smith on Baseball.* Chicago: Ivan R. Dee, 2000.

Thorn, John with Pete Palmer, Michael Gershman and David Pietrusza. *Total Baseball.* (Note: Several editions). New York: Viking, 1997 et al.

Thorn, John. *The Armchair Book of Baseball.* New York: Charles Scribner's Sons, 1985.

Torre, Joe and Tom Verducci. *Chasing the Dream: My Lifelong Journey to the World Series.* New York: Bantam Books, 1997.

Van Wieren, Pete with Jack Wilkinson. *Of Mikes and Men.* Chicago: Triumph Books, 2010.

Victor, Walter. *Brave at Heart, as told to Anne B. and Sidney R. Jones.* Macon, Georgia: Indigo Publishing Group, 2007.

Wilkinson, Jack. *Game of My Life: Atlanta Braves.* Champaign, Illinois: Sports Publishing, 2007.

Will, George F. *Men at Work: The Craft of Baseball.* New York: Harper Perennial, 1992.